ALL ABOUT
THE CHIHUAHUA

ALL ABOUT
THE CHIHUAHUA

MONA HUXHAM

PELHAM BOOKS

First published in Great Britain by PELHAM BOOKS LTD
52 Bedford Square, London WC1B 3EF
1976

ISBN 0 7207 0891 5

Set and printed in Great Britain by
A. Wheaton & Co., Exeter

To my husband and children who enjoyed and loved our Chihuahuas, and perhaps more especially to Quentin who paid me one penny (old money) for his 'Bunny', hence her name Emmrill Pennyworth. Bunny was his partner in crime all the time he was growing up and she also produced Emmrill Halfpenny for him. She lived a long and active life so he would appear to have had his 'money's worth'.

CONTENTS

LIST OF ILLUSTRATIONS

PLATES
(between pages 64 and 65)

Picture credits: 2 – C. S. Wedlock; 3 – Murray; 7 and 9 – Sally Anne Thompson; 6, 15, 17 and 19 – Thomas Fall; 8, 16 and 21 – C. M. Cooke & Son.

LINE ILLUSTRATIONS

ACKNOWLEDGEMENTS

I feel I must first of all thank my husband for introducing me to the Chihuahua and also for the presents of Chihuahuas he has made to me over the years.

Thanks too must go to my five children who have all loved the Chis as pets over the years. Through their interest we have all shared and enjoyed the fun and amusement that was to be found in our home from having our Chihuahuas in close contact.

To the many little Chihuahuas that have been such a delight over the last twenty-three years: Driada, Peta, Honey, Rocky, Peppie, Zara, Honora, Candy, Fudge, Sandy, Big Ears, Roguey, Bunny, Tu Tu, Beauty, Busy, Little Rock, Roxiana, Hogey, Merry, Tuppence, Halfpenny, Gold Dust, Humfri, Sweetie, Swagger, Beckie, Hubert, Champers, etc. Some were champions, many big prize-winners, some even Best of Breed at Cruft's. Others were known as pillars of the breed—but all were much-loved pets who earned our affection and respect because of their devotion to us, their complete loyalty and their appreciation of the home comforts they enjoyed in our house. The only way they are small is in their stature; apart from that no one could ask for more in a friend and constant companion. Above all, we love them for their brilliant sense of fun.

My thanks and grateful acknowledgement must go to the Kennel Club for permission to include the Standard of the Breed and for all the references to Kennel Club affairs. Also for the information which I have been able to extract from the Kennel Club *Stud Books* in order to make this book more interesting by adding details of Champions. The American Kennel Club and the Société Centrale Canine must also be mentioned here.

To the authors of all the books I read during my preparation for this book, especially to Dr Michael Coe of Yale University, U.S.A., and to Dr Warwick Bray of the University of London, who is a lecturer in American Archaeology at the University Institute of Archaeology and who gave me added help in my research. Dr Coe gave me the names of people who were actually involved in digging the Aztec graves and Dr Bray put me in touch with the *Book of the Life of the Ancient Mexicans* from which the picture of the dog with the Aztec corpse has been reproduced.

Grateful thanks to the staff of the Anthropological Institute for allowing me to use their very extensive library of ancient cultures, and to the British Museum where Dr Bierbriar gave me so much help in reading matter on dogs in ancient times, especially Dr Arkell's article and the very important work, from my point of view, of Dr Kathleen Haddon on dog cemeteries in Egypt. Thanks to Miss Crawford of the Egyptian Exploration Society for allowing me access to their copy of the book *Cemeteries of Abydos*.

To Mr McNaughton of the Institute of Anthropology for his help in finding the rare copy of Delia Nuttall's book and also for his help over Diego Muñoz Camargo and Dr Arkell, etc.

A very big thank you to Mr Evans for his quite perfect photograph of the extract from the *Codex Magliabecchiano* from the original facsimile.

To Dick Dickerson of the Chihuahua Club of America for supplying Ida Garrett's article and other valuable information on the breed in America in the early days. I am indeed proud to be made an honorary life member of this club, which was the very first club for the breed and which recently celebrated its fiftieth anniversary.

To the Editor of *Our Dogs* for several quotations and in case any information I derived whilst Chihuahua Breed Correspondent may have been referred to in this book.

An especially warm thank you to Miss Sally Anne Thompson for her very fine cover picture and for all her other photographs. I am also grateful for those photographs so kindly lent to me by the owners of the Chis appearing in the book. Thanks, too, to Thomas Fall Ltd and C. M. Cooke & Sons for allowing me to reproduce their splendid photographs.

A very special word of thanks to Mr and Mrs Keith Murray who gave so much of their time and hospitality when my daughter and I were photographing their enchanting puppies, and for Mr Murray's own photographs which I have been delighted to include.

Thanks to my daughter Elizabeth Osman for taking those photos, and to Caroline Huxham for her line drawings, especially the illustrated standard which she and I put together from a composite group of dog pictures. This was originally done for the British Chihuahua Club's Handbook, so I know the Club will approve of my including it, as they consider it a true model of the breed and one that breeders and judges should keep in mind always.

INTRODUCTION

It will be said that, with my long experience in dogs in general, and Chihuahuas in particular, I have not given enough information in this book on resuscitating puppies, timing whelping pains and watching the first puppies being born, etc. In the case of other breeds, I could safely encourage breeders to buy good bitches and breed them regularly, and even suggest that they could make a little money out of their hobby. So if it is my reader's intention to secure a few good Chihuahua bitches, use a local stud dog and sit back and count the profits then I'm going to say here, in the very beginning, that profit in kind will be a very unlikely outcome. Profit in experience and the constant niggling of looking forward to the approaching whelping with apprehension and regret are more likely to be your lot—regret that you didn't call the vet earlier, regret that you didn't use the stud dog with the super head, regret that you mated your bitch at all, and even regret that you ever bought a Chihuahua in the first place. This would be the feeling of a breeder whose reason for going into the breed was purely monetary. This book will be of more use to someone who bought a Chihuahua bitch because she fell in love with it, was persuaded to mate her to a reigning champion, much against her will, and then, when faced with the possible complications of a difficult whelping, would feel the £30 or so spent on a Caesarean operation to save her precious little bitch, and ensure the safe birth of her one and only offspring, well worth the money. There would never be any question raised about the expense of the heating pad in the bed, the overhead infra-red lamp and only the best possible food being acceptable.

Chihuahuas, once they are born, can be as strong and husky as any of the other breeds – it is getting them born that is the problem. My advice to anyone starting in the breed is to enjoy all the pleasures of owning a Chihuahua, but when it comes to breeding from the tiny ones put the responsibility with your veterinary surgeon. If he thinks your bitch can breed with his help, then it is fair enough to let him take over on the day the pups are due.

11

Labour should get the milk glands going and the bitch will become maternal. But if there is the slightest risk of difficulty, the best solution is to decide on a Caesarean section before any trouble begins. Then the only worry is making sure the bitch has the puppies sucking from her when she comes out of the anaesthetic. Once the pups are born, there is rarely any trouble with resuscitation as they seem to have a strong grip on life. A vigorous shaking, as advised with other breeds, could misplace something, so the mucus must be drained and only the gentlest wiping away should be attempted. This procedure won't apply so much to the bigger bitches, who probably shell out the pups as well as any, but more to the 'tinies' of three to four pounds, which is the size I find so delightful to own.

You can also forget anything you may have heard about dogs being placed on this earth by our Creator to be the servant of man. God must have had a change of heart in the case of the Chihuahua, for our little friend thinks he was sent into this world so that man can be *his* servant, and he acts accordingly. Whether living with the Mexican Indians or the housewife in suburbia, the Chihuahua will expect the warmest or coolest place according to the temperature, the choicest food and the most attention.

Mention of the Mexican Indians brings me to the many versions of the actual country responsible for the Chihuahua's origin. Mexico has always been the favourite and the breed is mostly referred to in reference books as 'the Mexican Chihuahua'. I have come across enough evidence, supported by statements of many eminent and responsible experts in this particular field, as well as enough illustrations, to make me quite satisfied that the Aztecs owned an ancestor of our present-day Chihuahua and that they have been maintained in some form or other right down the centuries. Columbus took a Great Dane with him on his voyage to discover America, and his letters regarding the dogs he found there can be believed. Only ten years before that famous voyage, in 1482, Botticelli is supposed to have painted his panels of the life of Moses in the Sistine Chapel, Rome. He painted a little dog with a head that could have belonged to an ancestor of the Chihuahua, but as the legs are hidden it could equally have been an Italian Greyhound, a breed akin to the whippet and the much larger greyhound which have been recognised for many centuries in Europe, as well as in Egypt where they were depicted as decoration

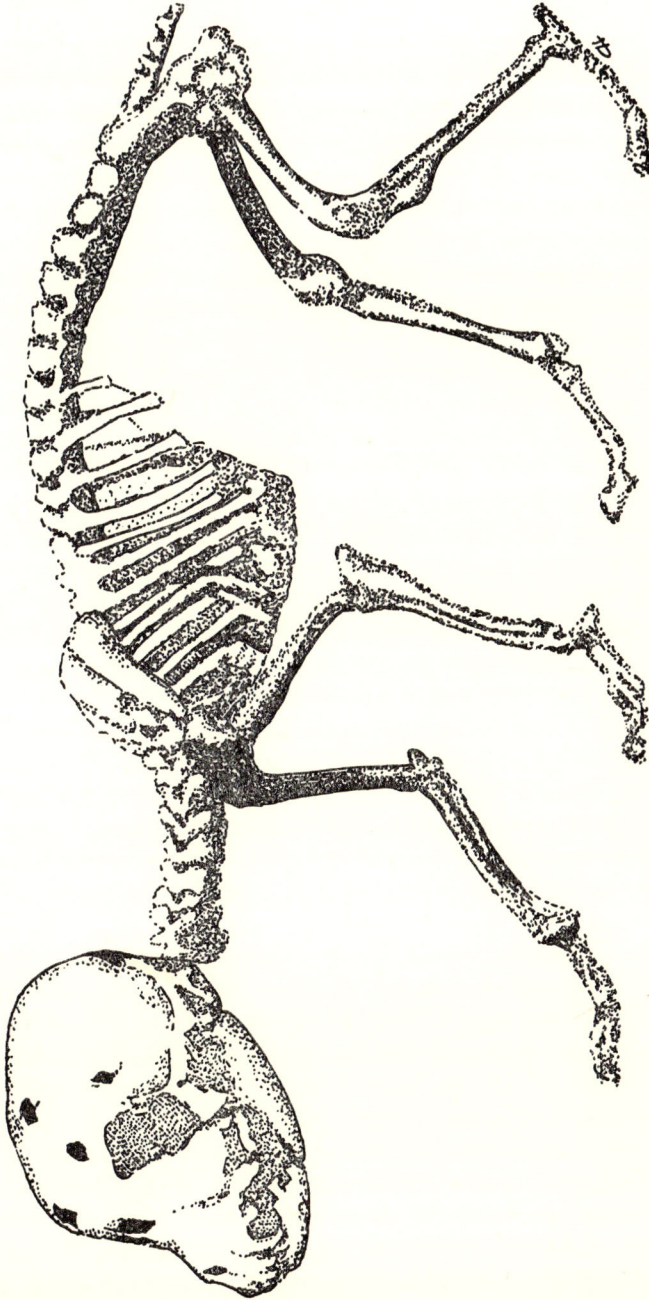

Fig. 1. Skeleton of a fully adult Chihuahua. Note the well-defined moleras, or holes, in the head, a peculiarity of the breed. This skeleton, which measures 7 inches nose to tail, can be seen at the National History Museum, Mexico.

on vases found in the ancient pyramids of the pharaohs. There is no way of knowing if the dog in Botticelli's Moses fresco had a molera, or hole, in its head which would, of course, make its connection with the Chihuahua more likely. There is proof, however, that there were tiny dogs in Mexico with several holes in the head, as seen in the skeleton of a tiny dog which was presented to the Museo de Historia Natural in Mexico City in 1910 which shows four moleras and is no more than seven inches from tip to tail.

In the very scholarly and expensively produced *The Life History and Magic of The Dog* by Dr Fernard Mery, the noted French veterinarian, there is a large reproduction of *The Sons of Moses* from the frescoes Botticelli painted in the Sistine Chapel. Dr Mery, who had thirty years' experience of canine medicine, says that without reasonable doubt the dog one of the boys is carrying is a crossbreed. He also shows a picture of the fresco in Florence attributed to Giotto (1267–1337) in which is depicted small black and white dogs with erect ears and of what he calls 'small greyhound type'. Botticelli lived until 1510 and could easily have gone back to Rome and added the dog or altered one he had painted on an earlier composition to look more like the dogs Columbus had brought back. It is true that the dog in question has a round head, bulging eyes and enormously long nails which all apply to the early Chihuahua. Writing about the Chihuahua, Dr Mery tells us that the Aztecs had two types of dogs, one of which was reared in flocks, fattened and sold in markets by the hundred. The second type was much smaller, had a globular head, a fine, close coat, and was the ancestor of the present-day minute Chihuahua. They were the beloved, tender companions of the Mexican Indians long before the arrival of the Conquistadors. So he concludes that the indigenous peoples of America had already domesticated the dog. They were, however, terrified by the fierce Mastiffs (devouring dogs) brought over by the Conquistadors, as they were so different from the dogs they were familiar with. The stylised dog in the Musée de l'Homme in Paris that was brought over from the museum of Tempoal is nearer the modern Chihuahua than the great Tibetan Mastiff. Paul Rivet, a director of the Musée de l'Homme, spent a lot of time in Mexico among the excavations and ruins of Mexican civilisations and so would make sure that the collections on show would be a true record of the country and its ethnology. This museum well merits a visit from people interested in tracing the ancient history of our breed.

Much has been written about the mummified body of a tiny dog that was found in an ancient Egyptian dog cemetery. Many writers would have us believe that this was the true ancestor of the Chihuahua. Whilst researching this book I came across an article published in the *Illustrated London News*, June 23rd, 1956, in which Dr H. A. Arkell refers to the way the ancient Egyptians mummified their dogs. This in turn led me to the Department of Antiquities at the British Museum where they referred me to the book *Cemeteries of Abydos* by Edward Neville, published by the Egyptian Exploration Society in 1910. Dr Bierbriar of the Department of Antiquities discovered that the book contained an article entitled 'Dog Cemeteries of Abydos' which had been written by Dr Kathleen Haddon. Apparently, Dr Haddon had joined an expedition to explore the well of Abydos and, while tunnelling at the bottom, she discovered large catacombs where literally thousands of dogs had been incarcerated. The dogs were buried there from the first century B.C. to the fourth century A.D., and during this period thousands of dogs' bones were deposited but not all of them were mummified. They were found piled up on the floor and looked as though they had been disturbed by robbers for they were all mixed up, but they were all bones of fairly large dogs. Dr Haddon made a detailed examination of eleven skulls and four whole skeletons which she found intact. All but one were of the pariah-type dog—large and very obviously of mixed ancestry. The odd man out, as it were, was the skull of a jackal. The skulls received were all of adult dogs, and one (No. VII) obviously belonged to a very old dog because the teeth were quite worn down, some were missing and others broken.

One of the specimens found was the mummified body of a tiny dog which was still in its wrappings, and Dr Haddon says that she found them very difficult to remove. The skull was $4\frac{1}{2}$ in. (115 mm) long and $2\frac{1}{4}$ in. (56 mm) wide across the zygomatic arches. The bones were not fused together and *the fontanel was slightly open.* All the milk teeth were present and the first molars could be seen lying below the surface in the lower jaw. The body had been embalmed by being macerated in a bath of natron, then dried slowly and wrapped in linen. The front legs were extended down the chest and the back legs bent up with the tail between them, the head being at right angles to the body. From the closing fontanel and state of the milk teeth Dr Haddon put the age of the puppy at ten weeks.

She was able to state with surety that the body was of a young puppy that would, in time, have grown to the same size as the rest of the skeletons found in the tomb. She lists the known breeds and says that the skeletons were of dogs showing features which established their relationship to some of the following breeds:

1. Tesam Dog—Curly tailed, as seen in the figure of Anubis (a dog worshipped by the Egyptians as a god). Often referred to as the Egyptian Greyhound.
2. Egyptian Pariah Dog—Similar in size to the wolf and jackal.
3. Egyptian Dog—Larger than the Egyptian Pariah.
4. Egyptian Spitz—Known only from one mummified skull from Asyut. This dog was considerably taller than the Pomeranian Spitz and more resembled a Dogue and the Abyssinian dog.

With the exception of the last, all the dogs found in Egypt were members of Dr Studer's group of southern dogs—Pariahs, Dingos, Greyhounds and Dogues, plus the jackal that Dr Haddon found among her specimens.

I spent many months investigating this subject and although I searched in all the obvious sources—encyclopaedias, libraries, museums, including the British Museum and Museum of Mankind, the Anthropological Institute, universities and many, many experts on the subject—I was quite unable to trace any tiny dog even remotely resembling the Chihuahua that could have come from Egypt.

CHAPTER 1

The Origin of the Chihuahua in Mexico

The Chihuahua is the tiniest dog in the world. This sweeping statement can be made because the Chihuahua is a pedigree breed registered with all the world's leading Kennel Clubs and all the lesser Clubs take their standards of all the registered breeds from these governing bodies. They include the English Kennel Club, the American Kennel Club, La Société Centrale Canine (France), and all the affiliated clubs of the Federation of Canine International. All these august bodies have laid down that the Chihuahua is the smallest dog because it has a top weight of six pounds. The Yorkshire Terrier, which is the next smallest, has a top weight of seven pounds. These limits are for show purposes and specimens used for breeding are often much heavier. The lower limit for the Chihuahua is two to four pounds. I have even owned them weighing only one pound at maturity, but they are far more of a responsibility at that size and not nearly so much fun to live with as the three to six pound ones who really are the most delightful little dogs to own or rather, to use the operative words, to be owned by.

I got to know the breed in 1949 and was intrigued by the minute size and immense character of these little creatures. My earliest impressions, however, were anything but favourable, as most of the dogs on exhibition at that time were so very unsound in their legs and I, as a breeder of terriers and poodles which in order to win in the showring had to be sound of limb, was appalled at their cow hocks, slipping stifles, bow fronts and terrible shoulders. I remember saying to my husband that they would be enchanting little dogs to own if only they could be bred with sound limbs. In those days I was a farmer's wife, mother of a growing family and breeder of poodles, and I found the effort of getting the family and their individual pets ready to go out a terrible headache. The children insisted on taking their poodles everywhere, and guess who had to brush them to try to make a good impression on the public eye. As my three elder children got more adventurous their pets did

17

likewise, and after a particularly muddy expedition into the bogs of Bramshill Forest looking for early primroses to present to my mother who was expected for the Easter holidays, I was heard to long for a smooth-coated breed as house pets. My Mama was the fondest of grandmothers and the children and the dogs adored her and showed their affection even before she got right out of the car. On that occasion she was wearing a new Easter outfit and I spent a miserable week-end (in the days prior to the automatic dry-cleaning machines of the ever-open local launderette) trying to get her suit fit to attend the christening of the fourth member of the family.

It was in 1952 that my husband came to my bench at the Ladies' Kennel Club Show at Olympia to say he had just seen a Chihuahua that had won a big variety class and seemed perfectly sound to him. As a life-long breeder of farm livestock he knew what to look for and I respected his opinion, so I went to have a look for myself and found the tiny figure of Dengers Don Armando of Belamie surrounded by such a huge crowd of onlookers that it took us quite a long time to struggle through them in order to speak to Mrs Dora Wells, his proud owner. Thinking we would be able to buy a puppy from her next litter, we handed her our name and address, only to be told that she had such a long list of orders that it would probably be a couple of years before she had anything available, but she promised to pass our name on to other breeders she was in touch with. We had forgotten all about the incident when one day, right out of the blue, we received a phone call from Mrs Joan Forster to the effect that she had a Chihuahua bitch ready for us at a cost of £75. At that time £75 would have bought a pedigree Guernsey cow whose milk yield would increase our monthly cheque from the Milk Marketing Board. Bearing this in mind, we agreed to go and see the puppy, but keeping a completely open mind. This state lasted until I saw the puppy that was held out to me and at that first sight of a tiny baby Chihuahua all my good resolutions went by the board. Hastily promising to pay my husband back out of my next litter of poodles—then making about £15 a piece—I became the owner of my first ever Chihuahua and I can assure you that my life has never been the same since.

With the puppy's pedigree and feeding instructions I was handed a leaflet explaining the origin of the breed as laid down by Mrs Forster, Mrs Wells and the other members of the club that had just been formed to promote the breed. This was the first indication I had that the breed had such a romantic and seemingly unknown background. Since those early days I have spent more time than I like to think delving into history books, both Mexican and Spanish, as well as all the known writings on the breed that I can find, and I am going to admit now that there is still as much conjecture as ever, for most of what has been written about the breed in one volume is promptly refuted in the next. So without bringing my own findings to a definite conclusion I have decided to put all the various opinions before you in as chronological an order as possible and let you draw your own conclusions as to how and when the Chihuahua was produced. I am also going to state here and now that however the breed started I for one am very, very glad somebody, however recently or in the mists of long-past history, had the forethought and good sense to think up this exquisite and unique breed so that we can have the benefit of its charms to cheer us through these none too easy times.

The information I was first given on the breed told me that the Chihuahua (pronounced chee-wah-wah) originated in Mexico and was most frequently found in the State of Chihuahua. Held in great esteem by the Aztecs, and possibly even before them by the Toltecs, the little dogs were a vital link in religious ceremonies. My further investigation added to this and gave the information that the Aztecs firmly believed that the dog was necessary to act as a guide for the dead during their journey through the underworld, so the Aztecs killed the dog and cremated it with the body of its human master and together they were expected to arrive at the other side of the River of Death. Without a dog the Aztecs thought the dead would not be able to find their way.

The dogs killed for this purpose were not the hairless, castrated and fattened Techichi which were kept purely for eating purposes and were found by Cortés and his Conquistadors (when they invaded Mexico) living in the yards surrounding the natives' houses together with turkeys, rabbits, chicken, partridges, quails, wild duck and pigeons. On feast days, the aristocrats ate turkey but the poorer people put slices of turkey on the top of a dish and filled it underneath with slices of the fattened hairless dogs which were much cheaper and more plentiful.

From my reading I do not feel that Cortés was uneducated, as his letters to Emperor Charles V are informative and concise. Even if they were written for him by a secretary, at least one of them was well informed and a very clear picture can be gathered from the description he gave of life in Mexico when he first arrived there.

Maxwell Riddle, one of America's most authoritative writers on the breed and a fellow judge and houseguest of the author's at the Staten Island Dog Show in New York some years ago, has a theory which he expounds in his book *This is the Chihuahua*. He believes the dog in Mexico at the time we are studying had not properly evolved from the wild state. He pictures the 'hutia' which is a rodent but which was often called a dog by the Conquistadors. This is probably because their word for dog, i.e. 'perro', was the same as the word the Mexicans used when referring to another rodent which they owned, namely the 'perro' or 'perro Chihua-hueno'. There is always much confusion when languages are translated as often a double meaning is used in the wrong sense, so that 'perro' the 'rodent' can easily be interpreted as 'perro' the 'dog'. Another cause for confusion in this instance is that the Aztecs had word-pictures and when their records might have meant to refer to a dog the picture to the uninitiated could have had a different meaning.

Before the Aztec civilisation, Mexico was inhabited by the Toltecs who took over from the earlier Maya culture. The Toltecs were a mild and learned race who venerated the dog. They had a dog-god called 'Tula' and they built a city in his name. They also built the pyramids of Cholula which in turn were used by the Aztecs as a holy place. When the Conquistadors pulled down this temple they used the stones to erect their own Christian Church of Los Remedios, and on some of these stones can be found Mexican picture-writing with engraved sketches of dogs which look very much as if they could be ancestors of the present-day Chihuahua —very small, short faced, with erect ears and not hairless. Similarly shown are pictures of the national dog—the Mexican Hairless, or Xoloizcuintli, which is the breed that Cortés tells us was fattened especially for the table. The Spaniards so enjoyed eating this dog that it is a wonder any of them survived. The modern name for this breed is Sholo.

At the present time, excavations are going on under the ruins of Mitla where remains of the Zapotec Indian culture are to be found and where, today, the finds of these excavations can be seen in the Frissell Museum. This site was originally supposed to have been

one of the finest religious centres of the Zapotec tribe and was
seized by the Mixtecs just prior to the Spanish Invasion. In the
ruins here are tombs round a huge plaza, temples, ball courts and
various buildings. The carvings here are very well preserved and
the picture-writing clearly shows the daily life and possessions of
the Zapotecs, who still today own the tiny dogs they have owned
over the centuries. After the Spanish Invasion the natives of Mexico
were treated badly; they were robbed of food and made to work
so hard that many died and some moved away out of range of the
conquerors' abuses and exploitation. So catastrophic was the decline
in the Indian population that it decreased from 16,871,408 in 1532
to 1,069,255 in 1608. Some Zapotecs were far enough away to
move even more and took their dogs and household goods with
them.

The Spanish passed a law making it illegal for dogs to be
castrated and fattened for food and also banned the practice of
killing off dogs to sacrifice to the gods, which had been the usual
practice when there was a shortage of humans to slake the un-
quenchable blood-thirst of the Indians' gods. As it was only the
heart of the victim that was required, the rest of the bodies were
just left to fall down from the high altar where the priests performed their revolting tasks.

The Conquistadors were not above sampling the flesh of the
dogs cooked for their own tables. They so enjoyed the taste that
they ate all that were available and the Indians were so poor themselves that they hardly had enough food for their own use let alone
to feed their dogs, so the numbers of dogs decreased even faster than
the human population. The only Indians who survived were those
able to find time to work their own pieces of land and grow crops
and keep animals as they had done before the Conquest.

The Tarascan Indians were a race who inhabited land on the
west coast, which is now known as the State of Michoacan. These
people were never conquered by the Aztecs as they were very
distinguished warriors. Their capital was Tzintzuntzan and their
last emperor was called Caltzontzin. The famous Mexican artist of
the twentieth century, Diego Rivera, painted many murals and
large paintings depicting the whole history of Mexico, and in
his painting of the Tarascan civilisation he has included three
Chihuahuas and three turkeys outside a native house. The dogs are
sitting on the steps leading up to the house and the turkeys are on

the ground below. The note which Rivera wrote about this picture says that the dogs and turkeys were natives of Mexico long before the Spanish Invasion and that turkey was the favourite dish of the Emperor Montezuma II, the ninth Aztec emperor.

Rivera paints the Mexican Hairless dog in many of his murals and frescoes. In his painting of the arrival of Hernando Cortés at Veracruz on April 22nd, 1519, he shows a hairless dog snarling at a Spanish dog. In his stupendous mural of the Grand Tenochtitlan (Mexican name for Mexico City) Rivera shows us a panoramic view of the Valley of Mexico with the capital of the Aztec empire as it was before the Invasion. Among the stalls at the market, depicted on the right-hand side of the centre, are two Mexican Hairless dogs and he shows these dogs again in his mural of the Maguey (parchment for writing on, made from the bark of the Amatl tree which is soaked to make it pliable). We see at the bottom of this painting a woman lying on her stomach and soaking strips of bark in a small pool; with her are two black hairless dogs lapping the water. Rivera says that these dogs were greatly esteemed by the Aztecs as foot warmers as they have a body temperature of 105–110°F which is far above the normal dog temperature of 101.5°F. These dogs, he tells us, are the rarest dogs in the world.

Diego Rivera was not only a first-class painter, he was also a very careful historian, and before he executed any of his historical works he studied the subject down to the smallest detail and enlisted the aid of other historians and professors of anthropology. He studied the *Codex Borbonicus* and the *Codex Terleroano Remensis*, which were Aztec picture-writings. So exact was Rivera in his attention to detail that he had the skeleton of Hernando Cortés taken to the Jesus Hospital in Mexico City and examined by the eminent scientists and anthropologists Miss Eulalia Guzman and Dr Alfonso Quiron Cuaron, who after making their examination agreed that Cortés was in fact nothing like the pictures of him found in history books and references. Instead of the handsome, arrogant, well-set-up gentleman, he was in fact only about four feet tall—a dwarf—with very serious physical deformities—a hunchback and a shortened leg. His skull measured only 7 inches (177 mm) which is much less than the normal $7\frac{1}{2}$ inches (191 mm). It appears that he was very self-conscious of his looks and refused to let anyone paint him. Hernando Cortés' heirs destroyed the true portrait of Cortés, which he had caused to be painted on the walls of the Jesus Hospital. In this portrait Cortés was depicted in an act of contrition showing all his many sins. After his death his heirs replaced this true portrait with one of Emperor Charles V. Rivera admits to being taken in by this hoax in earlier works but he assured his public that in his paintings they were seeing the true Cortés.

A reference is made to Cortés in a document found in Ixcateopan. It states that Hernando Cortés had no land, was short of stature, a hunchback, bow-legged and ugly. The two professors who examined his remains confirm this.

If Rivera is proved to be correct in his assumption on this occasion, having given the feature so much careful study, there is good reason to believe him when he shows us tiny little red/brown dogs with erect ears sitting on the doorstep of a house belonging to the Tarascan natives, and the many instances of the Mexican Hairless which he shows as several sizes bigger and always black. In the early history he shows them on the small side with erect ears, but in his painting of the Constitution of 1857 he shows the dogs again but with ears hanging down and much larger, but still seen to be hairless and with a very long muzzle. Anyone who can visit the murals and frescoes in the National Palace in Mexico City, where the President lives and from where the government is run, can see for themselves. In this way we can let Rivera look at the history books for us and decide what is to be believed.

In the Mexican National Museum of Anthropology can be seen pottery models of a tiny red dog exactly like the ones Rivera had depicted, but these are very, very old. No. 134 in the catalogue depicts a red dog in a reclining position—it is life-size and only $5\frac{1}{2}$ inches (14 cm) high. It is made of clay and was found at Colima. I was lucky enough to be able to obtain a present-day copy of a pottery dog of similar shape. It is very like that owned by Dr Waldher Christen, the German collector, and he has had his certified as being more than 500 years and possibly 2000 years old by Dr Dusselhoff, the Director of the Museum of Ethnology in Berlin. These dogs are not good replicas of the Chihuahua as we know it today, but there is no other dog it so nearly resembles, so we must accept the fact that even in early times—at least before the Spanish Conquest—there were at least two distinct types of dogs in Mexico—the hairless, which was castrated and used as food; and the tiny dog, too small to make much of a meal, which was a highly regarded pet and was killed to provide a guide through the underworld.

When I first acquired the pottery model of the Mexican dog I can't say anyone in my family was enamoured with it from an aesthetic point of view. My poodles were horrified by it and screamed at it in a high-pitched shriek so we usually put it on a high shelf where they couldn't see it. The Chihuahuas on the other hand sniffed at it, wagged their tails and accepted it as one of themselves. We believed that they decided the model was 'family' and so sacrosanct. This is a peculiarity that anyone who has only one Chihuahua won't know about. When I only had my first one, Driada, she lived with the poodles and thought she was a poodle until one day, when visiting the chemist, she saw herself in the mirror behind the shelves at the bottom of a showcase. She screamed with rage at the strange dog as she always did if we passed any dog other than a poodle. When we got home I made a point of showing her her reflection and after a time she became reconciled to it. Feeling sorry for her, I decided to get another Chihuahua and answered an advertisement from someone on the east coast, which meant a very long journey. We compromised by agreeing to meet on Waterloo Station, and not wanting to let anyone else have the opportunity of forestalling me as the breed was then so rare and so difficult to find, I set off there and then.

When the transaction had been concluded and we had refreshed ourselves with British Rail's pitiful style of refreshments, I found I was returning on the last train and would not arrive home until the early hours. I knew I would be in trouble, arriving home so late and waking my farmer husband who had to be up at 5 a.m., so when I did get home I was very worried by the reception my new Chihuahua would get from my other one who always made such a fuss when she met other breeds of dogs except poodles. My only way in was through the kitchen door as the front door was barred and bolted. I tried to hide Pepita, my new acquisition, but it was no use. Driada rushed to greet me and hurled herself against me so I had to put Pepita down in order to pick up Driada and stop her barking in excitement. I then expected her to make the most horrible din when she saw the stranger, but to my great surprise she simply walked round the stranger, sniffed at her gently, and after a few circling movements suddenly started to wag her tail and give the newcomer the most enthusiastic welcome. From that moment they were the best of friends and did everything together. That was the word for it, 'together'. She must have recognised her own breed and was obviously pleased to find it. They were fully adult but never had the slightest disagreement ever, and the way they sided together against the poodles, who hitherto had been Driada's constant companions, was very remarkable.

In no time at all they had the whole establishment working to their demands. The two of them teamed up and turned themselves into a two-man cattle-driving gang. Every morning, after milking and feeding, the seventy-strong herd of cows would be turned out of the milking parlour into an adjoining meadow and left there whilst the cow-men went home to breakfast. They would then lie down quietly to chew the cud and digest the recent meal. This did not suit the Chihuahuas at all and the moment they were let out of the house for their first 'outs' they would make a bee-line for the home-meadow and worry and pester the poor cows until they would get up on their feet for a bit of peace. The Chis would run round each cow, bark into its face quite fiercely and then chase one another round the cow so that it would get up and be ready to get out of that field as soon as possible. When they were all up on their feet the two little minxes would run back to the house, bark to be let in and then make an unholy noise while they boasted of their efforts. The other dogs we had never went near the cows unless we were with them. The Chihuahuas were born to be house pets, not workers, but they had got this idea or instinct from somewhere and carried out what they took to be their duty with the greatest determination every day from then on, unless they were confined in the nursery. Pepita only had one puppy in her lifetime and so the day came when we decided she could go as a house pet to a local admirer. Once she went away Driada stopped going to round up the cows. She never tried to get one of my other Chihuahuas to go with her even though she was the matriarch and we had many of her children, grandchildren and great-grandchildren, who were all capable of doing so if they had been encouraged, but she never did and none of the others ever took any notice of the cattle.

There is no doubt at all that we are dealing with a most unusual and amazingly intelligent animal who, right through the centuries, has been able to keep fairly pure-bred because of its very tiny size, making it well-nigh impossible for it to be bred to any larger breed. There is some suggestion that the mating of the Chihuahua with the Mexican Hairless might have produced the Chinese Crested— a breed of very small size, with no hair except for a flowing tail and crest of long silky hair. It is true that there is some ancestry behind the Chinese Crested which has hair because one of the breed's failings is to have litters of some hairless and some covered with hair to the extent that they are called 'puff balls'. Said to have originated in China, they have been bred in North America for many years—almost as long as the Chihuahua.

Maxwell Riddle would have us believe that the natives of Mesoamerica, which is a word to cover all the cultures of the part of the world now known as Mexico, and which in the days of the Conquistadors consisted of many different cities and cultures some of which were subjugated by the Aztecs and some which were not, had no knowledge of dogs.

The Olmec culture is linked with the origins of the Zapotecs and the Toltecs who, when they were driven from their first city, went to the Gulf Coast to the regions of the Olmecs who had been evolving south of Veracruz and north of Tabasco since 1500 B.C. Veracruz was the port where Cortés landed when he arrived to conquer Mexico and make it into 'New Spain'. In the Mexican National Museum of Anthropology can be seen toys made in the form of jaguars and dogs on wheels which were copied by other cultures right down through the ages. Mr Riddle says that the Mexicans were too primitive to know about the wheel, but the toys prove otherwise. The fact is that the Mexicans felt that as they worshipped the sun above all else, to depict the wheel in their everyday life would be a form of insult to their god, so they did without. The Mayas, who inhabited Mexico about the period 200 B.C. to 200 A.D., had whistles made in the form of lizards, jaguars, frogs, dogs, dolphins, squirrels, scorpions and snakes. They also did picture-writing and their codices were the *Dresden Codex*, which shows the equinoxes, the lunar seasons and solstices, and the *Tro-Cortesian Codex*, which shows their numbering system and astronomical observations and their calendar, including the *day of the dog*.

Cortés may have been a soldier and gold hunter above all, but Fray Bernardino de Sahagun (*c.* 1499–1590) was a scholar of remarkable ability and foresight who deplored the destruction of all that was best in the many civilisations that abounded in Mesoamerica. He learned their languages enough to be able to translate some of their codices, some of which he found after they had been hidden by the Indians and others which were remembered by the Indians and copied for him. He saw the need for understanding the vanquished people before replacing their lost religions with the Christian one, and when ancient buildings were torn down and new Spanish-type ones built over the sites he kept records of what had been before. He also made a full list of all the flora and fauna (including dogs) and saved many documents and objects to help future generations from forgetting Mexican lore and history completely.

His works, in which he records all he found during his long and close association with the country, are one of the best treatises in the world on the ethnology of the region.

Burial places have been revealed by modern development building and when the excavations were made for the underground railway in Mexico City a lot of the old architecture was revealed so well preserved that it has been possible to reassemble much of it. The wall-pictures show life in the old city and a student of history can follow any path he wishes in his own particular interests—in our case 'dogs'—and some very interesting discoveries have been made. When the wall-pictures are examined a very good idea of the life-style of their origin can be imagined. In one instance, instead of the usual method of incarcerating the dead in tombs or in vaults, with all the trappings of death included such as food, jewels, clothes, bows and arrows, and dogs for the journey through the vale of death, there can be seen another method which was to wrap the deceased in mats or blankets, tying them round and placing the bodies, either flexed or in an extended position, inside pits dug in the ground. The bodies were sprinkled with red paint or cinnabar and accompanied with offerings of food and personal objects for use in the hereafter and amongst them is a little red dog with his legs extended in the same way.

Other dog figures have been found in tombs of great antiquity, namely those at Colima (Catalogue No. 2 – 5447 in the Mexican National Museum of Anthropology).

Chichen Itza, in the Yucatán's peninsular, was the site of one of Mexico's largest pyramid masses, covering about six miles. In

1885 Edward Thompson, a vigorous young American Consul, purchased the whole of Chichen Itza from some Mayan Indians for seventy-five dollars and presided over his ancient empire for thirty-nine years. In 1904 he began exploration of one of the sacred cenotes to verify the legends of human sacrifices and, from the vast amount of skeletons he unearthed and the store-house of treasures and ritualistic offerings he recovered, he was able to fill displays in many museums in America and Mexico. He also revealed the colonnaded Great Market and the great Ball Court, and the Temple of Warriors, the walls of which are covered with pictures of animals, including dogs, as were the columns in the Group of a Thousand Columns. What happened to suddenly destroy this vast complex is unknown. Suggested causes are agricultural collapse, epidemic disease, earthquakes or an unbalanced sex ratio. It may just have been the arrival of the Conquistadors but in this instance their coming is not so evidenced as it is in other ruins where Christian churches were built to completely eradicate what was there before. A few natives stayed on, camping out in the rooms of forgotten palaces and when the invaders came they were able to retreat to the Caves of Balancanche, three miles east of Chichen Itza. These caves were uncovered in 1959 after being sealed up for hundreds of years. Inside were found ritual objects and a holy altar dedicated to Tlaloc, the Toltec god of rain. These were found just as they had been left by the priests and the worshippers.

More and more hidden ruins of the past are continually coming to light, so it is politic to keep an open mind about what dogs the natives of Mexico owned before the Conquest. That they were unacquainted with dogs as 'dogs' has been proved wrong. Montezuma II had a very well-stocked zoo of unusual animals which impressed even Cortés with the rarity of the beasts and the knowledge the Mexicans had of them. They had parrots, parakeets and macaws whose feathers they used in their head-dresses (quetzal); they knew the deer, rabbit and hare and had sporting hunts to catch them. They had giant lizards and turtles—they even had a temple to the turtles where sculptures of them adorned the walls (they knew both land and sea variety); they kept monkeys and used their skins for clothes and they also had turkeys and dogs which they kept right down through the ages. When the country was opened up with the coming of the railways and it was possible for travellers to explore the hitherto unknown areas of the country, it was a matter of great surprise to them to find that so many of the natives had domesticated dogs—not kept for food but as household pets and as rat-catchers. Rats were always great nuisances as they invaded the corn stores and such. Chihuahuas, although small, are excellent mouse-catchers as their reflexes are so quick—I would not put one to a rat as size for size they would not be equal opponents, but, no doubt, the natives finding rats in their corn would think otherwise.

I am indebted to Dr Michael Coe, Assistant Professor of Anthropology at Yale University, U.S.A., for the information about the 390 skeletons that were found in a burial ground in Chupicuaro, the complex which lay above the Lerna River in the state of Guanajuato, about eighty miles north-west of the Valley of Mexico. These skeletons belonged to the late formative period 300 B.C. to 300 A.D., a thousand years before the coming of the Aztecs to the City of Mexico. Almost all of these bodies had been laid on their backs in simple graves with abundant offerings of pottery figurines, jade, and various clay objects. The later Mexicans believed that the owner's dog would help his soul across their equivalent of the Styx, and we find at Chupicuaro that dogs were also interred, many of them with great care. Were these little dogs the ancestors of the Chihuahua found in Mexico today? Colonel and Mrs Hilary Harmar, when they searched for Chihuahuas all over Mexico in the 1950s, found more in the village of Valle de Allende than anywhere else. San Miguel de Allende is the present name for the district and where the State of Guanajuato is still to be found. The capital city of this state is also called Guanajuato: it has been declared a national monument and is a good place to excavate and investigate the background of the native dogs. People in these parts have Chihuahua dogs in every house and no one living can remember a time when there were none of these little dogs there. These dogs will be found to have all the idiosyncrasies of the Chihuahua breed—large round eyes, long backs, long claw-like nails, a molera in the head, and wide, flat, furry 'badger' tails. They are in all colours and are of a sturdier type than those found in Mexico City and farther south.

Dr Coe also elaborates on the clay figures of dogs found in Colima and Jalisco on the west coast. He affirms that the little pot-bellied dogs that these represent belong to the hairless breed that the Mexicans specially fattened for consumption by forced feeding, like Strasbourg geese.

Bernal Diaz, who accompanied Cortés when he invaded Mexico and fought alongside him, afterwards wrote the most complete and authentic report on what he saw personally and which is even more to be believed than that of Fray Bernardino de Sahagun. Diaz says that when Cortés landed at the Port of San Juan de Ultua on Holy Thursday 1519, two huge canoes arrived with Indians who had come to see what the strangers were seeking. When told that they wanted to trade for gold, the Indians returned a few days later, after Cortés and Diaz and their men had landed, and brought a golden disc like the sun, a silver disc like the moon with figures on it, a helmet full of gold ingots of very fine quality, twenty ducks made of gold and of very fine workmanship, some ornaments *in the shape of their native dogs* and many others in the shape of tigers, lions and monkeys. I print this to show those people who doubt that there actually were dogs in Mexico before the arrival of the Spanish. Diaz also wrote at length of the little hairless dogs that were found on market stalls.

An interesting fact about Bernal Diaz is that he took a grey-hound with him when he accompanied Cortés' predecessor on his exploration of Mexico. When the ship landed, the greyhound was sent off to hunt and was not found again until Diaz returned to Mexico with Cortés, which was quite some time later.

Proof of the presence of a different type of dog to the Mexican Hairless will be found in the *Codex Magliabecchiano*, the original of which is in Florence, Italy. This depicts a corpse of an important chieftain sitting upright with legs outstretched, the body wrapped with coloured blankets and winding sheets secured with cords. The corpse was further adorned with insignia made of paper and feathers (richer men were hung with jewellery). A little jade stone was placed in the mouth to placate the ravenous beasts of the Seventh Hell and *a little yellow dog was killed and laid across the knees of the bundle.*

I was fortunate enough to be able to examine the facsimile of this manuscript in the library of the Royal Anthropological Institute and it can be imagined with what eagerness I examined the full, coloured picture-writing contained in this priceless volume, namely *The Book of the Life of the Ancient Mexicans* (*Their Rites and Superstitions*) by Delia Nuttall, published by the University of

California, Berkeley, in 1903. This first part of Miss Nuttall's work, which was presented to the Institute by the Haddon Library, Cambridge, U.S.A., is in Spanish but has English explanations. Miss Nuttall made the discovery of this very important manuscript when researching American history in the Biblioteca Nationale Centrale, Florence, Italy, in 1890. The head of the library told her he had found a very old and important item amongst the collection, which was founded by Antonio Magliabecchi and presented by him to his native city of Florence. The manuscript has been in Florence since 1714 but had been known in Spain since 1601 where it was considered of paramount importance.

It was in 1601 that Emperor Charles V ordered Antonio de Herrera, the royal historian and chronicler, to publish his *Descripcion de las Indias Occidentales.* Some identical pictures of deities—i.e. those appearing on pages 32, 33, 34, 52, 53 and 61 of the Magliabecchi manuscript—were used in Herrera's work and, according to Miss Nuttall, who in her day was one of the world's leading experts on the subject, could not have been found in any other Mexican manuscript. Miss Nuttall brought to light this anonymous Hispano-Mexican manuscript and with the permission of the Italian government she was allowed to photograph and chromo-lithograph it—a most expensive business in those days and from which we are able to benefit with the picture I have been allowed to include in this work. Miss Nuttall's work was published by the Fund for Archaeological Research in Mexico and was placed at the disposal of the Department of Anthropology of the University of California by Mrs William Crocker and Mrs Whitelaw-Reid. To Chihuahua enthusiasts this find is of tremendous importance as it proves, without any doubt, that the so-called fantasies of the early breeders' imaginings were based on fact.

On the frontispiece of Herrera's work is the picture of one of the Pulque gods and there is a picture of a dog with large ears, big eyes and a long furry tail. The mouth is open and you can see the teeth and a long red tongue sticking out—this makes it a dog and not a squirrel.

This picture is in Miss Nuttall's book and she states that there can be no doubt that the drawings in the manuscript were done by a Mexican whose work is characterised by an exceptionally clear execution of outline and detail and a perfect familiarity with the conventionalism of native art.

Emperor Maximilian, the ill-fated Hapsburg prince who was sent to rule Mexico by the French rulers of that time, Napoleon III and his wife Eugénie, lived in a palace called Chapultepec which stood in Mexico City. He and his Belgian wife Carlotta had their home full of little Mexican dogs of all colours. Maximilian was imprisoned by Juarez and Carlotta returned to Europe to try to get help for him—soldiers to help him put down the rebellion. Unfortunately, before she could return Maximilian met his death before a firing squad and Carlotta, already deranged, never saw her husband or her little dogs again. Visitors to her court had been charmed by these little dogs. The Emperor and Empress had found them in the park of the royal palace when they arrived and they bred them at their country house at Cuernavaca. These dogs were also found in most of the presidential palaces.

It has been proved that all through the centuries tiny dogs were an essential adjunct to the household in most of the regions of the Allende Valley. Some Indians of the poorer type also clung to the old religious beliefs of the dog guiding their dead through the 'Styx', and although they prayed at the altars in Christian churches, they never lost sight of the fact that every Christian church was built on top of their old religious places, and that in many cases their dead ancestors were buried beneath them in the Aztec sites and in the even older Mayan sites. The invaders had hoped to completely obliterate the early Mexican places of worship, but the Indians were mostly illiterate and could not understand the Spanish let alone the Latin in which the Christian services were carried out. The old Mexican religion, which was partly Mayan, partly Toltec and adopted and injected with the vile cruelty of the Aztecs, was so harsh that it demanded daily human sacrifices to placate the gods Huichilobus and Tezcatlipoca whom the Aztecs believed would prevent the sun from rising and make their daily life impossible. Even after his capture and imprisonment by Cortés, the mighty king of the Aztecs Montezuma II refused to stop sacrificing human life and had the still-beating hearts that had been cut out of the chests of the sacrificial victims offered up to his ghastly gods. In the end, Cortés' priests built a Christian altar with the Cross above it in the same hall as the blood sacrifices were performed in the hope that the Indians would be converted to Christianity as the preferable of the two religions.

When human victims were in short supply, their little house-dogs were slaughtered instead. This practice continued even after the Spanish Conquest, much to the distress of Diego Muñoz Carmargo who, at the end of the sixteenth century, found Indians still sacrificing to the god Thaloc and took the matter up with the authorities to have this error extirpated. This information is contained in Jacques Soustelle's book *The Daily Life of the Aztecs*, which was published in French in Paris in 1955. He quotes from the *Mendoza Codex*, of which a copy, edited by James Cooper Clark in 1938 and published by Waterlow & Sons, London, is in the Bodleian Library. This codex was originally made of deerskin and took the form of long strips folded like a concertina and painted in the most vivid colours—the Aztecs being experts at making dyes from the plants and substances they had around them. The codex we are concerned with in this instance was drawn up by native scribes at the command of the Viceroy Antonio de Mendoza (1535–1550). He sent it with other treasures to the Emperor Charles V. On the way to Spain the ship was seized by a French privateer and so the precious *Mendoza Codex* came into the possession of André Theret, the leading French cosmographer. Mentioned in this codex is the Aztec calendar with a day dedicated to the dog-god 'Xolotl'.

Orozoco y Berra describes the Aztec dogs in his *Historia Antigua y de la Conquisto de Mexico*, and Charles Gallenkamp, an exceptionally well-qualified anthropologist at the University of New Mexico, has researched extensively in Mexico and is a member of the Mayan Research Fund, a research associate of the Instituto Interamericano, and adviser to the Department of Anthropology of the Houston Museum of National History, Texas. Mr Gallenkamp attempts to show how early man of the Pleistocene geological period first arrived on the American continent during the Ice Age. He tells us that by the seventh century A.D., the Indians had cultivated at least twenty different food-bearing plants. They had discovered ceramics and gold, *and had domesticated the dog*. They also kept turkey, llama, alpaca, ducks and bees. The number of ruined cities attests to Herculean feats of construction—tons of granite placed in position on a scale of building so massive that it defies the imagination. Temples, fortresses, houses, and even palaces point to the flourishing culture that can be traced back to pre-Columbian times.

In the sixteenth century, Father Joseph De Acosta, a very learned man and a member of the Council of the Indies, questioned some of the surviving Conquistadors about dogs. In his *Natural and Moral History of the Indies*, published in 1590, we read :

'Dogges have so multiplied in numbers and bignes that they are to this day the scourge and affliction of the Land for they eat the sheepe and go in troupes through the fields. Such that kill them are rewarded like to them that kill wolves in Spain. At the first there were no dogges in the Indies except some little dogges called 'Alco'. The Indians do so love these little dogges that they will spare their meate to feed them, so, as when they travel in the countrie they carry them with them upon their shoulders or in their besomes, and when they are sicke they keep them with them, without any use, but, only for company.'

Montezuma and his people loved their dogs and even sacrificed slave boys to feed them. The more pampered of these little dogs—especially those belonging to Montezuma's sister—were fed only on the minced testicles of these boys. It would seem to be the depth of degradation except for the fact that some sacrifice or other was made every single day in order that the moon would follow the sun in the correct order, and the dogs would act as vultures cleaning up the mess.

Not all the people of Mexico were conquered by Cortés and the ones that escaped hid in the barren hills of the north where, even today, few people have ever penetrated. This is where some of the dogs were hidden and because of their extremely tiny size making it well nigh impossible for a larger breed to mate with it, the breed was kept fairly pure. Because their religion demanded it, the dog was bred and kept for use in the burial of the dead for, as the Spanish priests had not been able to reach them with the word of God, the natives continued in the pagan ways of their forebears and carried on as they had for centuries. Even today these beliefs are still a part of life for some of these Indians hidden away in the hard-to-reach safety of their mountain homes.

Very little was ever heard about the breed outside Mexico, but at the end of the nineteenth century the celebrated opera singer, Madame Adelina Patti, was making a tour of Mexico and was entertained to a banquet by the president of that time, General Porfirio Diaz. General Diaz presented Madame Patti with an enormous bouquet of dahlias, a flower of Mexican origin, and in the centre was a tiny male Chihuahua, again originating in Mexico. Madame Patti soon learned how delightful it was to own such a tiny gem of a dog. She travelled the world and took Bonito with her. Bonito was black and tan and he was such an amazing little character that everywhere the famous singer travelled her pet got nearly as much attention as she did. When Bonito died after a long, adventurous life, Madame Adelina had great difficulty finding a replacement for him. Nothing would do but another Chihuahua, for this famous lady was never to be without one for the remainder of her life, and eventually she obtained Rigi, a fawn. Madame Patti always told admirers of her Chihuahuas the story of their origin as told her by General Diaz, which was that they were descended from dogs owned by the Toltecs who did not kill them for food or for sacrificial purposes. When the Aztecs drove the Toltecs out of Tenochtitlan, the Toltecs sought haven in the city of Cholula and they took with them their possessions and household animals, including dogs, birds, etc.

CHAPTER 2

The Chihuahua in America

Because of great difficulty with the terrain, it was a long time before a railway was constructed in Mexico. The British-owned Mexican Railway Co. at last managed to complete the railway they had started in 1872. In 1880–81 a track of seven hundred miles was completed. By 1911 this was extended to twelve thousand miles and there were seven points of entry into the U.S.A. Trade increased from 699,000 tons to 1,620,000 tons and this brought many rich and other not-so-rich Americans rushing to the Mexican border either to trade or to take their holidays touring the otherwise impregnable mountainous forests and deserts of the Sierras.

Many tourists took home stories of how they had seen very tiny dogs running about the wide open desert country. There were tales that these little 'dogs' lived in snake-holes in the greatest amity with the snakes. When the trains were stopped or going very quietly it was thought that the barking of these little animals could be heard. The fact of their existence became known far and wide and many people set out to try to find the little animals that had been seen from the trains in order to take them home and try to make pets of them. Many years later, however, it was proved without any doubt that the little animals seen from the trains were actually small rodents similar to the fennecs of the North African desert, which with their large ears and funny barking kind of voice could easily have become mixed in people's minds.

One group of travellers left the railway and continued their journey on horseback. In a ruined building they found some peons of a very poor type who had some very tiny dogs which they were carrying about and feeding on their own meagre rations. The Americans found themselves more interested in the dogs than the ruins and after only a very short bargaining session they managed to persuade the Indians to sell their pets. Returning home, they had great difficulty keeping these little creatures alive as they were very thin, undernourished and very subject to colds and chills.

36

When they died, as they did only too soon, their frantic owners went back to Mexico at the first opportunity to replace their rare and delicate little dogs.

After a time it became the habit of certain American dog-lovers living near the border to organise trips across in order to look for more little dogs. This fact was not lost on the Indians, who collected specimens and stood around at most of the railway terminals proffering their tiny merchandise. They soon realised too, that the tinier the dogs were the more attractive they were to the buyers and many a tiny puppy was passed over as a fully grown one. In time, however, the buyers became more choosy and the Indians set about breeding their dogs from the smallest stock possible with the result that some of them grew to be only one or two pounds at maturity.

In 1888, one of the passengers on a train to El Paso was Mr James Watson, the eminent American dog judge and fancier, who was on his first judging trip to the west coast from his home in Philadelphia on the east coast. He was only intending to cross the Mexican border in order to boast that he had been into Mexico, but while there he spotted a Mexican standing with a very small dog in his hand. He used his small amount of Spanish to ask the cost, which he learnt would be five dollars. As he was taking out the money to pay, another man rushed up saying that he could speak English. He told Watson that the Mexican would take three dollars, which he did. Watson said afterwards that the purchase rankled on his conscience for many years until, eventually, he confided in a 'doggy' Father of the church, who told him he was justified in paying the three dollars. Watson said that he had never seen anything like this little Manzanita, as she was named. Her coat was like beaver fur, both as to colour and texture, and she was so small that he carried her in his coat pocket till he got to Los Angeles where he bought the smallest size chip basket, in which she had plenty of room. A boy at the San Francisco show exclaimed at the sight of her : 'Oh, an Arizona dog', and a gentleman in Germanstown stopped Watson one day and said he had not seen one of these dogs since he had been in Arizona a few years ago. When Manzanita (the name means a shrub met with in the Sierras which in addition to its grey foliage and light red bark is remarkable for its toughness) died, Watson missed her so much that he tried all ways to get some other specimen from Arizona. However, it was not until he was able to return to Mexico that he found another little dog. He first tried Santa Fe, but without success. He moved on to El Paso where he had been lucky before and sure enough he was able to pick up several—in fact half a dozen of various types—one was a terrier type which he named Juarez Belle and which later became a champion. She was pure white and beautifully built, having perfect feet and forelegs; others had shorter legs and longer bodies. Then he got a litter of three—all black and white and all varying in coat, one smooth, one furry and one with a sort of Maltese coat. From another litter he found a very small dog of liver and white colour. Most of these dogs, however, succumbed to the cold of the winter. (I can vouch for the intense cold of the Philadelphia winter, having been snowed in there for five weeks. With central heating and television it was quite comfortable but before such heating it would have been difficult to rear such tiny dogs.)

Watson had to make a return trip to the south and he visited El Paso and Juarez. Finally, he succeeded in obtaining the best example of the breed he had ever seen—a small, smooth-coated dog of seven months of age, weighing less than sixteen ounces on the drug-store scales. This little dog was all white except for a black spot at the root of the tail. Again misfortune struck, for Watson lost this little dog while carrying it about in a basket in Philadelphia. He put the basket down for a moment while paying some business calls and that was the last he saw of his best Chihuahua.

James Watson was an author as well as a judge and in 1914 he wrote an article entitled 'The Chihuahua Dog' which was published in *Country Life in America*. He is also reputed to have written an article on the breed in the Kennel Register for May 1888 which was merely signed 'J.W.'.

Although he had this much experience of Chihuahuas, Watson does not seem to be really conversant with them as he makes no mention of them at all in his mammoth work *The Dog Book* which is, or was, considered the standard work on the subject of dogs as it was the first one to be published in America. According to Maxwell Riddle, Watson was a 'hard-head'—he read many stories that were being concocted about the origin of many dog breeds and exploded them. He found out how many dog breeds had been developed, he traced their course better than any writer had ever done, but he never mentioned the Chihuahua in his two-volume book which was published in 1906. Watson always looked for the molera in order to prove the origin of the Chihuahuas he bought, and although they may have been of various coats, colours, sizes and types, they *all* had the 'hole in the head'.

The first Chihuahua to be registered in America was called 'Midget', bred and owned by H. Raynor of El Paso, Texas. Midget was born in 1903 by Pluto out of Blanca and registered in 1904. Raynor registered four more Chihuahuas that year and J. M. Lee of Los Angeles, California, registered one.

The American Kennel Club's correspondence on recognising the new breed has been lost but the records are there to show that the first American Champion was Beppie, owned by Mrs L. A. McLean of Hackensack, New Jersey. Beppie was from a litter sired by Bonito, a litter mate of Midget, the first registered Chihuahua. Another early champion was James Watson's bitch Juarez Belle, which he called a 'terrier type'. Doubtless because of their extreme delicacy there were only a few records of Chihuahuas in the twenty years that followed. There were other toy breeds that were extremely popular, but the Chihuahua seemed to lack promoters and there was no clear standard or blue-print available, probably through lack of knowledge.

We must wait until 1923 to see the breed arrive properly with the organisation of the Chihuahua Club of America. From that time, progress has been rapid and today the Chihuahua is among the 'Top Ten' in registration with the American Kennel Club. Mr Riddle has calculated that some 2500 Chihuahua puppies are born in America each month.

Luckily, the Club was able to formulate a standard and since that time all the Chihuahua clubs in the world have based their own breed description on that first American one.

A most noted sire in the breed and the first one to really make an impression on his offspring was called Caranza. He was owned by the partnership of Wister and Stewart and had been obtained in Mexico early in the nineteen-hundreds when Owen Wister, author of *The Virginian* of television fame, and in those days well known for his writing and painting, was on a visit to Mexico with his companion Charles Stewart to obtain local colour for his books and painting. In a very mountainous area they found some Chihuahuas and were fascinated by them. They spent a lot of time searching for these little dogs with a view to breeding them as a hobby on their return to Philadelphia. It is possible that they knew James Watson as they both hailed from the same state, but whatever the reason there is no doubt that they gave careful study to the breed and ended by purchasing Caranza and quite a few others. Their plan must have been successful, and on their return they sorted out the dogs between them—Charles Stewart, who lived with his wife on the Wister estate, was given the inferior ones, while Wister kept Caranza as a pet and 'chief' of the Chihuahuas in his own beautiful home.

Mrs Ida Garrett, one of the founder members of the Chihuahua Club of America, of which Charles Stewart was another, visited the Wister-Stewart Kennels and was most impressed with Caranza. She describes him in detail as follows:

Caranza was about $2\frac{1}{2}$ or 3 lbs, of a dark, fiery red, a long-haired dog, his tail like that of a squirrel. His head was perfect by the Standard we have today. His eyes were ruby red, ears fringed not unlike those of the Papillon. He was a 'Ducky' type—shorter on the legs than length of back. I think he was the most loving and beautiful creature in dog flesh I ever saw.

Caranza met his death in a most tragic way after he had started one of the finest strains of Chihuahuas in the world. A great oak tree had been felled by a terrible storm and was left lying in the Wister estate. The little dog worked his way through the branches to the trunk of the tree towards the upturned roots. To his half-blind Great Dane friend he must have looked much like a squirrel, for he grabbed Caranza and killed him. The tragedy must have upset the Dane for he also died soon afterwards.

It was fortunate that Caranza's fame had been spread about and that he had already been used by most of the leading breeders who all agreed with Mrs Garrett that he was a perfect specimen.

A Mrs Ann Radcliffe bought a dog from the Wister-Stewart partnership. She registered him with the Kennel Club as Meron. He was a close-coated fawn with creamy under parts to his body. He had no pedigree but was by Caranza, who in turn was by Duke out of Deano. Mrs Radcliffe registered the first Little Meron on his wins and made him a champion. He in turn sired Ch. Little Meron III bred by Mrs H. Diehl of San Antonio, Texas, out of an imported dam, Lady Goldie (ex Dona Mignon by Don Oro).

Mrs Garrett bought Little Meron III for a price well in the hundreds of dollars and made him a champion in three straight shows, registering him on his ten point wins. This outstanding Meron was very much like his sire but better in type, sturdier and darker in colour. Many superb champions are among his grandsons and granddaughters and their progeny. It is believed that the Merons have contributed more of the best type of Chihuahua to the breed than all the other families put together.

The Wister and Stewart partnership did not register their dogs as they did not believe in it, but after Mrs Radcliffe registered her first purchase from them they changed their minds.

At the Chihuahua Specialty Show in Chicago in 1935 sixteen champions entered the ring to compete for Best of Breed and every one of them was a Meron, sons or grandsons of Ch. Little Meron, a four-pound Best of Breed winner then nearly five years old.

There are still some breeders who refuse to acknowledge the long-coated Chihuahua as a pure bred, but it is an established fact that the Merons throw more long coats than any other strain and the Merons remain the foundation strain of the breed. (This I can vouch for as the first dog I imported from the United States, Emmrill Son-ko's Red Rocket, was of very strong Meron lines and when he was mated to his smooth-coat daughter out of a smooth-coat mother from a strain that had never before produced a long coat, I had a very beautiful long-coat bitch who was the dam of my first long-coat champion, Champion Emmrill Fudge, said by the judges who wrote about him to have had the perfect head.)

Another famous strain, the Perritos, was also responsible for some more great Chihuahuas. The first Perrito was purchased in Mexico by Dr Speare of the U.S. Navy at the cost of a few hundred dollars in gold, but his sire and dam passed to an American family for six hundred dollars in gold when he was well into middle life. A Mrs Atwood, a Mexican lady living in New York, paid one thousand five hundred dollars for her Chola, and a Col. Baynor, living in Texas, wanted to buy Mrs Garrett's Juanita for five hundred dollars. A big change from the three dollars James Watson paid for his first one.

After making him a champion Mrs Ann Radcliffe sold Little Meron to Mrs H. Diehl of Texas. From Mrs Garrett, Mrs Diehl purchased a daughter of Perrito II, whose dam, Champion Sonora, was a Caranza granddaughter and was bred by the Wister-

Stewarts. Out of this Perrito bitch mated to Ch. Little Meron, Mrs Diehl produced a litter of five small, lovely puppies correct in head and body conformation, three of which were smooth coated and two long haired. The best smooth was secured by Mr Paul Mourmans which helped him to found his kennel of Miniatura. Paul Mourmans was a rather poor musician who did not enjoy very good health. Through the help of Mrs Garrett and a vet in New Orleans he was able to breed some outstanding examples in Ch. Little Pipo and Little Litina of Miniatura, and a Miniatura in the background of any pedigree is a sign of the highest possible quality.

Mrs Ida Garrett was a journalist as well as a breeder and we are indebted to her for her very informative books and literature on the breed which are the source of these paragraphs. Ch. Lady Vita was imported by Mrs Garrett and mated with her El Capitan to produce some of her best Chihuahuas. With her famous Perrito II she founded a line that was second to none. Perrito II was a tiny dog, not over two pounds in weight and lemon in colour; he lived for only eight years and sired twelve litters each of four puppies. He was born in 1920 and headed a list of eleven Perritos registered over a period of seven years. Perrito VI sired the famous Ch. Si-Si Oro Principe in 1930, possibly the last to be registered by a Perrito sire of direct descent. Perrito X and his son El Feljo should both have had their day on the bench, according to Mrs Garrett who declared them to be two of the best of their day or the present. Perrito X was a three-pound salmon-coloured dog with ruby eyes.

In the same period, early 1920s, Mrs Bertha Peaster of Phila-delphia started the La Rex Doll strain with Sonora, a three-pound bitch purchased from Wister-Stewart. Mated to Mrs Atwood's imported Chiquelo, Sonora produced five puppies. The bitches were retained as foundation dams for this famous strain. A male out of this litter, Peaster's Little Chiquelo, was bred to Mrs Alling's Chi Tanta Royal and produced that grand little sensation of the show benches, Ch. Peaster's Little Pedro, a solid fawn weighing about a pound and a half. Little Pedro is the sire of many La Rex Doll Chihuahuas and he and Ch. Little Meron III have probably sired more than any other males in the breed. Ch. Peaster's Little Conchita was mated to Candy Kid, one of the best type, according to Mrs Garrett, both his parents being imported from Mexico. From this mating came La Rex Doll Donna Ana, found in so many of the best pedigrees of latter day. Mrs Peaster also owned a strain from a male called Slim imported from Mexico by Dr Speare, and when this dog was mated into the Meron line some of the very finest type were produced.

Mention of the Chihuahuas of Texas recalls Mrs M. E. Hood with her very good strain and also the Attas line.

In the early 1930s many new strains appeared. Three famous ones were: the La Oro line, bred from Meron; and Perrito and Miniatura stock, which were mentioned above. The La Oros were bred by Mrs Anna B. Vinyard who was known by many of us from her trips abroad where she showed her dogs fearlessly in all the countries she was able to do so except, of course, Britain where the quarantine restrictions kept her away. The most famous of the La Oro strain was Ch. Si-Si Oro Principe who was born 20th March 1930 in Mrs Vinyard's kennels in Cincinnati, Ohio. He was by Perrito VI ex Aieda A and he in turn sired eleven champions —an amazing record for a period when there were far fewer dog shows in America than there are today and air travel had not become a popular mode of getting from place to place. Si-Si is credited with possessing most of the good qualities—from his Meron great-grandsire he got his full, typy head and true Chihuahua expression, from the Perrito line he got his aggressiveness and excellent showmanship and from Ch. Villa and Ch. Chiquito his other great-grandsires he got the other qualities which gave him his greatness.

By combining all these strains in the way she did, Mrs Vinyard called a halt to the development of great single-family strains as they had been, but Si-Si himself sired Ch. Bebita de Oro Gitanilla, which translated means 'gold baby of gypsy girl'. In 1937, this bitch was placed second best American-Bred Toy in the United States after only three months of showing. She held the record for winning the largest toy group in Chicago that same year and also the next six straight groups in which she was shown. Under the American methods of making champions it is not as difficult to qualify as it is in Britain, but to win groups in this way shows that she must have been something quite outstanding for she would have had to compete against every other toy Best of Breed.

About this time, Mrs Evelyn Brush acquired Sneath's Chiquito and commenced her strain of Don Rubio Chihuahuas. Sneath's Chiquito was a splashed black, white and seal, with a slender, long body and was a wonderful sire. Ch. Brush's Don Rubio was registered on his many California wins and for many years was known as the Chihuahua that had won more trophies than any other show dog, until the advent of the late Ch. Meronette Grudier. Rubio was by Juano ex Teracina by Tommy Tucker and out of Merilla (ex Salamanda by Bab's Bobo). Rubio was red fawn, of medium size, with a good head and ears, rather long legs and very aggressive. He is the foundation stud of a long line of solid reds, many of which are more typy than their famous ancestor. To influence colour in this way is a most desired quality as it is almost impossible, even in these days, to know what colour any litter will be even if bred from two or three generations of one colour. Only black and tans seem to have this quality.

No record of famous American dogs would be complete without mention of Don Apache. He himself was far from a show type, being large and six pounds in weight, but he possessed very large expressive eyes, a broad head and unusually large flaring ears, and these good features he consistently transmitted to his 'get'. An abundant ruff, furry tail and heavy coat are also features of Don Apache's strain. He was out of Perrita Cherry Blossom and sired by a son of Si-Si, Ch. Oro De Lay, a pure Perrito. When crossed with the progeny of Little Meron IV exceptionally fine stock has appeared, such as Ch. Meronette Grudier, whose record of wins has seldom been topped, and her twin sister Ch. Meronella Grudier, another of quite outstanding quality.

The Perralto line also owes some of its quality to the Perritos. Top stud for many years was Perralto out of Mattalee (ex Maritza by Ch. Chum of Fleurette) and sired by the famous El Feljo (ex Mitta Mira by Ch. Perrito X). Montoyo II and Poncho Villa Cola passed on for their breeder Mrs Mayme Cole-Holmes the Perralto type and characteristics which include fine domed heads, cobby bodies and diminutive size.

One of the most important breeding policies, which resulted in the founding of a pure long-coated strain, was that of the Don Sergios which was started in the early 1930s with the mating of a bitch named Quita, owned by Miss Sarah Holland of Duxbury, Massachusetts, to Mrs. L. Palmer's fine little apricot stud El Feljo. This mating produced the first Don Sergio, a white and chocolate marked long coat who never grew more than three pounds in weight. He possessed a truly wonderful head, ruby eyes, large fringed ears and a beautiful plumed tail. He was acquired by a Mr and Mrs John T. Kinsman of Chicago and Boca Raton, Florida, when he was about a year old. He had sired a few puppies in his original home but was not used again for six years as he had been bought as a pet. Luckily, among the stock he had already sired were five champion long coats, two of which were show stoppers. One of these, Sela Donna, bred by Mrs Kinsman's sister, Mrs McCoy, was a flyer, winning nine straight shows including an International. The other, Ch. Don Sergio of Boca Raton, won the highest award offered by the Chihuahua Club of America—the trophy for most Best of Breed wins. In 1930 a bitch named Cheateau was bought by a Mr Louis Weitz of Chicago from a native breeder of long coats in Columbia who in turn had got her from a breeder in Brazil. She was the only Chihuahua of this blood in the United States except for her own stock. Cheateau was mated with Don Sergio and produced Donna Anita, who in turn was mated back to her sire and produced Brazilian Brown Chiquita, who again was mated back to her sire and grandsire to produce the lovely Ch. Brazilian Brown Joy in 1939. This cross with Brazilian blood greatly strengthened and beautified the strain which remains, even today, the only absolutely pure long-coat line of Chihuahuas.

CHAPTER 3

The Chihuahua Arrives in Britain

We know that Madame Adelina Patti brought her little Bonito to England. Bonito was the black and tan Chihuahua dog which President Porfirio Diaz had presented to her in a bouquet of dahlias in 1900, and this was one of the early arrivals of the breed in this country.

At the turn of the century, a Mr Rentoul Symon imported a little dog called Chadro who was fawn with pale points and grew to be four pounds. He was acquired by Mrs Lilburn MacEwan and had big round eyes, large flared ears and was a very typical specimen.

People wanted the very tiny ones such as a twenty-three ounce bitch that was greatly admired. Captain Mayne Reid, who had studied the breed in Mexico, considered that the tiniest of all were the greatest prized in the Mexican capital. He decided that if any were taken away from their natural environment and bred in another part of the world the progeny would increase in size and bulk and become, as the Mexicans said, 'degenerado'. Captain Mayne Reid thought it possible that the climate and soil of Mexico had something to do with this—it was supposed that the high table-lands of Chihuahua could have an effect on growth, and many thought it was impossible to maintain the small size for many generations away from that barren, bleak country.

Lady Fairbairn imported Feo, a tiny white dog with black patches on his head, and the Hon. Mrs Bourke also had a tiny one but of a delicate fawn colour. A favoured colour at the turn of the century was blue with tan markings, but as for size, the smaller the better was really the criterion in those days.

In 1904, Miss Rosina Casselli wrote an article on Chihuahuas in the August 6th issue of *Our Dogs*. This was the first information many of the dog public had had and, even if some of her assumptions are far-fetched and fantastic, she was able to throw some light on many aspects of the breed that had hitherto been unknown. Miss Casselli had a performing troupe of tiny Chihuahuas which

she had trained. Her Chihuahuas brought her and the breed much
acclaim and made a lot of people conversant with them who otherwise would have been ignorant of the existence of such a tiny and
charming breed. Her words, however, must be read with an open
mind as she makes statements with which the author cannot agree
and which later knowledge disclaims. She says:

> Regarding the Chihuahua dogs I am in a position to be well
> posted. Of all the canine breeds these are probably the least
> known or understood. These little dogs of Mexico, which were
> in their natural state a distinctly wild race of dogs, are very
> shy, and, for their size, very savage.
>
> They inhabit only a limited section of the mountainous state
> of Chihuahua, from which the dogs derive their name. It is
> believed that these wild dogs are now extinct although they
> are reported by the natives to have been seen up to about
> fifteen years ago and it is barely possible that they might still
> be found in some undisturbed spot.
>
> These dogs were noted, not only for their extreme smallness,
> but other peculiarities which they possess.
>
> Their legs were very slender and their toe-nails very long
> and strong and very serviceable to them in making their homes
> as they lived in holes in the ground. Apart from their size their
> most striking feature was their head, which was very round
> and from which projected a very short and pointed nose and
> large standing ears. There was also a peculiar skull formation,
> found only in this race. In colour they varied somewhat in
> shade, it was a thorough mixture of reddish black and fawn in
> which both vary considerably in different specimens. The hair
> was short, fine and thick and the wild dogs, even when taken
> young, could not be domesticated neither would they live any
> great length of time in captivity.
>
> The Indians, however, had a way of taking these dogs and
> crossing them with the small specimen of the domesticated
> Indian dog, and, in this manner produced a domesticated
> Chihuahua dog which was kept replenished from the wild
> stock as much as possible. Although the type was to a certain
> extent modified and varied, the finer specimens retain it in a
> most prominent way. Until the opening up of the Mexican
> Central Railroad in about the year 1887, and which passes

through the section in which the wild dogs were most plentiful, there were plenty of fine specimens to be had, as prior to this time this section was difficult to reach being in a wild country hundreds of miles from so-called civilisation. The completion of the road, however, brought hordes of tourists and others who rapidly thinned out the dogs and scattered them in all directions, with the final result that today it is a piece of good luck to secure a really fine specimen.

Although the wild stock is no longer available, the type is so fixed that very fine specimens still crop up here and there but there is no certainty when or where such stock can be found, as the natives, although they reaped a rich harvest for a time, failed to provide for the future as they, with their experience, might have done. I have often been asked why it was that the breed has not been taken in hand by fancy dog breeders. My answer to this is that it was not for want of effort or interest, but failure to get genuine specimens the real cause. There are many difficulties in the way. In the first place they are very difficult to breed and a thorough understanding of these dogs in particular must be had. Without experience of them, breeding is a most difficult matter, as the chances are all on the side that the mother would die in giving birth to her litter and, even if she survives the ordeal, she is likely to destroy her young and for a time precautions must be used to prevent this.

Again the Chihuahua dogs are very exclusive in their affections and, as a rule, will choose a favourite among those that care for them and become extremely attached and, once such an attachment is formed it is very difficult to break off, and to turn them over to strangers is apt to be a fatal process. When procured at a proper age they are apt to be made a great deal of and spoiled, for they are very affectionate and demand all sorts of attention. If they don't get it they will pout and mope around for hours and seem to try to make their bodily suffering equal to their mental by hiding in the coldest and draughtiest spots they can find. Neglect of attention soon tells on them and it is that more than anything else that has produced the very general idea that these dogs can't exist out of their native climate. Such, however, is not the case, as they can stand any climate and are strongly constituted. I have never known one to have distemper. Both my Brazilian dogs had it and I lost one, and just got the other through by a miracle.

The Chihuahua dogs slept in the small box with these for nearly three weeks before we knew what was the matter and not one of them got a touch of it. No one should acquire a Chihuahua dog unless inclined to pander to their whims and notions and intend to continue to do so. Dog trainers are almost united in their belief that small dogs are useless as performing dogs, but those who have seen my troupe perform must of necessity alter their opinion and admit that the Chihuahua dogs are marvels of intelligence.

I knew Miss Viva Montgomerie who told me that she was born in 1879 and had been interested in dogs, especially Chihuahuas, all her life. She died in 1959 so was able to see the breed develop. She had travelled in America and saw her first Chihuahuas at a dog show in New Jersey. She was told that the breed lived in snake holes in the desert and dwelt side by side with the snakes quite amicably. She was also told that they could climb trees and she was always most concerned if she saw Chihuahuas with the dew claws removed as she felt this would stop them being able to climb. The prices the owners put on their dogs were so high that she was afraid to try to buy one, but she was very delighted to receive a couple as presents soon after she got back to this country. She did not receive pedigree stock but was able to breed several litters from her pair and she gave one puppy to a cousin who lived in Heckfield, the next village to Hartley Wintney where I lived for twenty-three years. Our parish magazine once ran a feature on the history of the parishes of Heckfield and Mattingley and everybody started searching through old letters and family papers. One lady unearthed a book written by her aunt which was about the Chihuahuas that she had owned in her youth. I couldn't find out if one of these Chihuahuas could have come from Miss Montgomerie as she was dead by this time, but the book contained stories of the delightful little dogs that had run about Heckfield during Edwardian times.

Viva Montgomerie also gave a Chihuahua to a relation who lived in Suffolk. This dog was called Tric for it was a tricolour and, although rather on the large side for some people's fancy, he was a most devoted and intelligent pet and never left his owner's side, in fact he was found on her bed when she died. A new home was found for him and he settled down quite amicably. But one day, during some very stormy weather, he got outdoors and disappeared and could not be found anywhere. Great was the consternation at his disappearance for he had made himself much liked in his new home and his owner was intensely aware of how coddled he had been for he had always snuggled into the rugs and covers of his first mistress's bed. To everyone's great joy and relief he was found quite safe and apparently sound in the kennel of a big dog who had shared his food and shelter with him. Tric was seen following this dog by a woman who thought he was too small to be out in such weather, so she took him home with her until the police informed the owner of his whereabouts. The owner then took him home with her and he lived to be eighteen. She always claimed that Chihuahuas were very tough and hardy if allowed to lead outdoor, sporting lives as hers did. Sometimes some of her Chihuahuas would go off hunting and disappear down rabbit holes and often had to be dug out just like terriers.

In 1904, Lady Violet Thesiger brought a tiny little bitch out of Mexico as a present for Lady Hillingdon, whose two sisters also had Chihuahuas.

The Hon. Mrs Gwendoline Bourke was visiting a dog dealer in 1897 when she found a tiny little cream bitch who climbed on her lap as though to beg her to take her away. She was about three and a half pounds in weight and Mrs Bourke bought her for £3 but neither she nor the dealer knew what kind of breed it was. Later, she saw the same breed at a Henley dog show and realised that she had a Chihuahua. One evening, while the family were playing croquet, the little dog was sitting in her basket at the end of the lawn. When the game was over they went to collect the dog but found she had disappeared. That night they found her body drowned in a fish-pond. Later, Mrs Bourke received a tiny black and tan from Lady Adele Essex who had brought three over from Mexico. However, this little creature's bulgy eyes did not appeal, and she gave her away to her cook who loved her dearly.

Many people who visited Mexico were fascinated by the tiny dogs and some brought them home smuggled in bags or muffs. Many died because they were not kept warm enough, others survived but were not recorded in any way except in fond memory by their owners.

Several noted dog authorities, including Mr Croxton-Smith and Mr Will Hally, wrote about the breed in well-known publications—Mr Croxton-Smith wrote in the *Sporting News* and Will Hally in *Our Dogs*. Will Hally wrote that Miss Lovett of the Leysfield Kennels had a Chihuahua dog in quarantine due to emerge in February 1924 and she was very anxious to start this breed in Britain. She had imported three bitches the year before but unfortunately they had died in quarantine. That was a big loss from every point of view for as Miss Lovett herself said: 'Chihuahuas are expensive little beasts to secure on the other side and so, unless some enterprising American thinks of sending over some with a view to establishing them here, I fear I will have to remain content with the one dog in the meantime.'

'I hear, however,' writes Mr Hally, 'that there is another kennel in England which has two bitches, so a little patience may eventually go a long way.

'Miss Lovett's idea was to secure three good bitches and another dog, while her ambitions include the importation of a brace of unrelated long-haired Chihuahuas.'

It would seem that poor Miss Lovett's high hopes did not materialise because nothing was heard of a foundation kennel until Mrs Powell's was started. Was Mrs Powell the owner of the two bitches mentioned by Will Hally? Anyway, in 1934, eleven years after Miss Lovett's abortive attempt, we find Mrs Powell importing a dog and bitch from the U.S.A. She had better luck too, for four days after the bitch arrived in the quarantine kennels she whelped four puppies, two of which survived.

On October 5th Mr Croxton-Smith wrote about the new arrivals under the paragraph heading of 'Exotic Little Strangers'.

In March 1937, he wrote another article for the *Sporting & Dramatic News* and illustrated it with a photo of the three Chihuahuas owned by Mrs Powell and they appeared to be very typical. The caption rather untruthfully said that they were the first of their kind seen here for forty years.

At the White City, London, in April 1938, on the occasion of the British Dog Breeders' Show, another photograph of Mrs Powell's dogs was taken, this time of a pair of light-coloured ones of about three years who, judged by present-day standards, were very good specimens with most typical heads.

Mrs Powell passed some of her Chihuahuas to Miss J. Macalister who had become very interested in the breed. At this time (1937), Mrs Powell had six imported dogs in her kennel: Idasconeja, a fawn; Betsy, a white and black; her leading stud dog, Hechicer Meron, a red fawn of top show quality who had won at all the leading shows in the States; Hechicer Meron's son; Duke of Wolf; and his sister who was a big winner before she left America. The Meron name shows that Mrs Powell was on the right lines and was knowledgeable about her breeding. She had started in Griffons and when she changed to Chihuahuas she took pains to cull out any undesirable features by giving away faulty specimens not to be bred from.

When the Second World War broke out, Mrs Powell was living in Kensington but as hostilities got more serious she moved her dogs to a new home at Clapham Common. The end of this lady's life-time interest in dogs came most tragically when her home received a direct hit in the bombing and all her little dogs perished. Mrs Powell herself became a helpless cripple and only outlived her dogs for a short time.

At the end of hostilities, Chihuahuas, like many other pedigree breeds, found themselves almost reduced to extinction. The only ones known were those that Mrs Powell had bred and sold. One of the buyers, Mrs Wilson of Burford, Oxfordshire, had a cream-coloured dog by Hechicer Meron out of Betsy. He was called Austral Followon and was born in 1940 and was still alive in 1948 when interest was aroused in the breed again. Another, born in 1938, was Austral Zorello owned by Mrs Gee. There was also Miss Macalister's Conchita of Manorgreen but she had a very bad defect —a wry mouth which had been the result of a broken jaw—and although efforts were made to mate her to Austral Followon these proved non-productive.

About this time, Mrs Marjorie Fearfield became interested in the breed but could not find any stock. She advertised in the dog papers asking if there was anyone who was interested in the breed. The result was most encouraging for she got dozens of replies, one of which was from Mrs Dora Wells who was later to make Belamie one of the famed names of the breed. Mrs Wells had been following up every bit of information that came her way and had found a dog belonging to a gentleman living in Hampstead. This little dog had suffered such shocks from the bombing that his heart was affected so he could not be used for breeding.

It soon became evident that the breed had come to a full stop and the only way to start it again was to import new stock from Mexico and America. Mrs Wells heard about a pair that were in quarantine kennels. These were a dog and bitch who had been the property of Lady T. A. Wernher in New York. The bitch was called Dona Sol and had been bought in puppyhood from her breeder Mrs Febles who later died without producing a pedigree for her. Lady Wernher had acquired the dog when he was fully grown and a champion; he was merely called Pedro. When Lady Wernher died, her husband and daughter brought the two little dogs to England and arranged for them to be left in boarding kennels following release from quarantine. They seemed to be of no interest to anybody until Mrs Wells heard about them and managed to persuade Miss Wernher to sell them to her. This she did without much ado and promised to send on the papers and pedigree for the dog when they came to light. About this time, Sir D. J. Wernher also died and in the upheaval after his death the papers got mislaid. The Kennel Club allowed them to be registered (as typical specimens of their breed) but with a Class 2 registration, with parents and grandparents unknown. Mrs Wells managed to breed a litter from them, but Dona Sol was not young and did not breed again. The only litter they produced consisted of two dogs and a bitch. The dogs were named Tizoc of Belamie and Chico of Belamie. The bitch succumbed to distemper when she was only seven months old. This was in the days before immunisation was able to take this awful worry away from breeders, so we will never know what standard this bitch could have reached. The two dogs, however, were destined to make history—Mrs Fearfield purchased Chico and Mrs Wells retained Tizoc. My first bitch, Jofos Driada, was by Tizoc mated to his own daughter, Gitana of Belamie. Eventually, Mrs Wells was able to get the pedigree of Pedro and was delighted to find that he was in fact Am. Ch. Mi Pedro Mia and she added the name of Belamie for good measure.

Mrs Fearfield started her line of Bowerhintons with Chico, and she bred many champions and was a leading light in the breed, being the first chairman of the British Chihuahua Club which was formed in 1949. The club then consisted of Mrs M. Fearfield, chairman; Mrs Gott, vice-president; Mrs Secker, Mrs Gott's daughter, vice-chairman; Miss Macalister, hon. secretary and treasurer; and a committee of Mrs Duckworth (Miss Macalister's sister), Mrs Jackson, Mrs Horner, Mrs Lydia Cross and Mrs Dora Wells.

The first meeting took place in the tea-room of Marshall & Snelgrove's shop in the afternoon of 22 May, 1949, when it was decided to call the club the 'British Chihuahua Club'.

Mrs Gott was a real pillar of the breed and set about importing the best stock from America and Mexico that she could find. To this end she corresponded with Major Mundey who, although he bred and exported far more Chihuahuas from Mexico than anyone else, was nevertheless in constant hot water with the authorities because he would insist that his dogs were produced by crossings with a kind of gopher, which wasn't a dog at all but a rodent. Nature would, of course, refuse to participate in such a practice, and even if it was possible that such a thing could happen, the outcome would be a hybrid that would not be able to reproduce. Perhaps this would account for the non-fertility of the most beautiful of all the stock that Mrs Gott obtained from the Major. She was called Tarahumara and was a quiet gentle creature with beautiful luminous eyes and huge flared ears. In contrast Tolteca, the dog that Major Mundey sold Mrs Gott, was a fiery little devil with a fierce South American temper and 'wild' in both senses of the word, but he was a great success as a stud force and was a prolific sire. He was mostly white with fawn markings.

Another of Mrs Gott's imports was a pair from the Sunstock Kennels of Mrs Stock of California. These were Sunstock Jollo, a dog, and Sunstock Systy, a bitch. Systy was a foundation bitch of unparalleled quality and produced some of the most frequently met names on the old pedigrees—Mrs Fearfield's Bowerhinton Margareta and Mrs Forster's Jofos Millinita. Both these bitches were mated to Bowerhinton Chico of Belamie with excellent results. They both produced champions although neither of them was very good looking.

Mrs Gott, whose registered prefix was Munsun (from Mundey and Sunstock), had several very serious outbreaks of distemper in her kennel at a time when the only protection against the disease was the old 'Field' vaccination. This consisted of giving the dogs a protective vaccine followed by an actual dose of the disease and then letting the best one win. This was often much more devastating in its destruction than if the dogs contracted the disease and were then given careful nursing. I found the Field method effective with farm terriers and cattle dogs who were a robust lot and quickly threw off any unpleasant consequences, but had I been faced with its use on anything as tiny and precious as baby Chihuahuas I know I would hesitate to put them to the danger. It was, at best, a touch and go method, and all too often, unfortunately, it was 'go'. Show-going was fraught with the hazards of contracting diseases, and those dedicated people who were pledged to try to promote the breed for all they were worth found themselves in an impossible position : to go to shows and bring back disease but get their Chihuahuas before the public, or to stay at home and keep them out of harm's way but never get their dogs seen. We do not realise just how lucky we are today with the very reliable vaccines that protect our youngest of young babies (the measles vaccine about which I have written further on) and the many television programmes that encourage anything rare to be exhibited to the general public from the safety of a TV studio. When my tiny dogs appeared on television everything possible was done to ensure that they were warm and fully protected in every way, even a special insurance policy was issued to cover any studio accident.

Mrs Lydia Cross, a very old friend of mine, was enchanted with the breed and managed to obtain one from a Canadian officer. She was delighted when she heard that there were possible mates for her bitch already in the country. Her little bitch was called Palace Bambi and she, in time, was mated to Sunstock Jollo. This mating produced a very pretty little red bitch called Chicata who was just about everything a Chihuahua should be and won regularly in the show ring. Mrs Cross parted with her eventually to Mrs M. Rider who had the Rowley Kennel of Alsatians. Mrs Rider mated her to Ch. Rozavel Diaz and she whelped Rowley Bronze Idol. When Palace Bambi was mated to Tizoc of Belamie she excelled herself by producing Palacecourt Queen Zamira and Jofos Ferronita also a consistent winner. Queen Zamira was the dam of Mixcoac, the black and tan bitch that started Mrs Anne Ellis-Hughes in the breed. Many years later, Chicata was mated to my Emmrill Son-ko's Red Rocket when she was over ten and, according to Peg Rider, she bred the best-headed puppy she had ever seen.

Mrs Horner, whose Denger's prefix was to become so famous in those early days, had several imports from America, the most noteworthy of them being a stud dog Pepito IX whose sire Jiggs was reputed to be the smallest stud dog in the U.S.A. Pepito IX produced a very fine type indeed as his most famous son Ch. Denger's Don Armando can well illustrate. Bought as a puppy by Mrs Dora Wells, he was shown by her quite fearlessly and always attracted huge crowds round his bench whenever he was shown.

Mrs Wells managed to acquire another bitch—a black and tan called Linda Mia II of Belamie. She was bought from a returned G.I bride and had already come through quarantine. At first her owner did not want to part with her and refused for over a year, then suddenly she agreed to let her go on condition that Mrs Wells took *all* her other dogs as well—a dachshund, a miniature poodle, and an American cocker—none of which were of the slightest interest to Mrs Wells, but their owner had become ill and found she couldn't cope. Linda Mia was originally bred by Mrs Pearl Robinson of San Antonio, Texas.

Major Mundey, who has been mentioned briefly earlier in the chapter, had been breeding his Chihuahuenos, as he would insist on calling them, for nearly thirty years. He claimed to have the only strain of dogs that had been consistently mated to a wild rodent-type creature and he maintained that whenever his dogs started to lose their type and increase their size he had to revert to another dose of the wild blood in order to preserve their type. This word 'type' is a very apt one, for the Major certainly bred a very distinctive 'type' and his writing on them appeared in dog journals all over the world, with the result that he had a very large demand for them. He exported them to America, Canada, Britain, Australia, and many other places where buyers were intrigued by his description of the breed and the fact that they were taking something 'wild'.

I think he must have read Miss Rosina Casselli's article on the breed and then tried to make a breed to conform to it, using the stock he found in the parts of Mexico he visited. He says that he had bought some little dogs from the natives and was later entertaining a friend who said that when he was out hunting he had shot a creature that looked very like the Major's dogs. A little later, this friend found another of these creatures and with the help of some natives managed to trap it. When caught, it had a mouse in its mouth and was so terrified that it died almost immediately. Major Mundey must have gone to the same district, found these little creatures and mated them into his own strain. That the creature must have been a dog is without doubt; the fact that it was carnivorous proves this. The rodents in Mexico are herbivorous and there is physical proof that if one species is mated to another it can only produce infertile offspring, which would be the end of the matter. It is far more likely that these were little Chihuahua-type dogs which had been abandoned after some of the many different types of disasters to which Mexico has been prone throughout its history. I feel that even though they were tiny and had been coddled to no small degree, the will to survive was possibly as strong in them then as we have proof it is today, and in some wild, inaccessible regions they have existed in a wild state, living off the land and becoming, as time went by, very fearful of anything strange, especially humans. I remember seeing some of the dogs that were brought over from Mexico in the late 1940s and early '50s, and a very unprepossessing lot they were too, with their long legs, very roached backs, terribly long neglected toe-nails (which some experts said should never be cut), etc. I do not doubt that Major Mundey bred dogs like these and after a time he did get a 'type' which would not endear him to the Mexican canine authorities. His idea was to make money out of the strain he had invented or caused to evolve. A few of them, like Tolteca, were quite presentable, but others were so crippled in the back legs that they had difficulty walking and their long ungainly legs and cruelly long toe-nails did nothing to assist.

By writing the far-fetched stories about his dogs in a lot of the foreign press he couldn't help but get on the wrong side of the Mexican Kennel Club who would naturally resent such statements, especially as they were contrary to all known genetic truths. They instructed Professor Baltran, the director responsible for *Mundo Canino*, the Club's magazine, to repudiate Major Mundey's claims.

Early in 1950, this journal invited all scientists, investigators, historians and laymen to supply them with all known facts and not legends about the breed. One of these stated his findings thus:

Doubtless the little Chihuahua dogs exist in the State of Chihuahua, particularly in the Valley of Allende, that is, in the town of Chihuahua itself and in the villages of the district.

Their origin is not savage [wild] nor do they breed in dens
or caves. Their alimentation [feeding] is the same as that of
other dogs, but it is advisable not to give them much meat
in the first year of their lives, so that they do not grow large.
  They are not rodents. (The italicisation is mine—author.)

Another of the correspondents made reference to the printed
works on the subject:

It is also believed that the origin of the word 'Chihuahua'
comes from the imitation of the bark of a dog, and because
for a long time past wild 'dogs' have lived in the hills of the
State of Chihuahua. They are not true dogs, but rodents
technically known as *Cynomys ludovicianus* and they have
been much confused with the little dogs of Chihuahua or
Chihuahuenos. We are dealing in consequence with a true
member of the 'canine species' whose savage origin is unknown. There is no evidence or record of the Chihuahua dog
having been seen in anything but a domesticated state.

A lady living in the town of Chihuahua, whose family resided for
many years on a ranch near the Valley of Allende where they bred
and raised many of these dogs, is quoted as saying: 'One thing to
know is that they are very sensitive to cold, and if they run loose
in the countryside they do not know how to find their own food.'
This confirms that they are not of wild origin but dogs with all
the handicaps of tameness.
  Professor Baltran himself made some very sweeping statements,
some of which could be denied right away and others which I
have been able to dispute from the small amount of study I have
been able to make. If Baltran had been *au fait* with his country's
history, instead of being primarily a scientist and interested in the
dog world to its exclusion, I think he could see the force of my
conclusions. He stated: 'It is the greatest lie in the world to say
that Chihuahua dogs can be captured in Mexico.' And referring
to an old jar, which had a picture on it which Major Mundey
insisted was a Chihuahua, he wrote:

The jar shown . . . corresponds with what the Spanish called
'barkless dogs' but which were nothing but 'racoons', an

animal previously unknown to them. If you visit our museums you can see these jars by the hundreds, classified as 'coons' and not as Chihuahua dogs. Now get your map and look over Mexican geography. Mundey says, 'The Chihuahuenos dig back into Mayan history!'. You know where the Mayan Empire was, 'Yucatán'. You know where Chihuahua is? On the U.S.A. border.

All the Chihuahua dogs now in Mexico originated in the U.S.A. The Aztecs never ate Chihuahua dogs. They ate the 'coons', just like the Negroes in your Southern States like to do. . . . Mexico has 25,000,000 inhabitants, and spreads over thousands of square kilometres, and I can swear to you that in all Mexico you cannot find over one hundred Chihuahua dogs. In *Mundo Canino* (the official publication of the Mexican Kennel Club) I published a letter signed by the Governor of the State of Chihuahua, denying that there are any wild dogs in all the territory of the State; an official document.

Major Mundey died in the early 1950s but maintained his opinion till his death. I am sure that there was a lot of truth in his belief that there were such small dogs in Mexico in ancient times, as we have much evidence to prove it. I do not, however, go along with his statement that he got his dogs by crossing with a rodent. I believe that what he was working with were true 'dogs' but that when he domesticated ones from the Indian breeders he got them too big and so had to go back to the native stock of the Indians in order to reduce size, for the advertised fact that he liked to boast all round the world was that his dogs were 'the smallest in the world'.

Charles Gallenkamp, in his book *Maya*, tells us that there were always dogs in Mexico and the early Mayans domesticated them, and since that time it has been possible to find certain peoples who had a special interest in tiny dogs.

The Toltecs had a dog known as the Techichi. Whether it was the same type as that kept by the Mayans is not known, but remains of small dogs have been found in burial grounds around Chichen Itza, the Pyramids of the Mayans in the Yucatán area, an eastern region.

Baltran maintained that in all of Mexico it would be impossible to find any dogs of this description that had not originated in the United States, but he was a member of the Mexican Kennel Club and, no doubt, would be referring to show dogs and ones registered with the Club. He would be unaware of how many little dogs known to the Mexicans as 'Chihuahuas' would be living in the country at any one time, just as the Kennel Club in Britain have no way of estimating how many Jack Russell Terriers there are, for instance, as they do not recognise this breed as a pedigree one, yet there is hardly a village or suburb which does not boast at least one of this very popular native breed.

Senora Dolores de Gonzalez was a noted breeder of Chihuahuas having bred them since 1911. Her famous prefix Altamira is known all over the world and many of her dogs have been shown in the U.S.A. and Canada. Early British fanciers, however, had no knowledge of the Senora and her lovely dogs and their only contact with the breed was through Major Mundey and the articles he had managed to get published in various journals around the world. Whenever one dealt with the Major—sometimes referred to as the 'Mad Major'—much time went by before the dog arrived and a much longer time before any 'papers' appeared. When they did arrive they were said by the Mexican Kennel Club to be 'not worth the paper they were printed on', and so naturally the Kennel Club here were not very willing to accept their said background and the dogs had to be given Class 2 registration and their antecedents entered as 'Unknown'. Diana Russell-Allen got very interested in the breed and when she saw Mrs Gott's 1948 imports she set about ordering some for herself and also contacted Major Mundey in Mexico. Diana was a very good friend of mine and it was with very great grief that I recently had to announce her death in my 'Breed Note Column' in *Our Dogs*. She had a marvellous sense of humour and the fund of stories of her early dogs would keep an audience spell-bound for hours. She was a writer too, and wrote many stories about Chihuahuas which were most beautifully illustrated by Miss Amherst Reid.

The first Chihuahuas Diana received from Mexico were anything but paragons of the breed. In fact, an early photograph of several of them standing side by side almost wrote the word OXO, and I don't need to tell what shape their forelegs had to be to do this! However, being a very determined lady and always having a very good 'eye' for what was right in dogs, horses and other livestock (Diana Russell-Allen had one of the most famous studs of Welsh Mountain Ponies and a vast sheep farm in Scotland), she soon put matters to right. With some very clever and carefully thought out breeding efforts and some new and much better quality blood from America it was not long before the Dalhabboch Chihuahuas were a power to be reckoned with. She introduced Sunstock blood by an admixture of Tolteca and Jollo and improved her line so much that she was to breed that very wonderful little bitch Anutica Aztec of Dalhabboch who was made world famous by being the cover picture for Hilary Harmar's *Chihuahuas* published by Foyles. On seeing this picture many people decided that they wanted to own a Chihuahua.

CHAPTER 4

Early British Breeders and Their Foundation Stock

1949 saw a nucleus of about five Chihuahuas in this country made up of Mrs Gott's breeding pair, Sunstock Jollo and Sunstock Systy, Mrs Wells's American Champions, Mi Pedro Juan of Belamie and Dona Sol of Belamie, and Mrs Lydia Cross's Palace Bambi. Mating these together, and with a few more importations during the next six years, put the Chihuahua right in the top group of the country's favourite dogs.

Mrs Gott was to breed the first puppy during this first era and in March 1949 Una of Phoenix was born. Not only was Phoenix the name of Mrs Gott's home, 'Phoenix Cottage', but it is also the name of a bird that rose from the ashes, as perhaps the Chihuahua did after World War II. Una was sold to Mrs B. A. Watkinson of York, who was a very generous benefactor to the British Chihuahua Club as she donated the die for the Club's badge, a most worthwhile gift in the early days of slender means.

The next year, Mrs G. Horner imported a dog, Pepito IX, and two bitches, Dona Pepita and Dona Chiquita de Perez Peron, from America. It was in 1950 too, that Mrs Horner took over the treasurership of the Club from Mrs Jessie Macalister who, unfortunately, had died shortly after having taken on the duty.

Many well-known, canine-world personalities became interested in helping the breed to get established, among them Mrs Phyllis Robson, the late famous canine journalist whose *Rambling Around* column was read wherever dogs were owned and bred; Mr Leo Wilson, Editor of *The Dog World* and a Fellow of the Zoological Society; and Miss Marjorie Cousens, the famous judge, breeder and organiser of the West of England Ladies' Kennel Society.

Mrs Marjorie Fearfield, M.B.E., as the Club's chairman, did everything she could to make the breed noticed in the right circles and with Bowerhinton Chico of Belamie won an 'Any Variety Not Classified Class for Novices' at Cruft's Dog Show in 1950. Mrs Gott and her daughter Mrs Secker got television coverage too, when

Mrs Secker appeared on the show 'Picture Page' which was presented by Joan Gilbert and Leslie Mitchell.

Mrs Gott wanted to keep the breed very rare and exclusive but Mrs Dora Wells had quite opposite views and did all she could to bring the breed to the notice of the public. Funds were very low—in fact an early balance sheet in October 1950 showed only £4 1s 9d in the kitty—so the enterprising members of the committee set about organising 'Bring and Buy' sales and raffles, and meetings were held in Mrs Robson's and Mrs Joan Forster's homes to save expense. A newsletter, entitled *Chihuahua News*, was published and was the eagerly read forerunner of *Chihuahua Chatter* which Mrs Beryl Mason and Mrs Eileen Goodchild were to make world famous for its regularity, style and abundant information.

The British Chihuahua Club had records of all the Chihuahuas in the country at this time and everybody knew everybody else's dogs. More and more Chihuahuas began to arrive from America, about another three came from Mexico, and some were brought from Canada by people returning after the war.

Funnily enough, not many were registered at the Kennel Club before this post-war era but now breeders really wanted to take the breed up seriously. They started applying to the Kennel Club for their own special 'prefixes' or 'affixes' which give the dogs they breed themselves a special name which the dogs would bear for life. A lot of 'Pepes' or 'Chicos' would be rather difficult to distinguish, but if the breeder lived in a house called 'Faraway' and this was chosen as a registered prefix he would pay an annual fee to the Kennel Club for the sole rights of this prefix and then no other dog in the country would be allowed to own the name of 'Faraway Chico' or 'Faraway Pepe'. It is a very serious offence at the Kennel Club to alter the name of a registered dog or bitch.

The first Chihuahua to be registered with the Kennel Club was Topsy, a sable-coloured bitch classified as 'Foreign Dog—Chihuahua'; she was registered on July 25th, 1907—owner, Mrs I. Boddy of Southsea, Hampshire. Where Topsy came from is not disclosed but as Southsea is next door to Portsmouth it is feasible that she could have been brought in from abroad in a sailor's pocket. There were quite a few Chihuahuas in the country that were purely kept as pets but they were not recorded. It was seventeen years before the next entry was made, when in 1924 Mrs Kovett of Buckinghamshire registered a black and tan male as

'Sorta Solo'. In 1925, a Mrs McColl of Earls Court, London, registered two bitches—Kinaultrae Lulu, who was bred by a Mrs R. Bedford by Tula Nigger out of Tula Palma, and Kinaultrae Novia, bred by Mrs Adams by Negretto out of Tula Nowada; Lulu was a black and white and Novia a fawn.

Up to 1940 only thirty-seven Chihuahuas were registered. Mrs Powell, whose dogs came next, was so critical of many of hers that she gave them away without papers rather than have them bred from—a practice that many people could follow even today as there are many faulty specimens that are used for breeding to the detriment of the breed generally. Anyway, in 1949 only eight Chihuahuas were registered, but from 1949 to 1957 1500 Chihuahuas were registered, 530 of them in 1957 alone. Now, in the 1970s, nearly 5000 are registered annually and this includes both coats for since 1965 they have been separated as two breeds with separate sets of Challenge Certificates (C.C.s).

Regrettably, in 1952 Mrs Dora Wells had to retire as hon. secretary of the British Chihuahua Club for health reasons but by then it was obvious that the breed had come to stay.

In 1951, Miss Russell-Allen imported from Major Mundey a full sister of Tolteca which, for such a tiny little dog, bore the over-long name of Dalhabboch Chichimeca Mundey. Another bitch, Quetzalcoatl Mundey, joined Dalhabboch, this time a sister to Mrs Gott's non-breeding Tara. The next year, two more came over from America but unfortunately both died in quarantine. However, in 1955, six came over and this time there must have been safety in numbers. They included some noted American strains and were namely, Dalhabboch Luce's Blue Snuggle Bunny, Anneray's Lady Magnolia, Luce's Lady Blue, Seko King, Luce's Little King Blue and Grosart's Corky. Seko King was getting on and had lost most of his teeth so that his tongue hung out, but he was the greatest asset as he stamped a most wonderful quality head on the Dalhabbochs. The Blues really established this rare colour in the strain and Corky was a champion producer. With these importations Miss Russell-Allen's kennel had a varied and useful nucleus. It was always noted for quality heads and good temperaments and some very pretty champions were produced.

In 1953, Mrs Thelma Gray of the famous Rozavel Corgis became interested in the breed and managed to obtain a bitch from the La Oro Kennel of Mrs Anna Vinyard of Cincinnati,

1. Corpse of an Aztec chieftain wrapped for cremation. A tiny red dog has been killed and placed with the body to guide the dead man's soul across the wide river to Mictlan, the place of the dead. (from the *Codex Magliabecchiano*—see Chapter 1)

2. Ch. Rowley Emmrill Lolita, first Chihuahua to win a Junior Warrant, dam of two champions, bred by the author and owned by Mrs M. Rider.

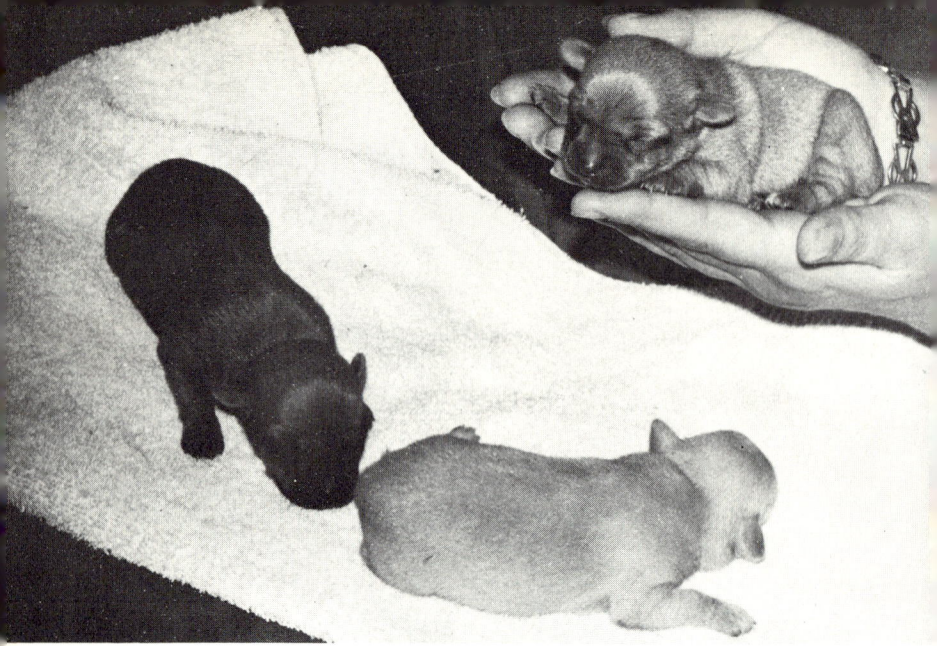

3. A litter of newly born Chihuahuas showing the variation in colour.

4. A young puppy being trained to stand calmly on the table in order to by judged.

5. Some of Mrs Murray's puppies playing 'tug-of-war' with a nylon show lead.

6. Emmrill Son-Ko's Red Rocket, imported by the author in 1955. A splendid stock-getter, and sire and grandsire of many champions.

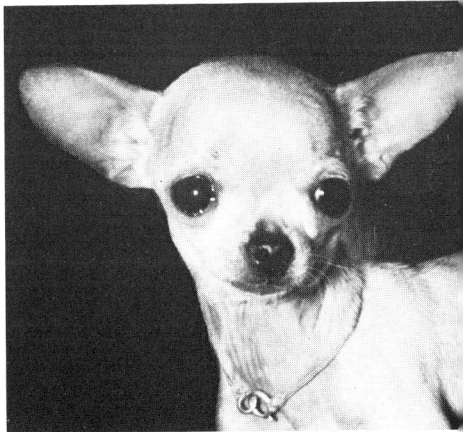

7. Dalhabboch Anutica Aztec, the most perfect-headed bitch, bred by Miss Diana Russell-Allen.

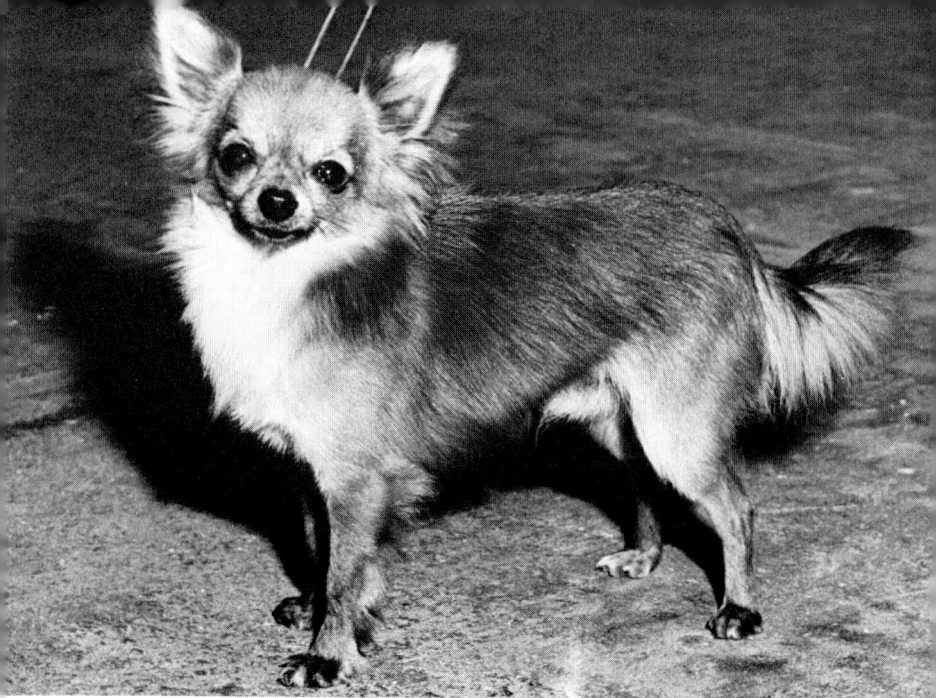

8. Ch. Emmrill Fudge, the red-sable long coat. Winner of nine C.C.s, two Res. C.C.s, and Best of Breed at Cruft's in 1964 under Mrs Thelma Gray. Three times best sire and winner of the coveted Cholderton Award of the Long-coat Chihuahua Club. Bred and owned by the author and grandson of her Emmrill Son-Ko's Red Rocket.

9. Ch. Rozavel Tarina Song, the highest winning long-coat Chihuahua in this country. Reserve Best in Show at Cruft's in 1973.

10. In warm weather this is an ideal carrying crate to take Chihuahuas about in as there is no fear of suffocation. A wooden or fibreglass travelling box is preferable in cold or windy weather.

11. An easy-to-erect portable play-pen, ideal for keeping your Chihuahuas out of harm's way. Especially good for house-training puppies.

12. Two of Beryl Mason's Rediviva long coats.

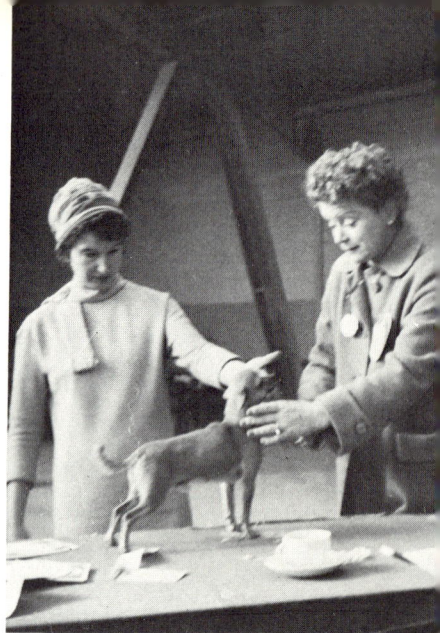

13. The author (*left*) judging Mrs Thelma Gray's Ch. Rozavel Humo at the Ladies' Kennel Club Show at Olympia in 1958. Notice the correct hindquarters.

14. Ch. Molimor Bronzel, bred by Mrs Mollie Moorhouse, Best of Breed smooth coat at Cruft's 1974 judged by the author.

15. Lady Margaret Drummond-Hay's first champion, Seggieden Jupiter.

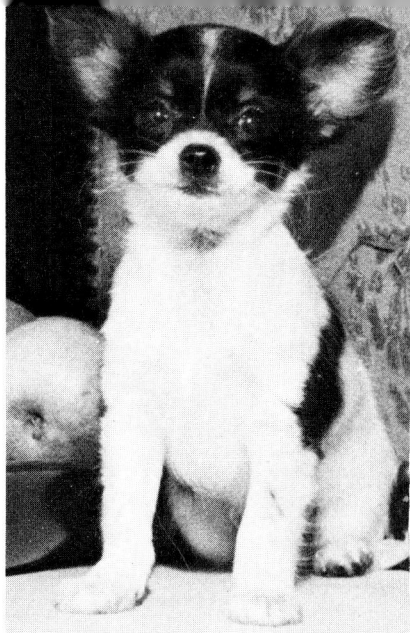

19. Ch. Valdama Honey-Suckle, bred and owned by Mrs V. Ashton. Best of Breed at Windsor Chihuahua Show in 1963 and at the South Wales Kennel Association Chihuahua Show the following year (both shows judged by the author).

20. Hedera Domino, a sweet little baby long coat, son of Ch. Emmrill Fudge, bred by Mr and Mrs J. Beacher.

21. Totland Tia Francesca, the Bitch C.C. winner when judged by the author at the 1974 Cruft's.

16. Emmrill Humfri, winner of two C.C.s and two Res. C.C.s. Judges' reports referred to him as the 'perfect long-coat Chihuahua'.

17. Ch. Molimor Talentina, the leading smooth-coat Chihuahua at the present time. Bred and owned by Mrs Mollie Moorhouse.

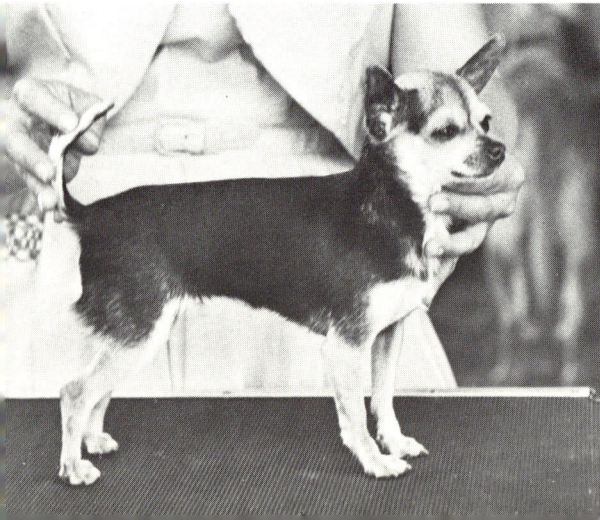

18. Am. Ch. Karlena's Mariposa, the two-and-a-half pound black and tan bitch, showing just how Chihuahuas should be 'stood to attention' on the judge's table at dog shows.

U.S.A. La Oro Sena de Oro was a daughter of Int. Ch. La Oro Alina de Tortilla de Oro, who had been campaigned and made a champion in eight different countries. She was mated to a dog called Salender's Darro Pharche before being flown to England and was clever enough to produce three sturdy dog puppies in the quarantine kennels. The one of note in this litter became Ch. Rozavel Diaz, a smart red puppy with a lovely temperament. He became Britain's first ever Chihuahua champion and the sire of the first litter of Chihuahuas I ever bred. Another bitch proved not in whelp and then La Oro Irra Pettina arrived mated to the same Darro Pharche. She produced but one puppy, luckily of excellent quality, who became Ch. Rozavel Francisco and he was to sire some top champions in both smooth coats and long coats.

After a judging appointment in Long Island, U.S.A., in 1955, Mrs Gray was able to tour the Chihuahua kennels and brought back with her seven bitches, five of which were mated before they left America. This expensive investment was to disappoint most cruelly for out of all this stock only one dog pup was produced and he proved to be sterile. Luckily, the gorgeous blue Shaw's Violet and her sister Constance made up for this.

Mrs Jean Rawson of the Brownridge Chihuahuas had a sister who when visiting America had brought her home a small chocolate and gold dog from Mrs Thelma Brandman of New York. Known as Brandman's Modelo, he was a beautiful specimen and was winning well at such events as the West of England Championship Show where he won the dog C.C. We enthusiasts were thrilled to watch him and were planning to book stud services to him, but dreadful tragedy struck and he had only mated one bitch before a lorry ran over him and killed him in the drive of his Yorkshire home. One wonders how people ever make themselves own another dog when they suffer so much over their loss but Jean tried hard to buy Rozavel Miguel, his only surviving son, from Mrs Thelma Gray but she, unfortunately, needed him in her own kennel where he produced some very useful specimens for her.

In 1954, Mrs Anna Vinyard paid us a visit and Rozavel Miguel, as a very young puppy, was the star of the party Mrs Gray gave for her. We all took our Chihuahuas for her inspection and she was very free with advice. She looked at my Jofos Driada and shuddered. She told me to take her home and love her and get myself something decent to breed from as it would be at least twelve generations before I could hope to breed out all her faults. I am glad now that I could not afford to take this (no doubt) good advice. Driada had cost enough for me to want to recoup some of the money with a litter, so I mated her to Rozavel Diaz and had five strong, healthy pups, each weighing six ounces and Driada weighing only five pounds herself. I kept the three bitches and sold the two dogs. One of the bitches, Emmrill Mielacita, when mated to my imported red dog, Emmrill Son-ko's Red Rocket, produced six pups—three dogs and three bitches—all red and all show winners. When Jofos Driada was first mated to Red Rocket she produced Ch. Rowley Emmrill Lolita and Emmrill Honora in one litter. Mrs Margaret Rider wanted Honora but I told her that Lolita was the better of the two and that I would give her Lolita just to prove my point. Lolita became a famous champion, sweeping the board and giving Peg the best fun she said she had ever had in dogs. Lolita died quite young of a very sudden illness but not before she had bred Ch. Rowley Umberto, sire of my Ch. Emmrill Fudge and several others, and Ch. Rowley Silver Cloud who was Best in Show at the British Chihuahua Club's Championship Show in April 1961.

Lolita was mated to Ch. Rozavel Humo (Ch. Rozavel Francisco ex Rozavel Shaw's Constance) to produce Ch. Rowley Umberto. I kept Honora and mated her back to her father Red Rocket (Rocky) and the in-breeding produced the first long coat that I had bred myself, namely Emmrill Candy. When Emmrill Candy was mated to her cousin Ch. Rowley Umberto she produced my delectable Ch. Emmrill Fudge who became a champion by winning his third Challenge Certificate at Cruft's under Mrs Thelma Gray. Altogether he won nine C.C.s and was a champion producer and such a splendid sire that he won the progeny shield year after year on the quality of his progeny judged at the Club show and also won the Cholderton award for the sire who produced the most first-prize winners.

Fudge held court at our house for nine years, but Rocky's time with us was tragically short. Both these dogs were 'people' in the best sense of the word and although losing them caused me some of my saddest moments, I would have hated not to have known them and would go through it again just for that rare quality of life that their company gave us.

When a standard of the breed was eventually forthcoming, I took stock of the Chihuahuas in my possession and decided that they needed a great deal of improvement. With this in mind I drew up a sort of 'blue-print' stating categorically what my own dogs needed to improve them. I showed this to Ben Burwell, one of America's well-known professionals who often visited this country, as, in exchange for two of my toy poodles, he had offered to try to find me a pair of Chihuahuas that would be suitable to mate together and of the quality I required. After a year, when I had almost forgotten that he was searching, he told me he had been unable to find the quality I needed in two specimens.

I had a theory that a lot of bitches had become bad breeders after flying across the Atlantic because of the actual flying, so I told Ben to just send me a male. It was not long before I received a cable to say that 'Rocky' would arrive in forty-eight hours. I spent most of this time trying to get him into a quarantine kennel, but it was such short notice. I was three-quarters of the way down the Ministry of Agriculture's list of quarantine kennels before I found one with room at Hatfield and I had great difficulty waiting for him to be settled in before travelling up there from my home in Hampshire to see him. It was love at first sight. Ben Burwell had excelled himself; he had sent me over everything I had asked for and more, for Rocky proved to be a tremendous little character. Mrs Dorothy Baesal of the Son-ko's Kennels where Rocky was bred wrote to tell me that he thought he was 'king' in her house. He was only seven months old when he arrived but he was soon 'king' wherever he went and after his release (from quarantine—which had seemed even more endless to me than it must have done to him) he lost no time in making himself popular with all the bitch owners, who were very eager to book stud services to him. Unfortunately, this was one function that he was not too clever about and it took a lot of time and patience before he became the prolific little force he was to become. Miss Penn Bull of the Kennel-garth Scottish Terriers has a side-line of assisting in cases of difficulty and she excelled herself with Rocky, and the owners of his champion children have her to thank for teaching him his duty so well.

Apart from his prowess as a stallion, Rocky was my constant companion, travelling in a bucket bag which was lined with a mohair scarf specially for his benefit. He came to church and cinema, travelled on the rack in his basket on train journeys, and on car journeys, if I was driving, in a special little container in case he fell off the seat. He chose his sleeping place with care—in the same box as my white, toy-poodle stud dog whose long thick coat made an ideal mattress. There would be the most ferocious growls from Rocky if the poodle so much as changed position and, if they happened to be going to a show, their travelling basket would move all round the floor with the extent of the 'aggro' that was going on. In fact they got on famously and when Rocky met with an untimely death my poodle was inconsolable.

Rocky was bright red with a small white blaze on his head. He had the most pleasing head and expression I have ever met on a Chihuahua and his round sturdy body was such a change after so many over-long and rather weak-looking shapes. He had good strong quarters and a very straight front. He was very individual and didn't really like going to shows. Being pregnant when I first showed him, I soon had to hand him over to somebody else but he always wanted to get back to me and hated having to stand in line in the ring. After my son was born, Rocky was very jealous and hated me nursing him. He got used to the idea though and I began to get some success in the ring with him—in fact he beat most of the champions of his day at some time but never won a C.C. At the last Cruft's he attended he was third in the Open Dog class and Ben Burwell was over, hoping to watch him in the ring at Blackpool, but Rocky died of heat stroke the day before he was due to be shown.

Because Rocky had sired several champions he was much in demand as a stud dog. I was afraid to overwork him so I imported Emmrill Buck's Peppie to help him cope. Peppie was well under three pounds; he was a very deep red with a good head and very good head carriage, but his self-coloured nose and eye rims robbed him of Rocky's wonderful expression. Peppie was by Am. Ch. Buck's Nifty Dude and his great grandsire was the famous Am. Ch. Don Vallijo who, in turn, was the sire of the famous Int. Ch. La Oro Alino de Tortilla de Oro.

Peppie came over with a bitch called Bonnie Lass to whom he had always been devoted, but to my disappointment and his great sorrow they were parted for the six months' quarantine period. He came over a plump, healthy little dog but at the end of his time in solitude he was a bag of bones. At some time during his stay there he must have had an accident for my vet discovered that he had had several broken ribs, one of which had punctured his stomach and another a lung. He was under treatment all the time I had him and improved enough to win Best of Breed for me. His best achievement, however, was to sire a beautiful litter for Miss May Tovey which contained Ch. Pedro of Yevot, who is found in so many pedigrees today, and Manuella and Gitana who have both made their mark on the breed, Gitana being renowned for producing the popular chocolate and gold colour. Pedro of Yevot sired the beautiful Ch. Heathtop Titania and Ch. Lippens Koko of Yevot bred by Mrs P. Blake and owned by Miss Tovey. Mrs Blake also bred Lippens Cracker Bang by Emmrill Son-ko's Red Rocket out of Rowley Cinderella (C.C. and Res. C.C. winner). Cracker Bang sired Mr and Mrs George Down's Ch. Weycombe Antonio out of Lippens Treacle. Mrs Blake imported Am. Ch. Lippens Son-ko's Ita Jet by Am. Ch. Son-ko's Don Jose, the same sire as Red Rocket, but whereas Rocky was out of Nanna's Bambi, from a very strong line indeed, it seems that Jet did not have such a good background, for Mrs Blake passed him on to Mrs Hilary Harmar. The poor little chap had to have an eye removed owing to injury, which didn't help matters. Mrs Harmar imported Am. Ch. Aztec Son-ko's Ita Max and later the long coat Int. Ch. Aztec Son-ko's Ita Stardust, winner of the first C.C. for long coats at Cruft's in 1965.

Mrs Celia Dugger sent a most gorgeous bitch called Dugger's Spice to Mr and Mrs Cross of the Kelsbro Yorkshire Terriers. Spice was a minute chocolate and tan and my own first view of her was when I judged her at Cruft's in 1956 and gave her a well-deserved C.C. and Best of Breed. I remember being delighted with her. The late McDonald Daly, the most eminent dog judge, canine author and television personality, said of her that she and my Emmrill Son-ko's Red Rocket were as like as two peas for quality and type and if mated together couldn't help producing some of the best Chihuahuas in the world. We tried in vain to bring off a mating between them but Spice was so small and screamed so much that I couldn't bear her being hurt, so I rang Mrs Cross and said I was sending her back unmated. I think they found she was too difficult to mate as she was sold to Mrs Kay Stuart and made a wonderful advertisement for her kennel.

Lady Margaret Drummond-Hay also fell for the charms of the

Chihuahua and imported quite a few at various times. One of her daughters, Miss Anneli Drummond-Hay, will be remembered as the famous rider of the well-known horse Merely-a-Monarch. The first pair Lady Margaret acquired were a white male called Kirstie's Little Strutter, and a brood bitch Pearson's Angela La Oro in whelp to Am. Ch. Allen's Snowball. Int. Ch. Seggieden Jupiter was one of those pups and he in turn sired Int. Ch. Seggieden Tiny Mite who got the C.C. from me at a Ladies' Kennel Club Show and was a consistent and well-deserved winner, being a much more refined and dainty type than his father.

Lady Margaret lived in Scotland, so too did Mrs Marjorie Mooney of the Winterlea prefix, whose home is in Dunoon, Argyllshire. Marjorie Mooney has always been a fearless importer when she needs to reinforce her dog collection, and quite early on she imported a very useful bitch in Bigo's Zoranna, who turned out to be a veritable 'gold-mine', as she put it. Bigo's Zoranna of Winterlea went back to Hound Shello, a famous American champion who was featured in all the books on the breed in that country. Not only did she produce Ch. Cisco Kid of Winterlea and Australian and New Zealand champions but also Winterlea Snow Queen who, in the 1950s, was the only Chihuahua puppy to ever win a Puppy Stakes class at a championship show. (A Puppy Stakes class is one open to puppies of every breed irrespective of size.) Through the years, Mrs Mooney has produced some of the most outstanding exhibits at our leading shows and is still a very strong force to be reckoned with. She has won Best of Breed under me at championships shows and generously spreads her dogs around for the benefit of other breeders. Lady Margaret Drummond-Hay, for instance, obtained from her Seggieden Little Heracles who was a strong addition to the stud force at Seggieden and his name is on the pedigree of many famous present-day winners.

1955 was the first year that the Kennel Club gave Chihuahua entries in its *Stud Book* for in 1954 six championship shows had awarded Challenge Certificates for Chihuahuas. At the Scottish Kennel Club, Mr Arthur Murray gave the dog C.C. to Mrs Thelma Gray's Rozavel Diaz and the bitch ticket to Mrs Fearfield's Bowerhinton Isabela.

At the West of England Ladies' Kennel Society's show in April, Mr Arthur Demaine judged the Chihuahua classes and found his C.C. winners in Mrs Jean Rawson's dog Brandman's Modelo and

Mrs Marjorie Fearfield's bitch Bowerhinton Isabela who got her second ticket.

Blackpool judge was Mr Tom Corbett and he gave Rozavel Diaz his second C.C. and Mrs Forster's imported Jofos Sadie her first ticket in bitches.

The next show to have Challenge Certificates for Chihuahuas was Leicester and here Mrs Thelma Gray judged and gave Denger's Don Armando his first dog ticket and Mrs Anne Ellis-Hughes came to the fore in bitches with her black and tan Mixcoac.

Birmingham followed and Mrs Marjorie Fearfield gave Denger's Don Armando his second ticket, winning two in quick succession. The bitch winner was a very beautiful little cream girl, Adella of Bendorwyn, bred and owned by Mrs Dorothy Benvie whose husband Mr A. G. Benvie took over the treasurership of the Club when Mrs G. Horner relinquished it. He was hon. treasurer when I was hon. secretary and he most nobly travelled down all the way from his home in Brechin, Scotland, to attend meetings; he was responsible for putting the Club's finances on the firm basis they have held ever since. Dorothy Benvie had bought Jofos Lucia of Bendorwyn and mated her to Belamie Zequi to produce the future Ch. Adella of Bendorwyn. Lucia was bred by Mrs Joan Forster of the Jofos Chihuahuas and she was by Bowerhinton Chico of Belamie (Am. Ch. Mi Pedro Mia and Dona Sol of Belamie) ex Jofos Millinita (Tolteca ex Sunstock Systy).

The last show of that year to present C.C.s to Chihuahuas was the Ladies' Kennel Club, and their judge Mr A. W. Fullwood crowned Rozavel Diaz with the title of 'champion'. This was a very great moment in the annals of the breed and, much as all the other exhibitors and early pioneers of the breed would have liked to have won this much coveted award with their own dogs, they were nevertheless generous with their congratulations to Mrs Gray when her lovely little red dog became the breed's first ever champion. He was this only by a few minutes though, for at the same show Mrs Fearfield's Isabela also became a champion and so the showing year ended with a champion in each sex.

No less than three entries in the 1955 *Stud Book*'s list of Chihuahua winners were bred by Mrs M. C. Beeson whose Beckanbee prefix was one of the most admired of those early days. Another interesting bitch to be included was Blaycroft Bruce's Lickie, owned by Mrs Vera Bostwick, bred by Mrs A. Henderson and brought into the country when the Bostwicks returned from Canada. Mrs Vera Bostwick and her husband soon became very involved with the Club. Since her husband's death Vera has become known to everyone interested in our breed for the splendid service she has given us with her wonderfully comprehensive stock of equipment and accessories devoted entirely to tiny toy breeds. I understand that she has built up a world-wide mail-order business and anyone who wishes to study the catalogue of her stock will be amazed at the very wide variety of items that have been designed and manufactured for this very specialised branch of the pet trade. We can be grateful that we have been able to enjoy such very necessary and welcome service and long may she and her helpers continue their very useful and cheerful service.

CHAPTER 5

Early Shows and Winners

When I bought my first Chihuahua in 1953, I asked to see a copy of the Standard of the Breed or a blue-print so that I could learn what points the breed had to have in order to be good enough to show. I was told that there was not a Breed Standard at that time. Everybody that had Chihuahuas then had different ideas about what made a good one. Some people had got Major Mundey's description of the breed and thought that we should make a Standard out of that. I knew that there was a Standard in America and got a copy from a friend over there. Then I set about making my own blue-print so that I knew what features to look for when buying a Chihuahua.

At that time, I was better known as a poodle breeder and was specialising in breeding very tiny black and brown ones. There had been toy-sized whites for many years but black toy-sized poodles were very rare. In America, the toy poodle was a 'fait accompli' but in Britain we were only allowed to call our tiny ones 'miniature poodles under 11 inches'. Be that as it may, I had been experimenting for some years and had produced some black toy-sized poodles that had done some winning and got themselves noticed. Ben Burwell, who was well known in America as a professional handler and also a breeder, happened to be visiting England soon after I acquired my first Chihuahuas. At the time, he was only interested in my tiny poodles and badly wanted me to sell him two rather fine dog puppies in the first litter I had bred from my first pair of under 11 inch ones. Of course I did not want to sell them, but Ben tried very hard to persuade me as he (with a much more experienced eye than mine) could tell that they were going to stay the right size. He tried upping the price but to no avail. My husband suggested that Ben try me with a Chihuahua. Ben said he thought a toy poodle such as the ones I had would buy two Chihuahuas in America. At this I was very interested and decided there and then to let Ben take my two dogs—a black and a brown

73

—and keep the bitch and try and get my own line from her. It was decided that Ben would try to find me a first-class breeding pair of Chihuahuas in exchange for the poodles, and that is how my first import was arranged. This was where my own particular blue-print came into use for I had to tell Ben exactly what sort of Chihuahuas I wanted. Colour didn't come into it but I insisted not just on the breed points of head, tail, molera, stop, etc., but, having been steeped in terriers and the soundness of construction that was necessary in poodles, I needed to have my Chihuahuas just as sound and I impressed on Ben the importance of good shoulders, sound quarters, level top-line and head carriage, and also on good mouths and strong ears—points that did not seem to bother many other breeders at that time judging from the number of soft and broken-down ears in the breed when I started.

Soon after this, Ben was lunching at the Kennel Club and happened to mention my requirements in the hearing of Mr Roger Boulton who was then the organiser for Cruft's Dog Show.

The outcome of this was that Mr Boulton was so interested in my requirements for a good Chihuahua that he invited me to judge the breed at Cruft's Dog Show the following year. This was in 1955, a full year before the actual engagement. The Committee of Cruft's very wisely ask all judges not to judge the breed for at least a year beforehand so that everybody can show. It is quite normal practice for an exhibitor not to show under a judge who has already judged his dog without giving it a prize. Cruft's Dog Show is the 'Mecca' of dogdom so most exhibitors would show there if they could. Nowadays, all exhibits have to win prizes at championship shows before qualifying for entry to Cruft's, but when I first judged there no such stipulation was in force and both coats could have been entered. As it happened, there were no long-coated Chihuahuas being exhibited at the 1956 Cruft's.

My first reaction on receiving such a greatly prized invitation was to write and say that I had never judged the breed and in fact had never judged a dog show in my life before but I would be only too pleased to try to find a judge from America who could officiate. However, Mr Boulton said that with a breed as new to Cruft's as the Chihuahua, knowledge of it was the most important requisite in his opinion and I would be doing him a great favour if I would accept the invitation. This letter is still in my possession as I realise that some people are a lifetime in a breed without being asked to judge at Cruft's and I had had real beginner's luck in being invited to judge there on my very first assignment.

My luck was even greater when I saw the wonderful quality of the entry. It was not difficult to pick out outstanding specimens. The hardest part of judging dogs is, in fact, sorting out a bunch of indifferent exhibits who do not have any of the qualities that you are looking for nor have anything really wrong and yet do not impress in any way at all. I was saved from such mediocrity by having the American-imported brown and gold Dugger's Spice, afterwards Ch. Dugger's Spice, who won no less than ten Challenge Certificates before the end of 1957.

When Mrs Dugger visited me recently on the occasion of the golden anniversary visit of the American Chihuahua Club to England, she told me that Ben Burwell had ordered a very beautiful Chihuahua from her to be sent to me after becoming an American champion. This little bitch was to be a pair with Rocky, I think. Unfortunately, however, the bitch was killed in a motor accident when being taken on the show circuit by a professional handler, and I knew nothing about it for all these years.

The other winners of my judging the breed at Cruft's in 1956 were the dog C.C. to Jofos Hockleyfell El Pepito shown by Mrs Joan Forster, bred by Squadron Leader and Mrs G. Wolff. Alice Wolff's long connection with Chihuahuas came to a very sad end when she was on her way to judge the entry at one of the summer social events that had been run by Mrs Joan Forster at the Polo Ground at Richmond Park. Mrs Wolff, who had retired to the West Country, was driving up to fulfil her engagement when she was involved in an accident from which she received fatal injuries. The tragic news was kept from the gathering so as not to mar their enjoyment, but Alice Wolff is sadly missed by her many friends in the breed.

Also making her appearance at this show was the gorgeous blue and gold bitch Ch. Rozavel Shaw's Violet, sister of Shaw's Constance, dam of Ch. Rozavel Humo, and she ran Dugger's Spice very close. At the Scottish Kennel Club's Show later that year, Miss Diana Russell-Allen reversed the placings in bitches and made Lady Margaret Drummond-Hay's Seggieden Jupiter Best Dog.

As mentioned before, a particularly tragic loss to the breed was the untimely death of the C.C. winning dog, Brandman's Modelo.

The only bitch he had mated was Mrs Gray's Rozavel La Oro
Sena de Oro and the result was one black and tan dog puppy,
Rozavel Miguel, who was out of the same dam as Rozavel Diaz,
the first champion in the breed, sired by Salender's Darro Pharche
owned by Anna Vinyard of La Oro. Diaz sired the first litter I bred
myself—a litter of five: three bitches and two dogs out of Jofos
Driada. The bitches were retained; one of them, Blancita, died
while undergoing Caesarian section. She was given an overdose of
anaesthetic after receiving several doses of pituitrin, a practice I
now abhor and warn everybody against as the effect of the drug
is so fierce it weakens the heart and the first whiff of the anaesthetic
is enough to kill the bitch. The other two were Mielacita and
Carmencita who, when mated to my imported Emmrill Son-ko's
Red Rocket, founded strains that are still to be found in the
pedigrees of many of today's winners. When Driada herself was
mated to Red Rocket she produced Ch. Rowley Emmrill Lolita,
the mother of Ch. Rowley Umberto, and Emmrill Honora the dam
of Ch. Emmrill Fudge's mother, Emmrill Candy, in one litter.

Diaz was a wonderful sire too, and he sired Mrs Anne Ellis-
Hughes' champion twins Ch. Maria Carmello of Wytchend, owned
by Mrs Raine of Phylrene prefix, and Jose Alfarez of Wytchend,
out of her winning bitch Mixcoac who won two Challenge Certificates and well deserved her title. Diaz sired another pair of
champion twins in Rozavel Gringo and Rozavel Mantilla out of
Rozavel La Oro Memoria de Oro. Diaz mated Rozavel Platina,
also a champion, and this produced Ch. Rozavel Bienvenida.

Miss Diana Russell-Allen bred a very nice cream dog in Ch.
Dalhabboch Rio Tinto King from mating her imported Seko
King of Dalhabboch to Veronica-Vi Dalhabboch. The same breed-
ing the next year, in 1957, produced Ch. Dalhabboch Sweet
Primrose and she in turn, when mated to the imported blue
smooth coat Luce's Little King Blue of Dalhabboch, produced
Ch. Dalhabboch Sweet Honesty. Both these bitches won under me
and they were a wonderful type. The beautiful head study of
Dalhabboch Anutica Aztec featured on the cover of Mrs Harmar's
book *Chihuahuas* (Foyles) will show the wonderful type that Miss
Russell-Allen achieved from mating Seko King to Dalhabboch
Munson Xochilt (Munson Temoc to Sunstock Systy). These early
highlights of the breed show how very rarely the true head type of
the breed is met with in the present time and what a huge debt is

owed to enthusiasts like the late Miss Diana Russell-Allen, who spared no expense to import only the best and which were always available to all at very reasonable stud fees. I am honoured to remember that she often used some Emmrill blood in her endeavours and she was particularly proud of her Dalhabboch Emmrill Dry Fly that I bred from Emmrill Son-ko Red Rocket's daughter, Emmrill Juanita, mated to Emmrill High Hopes by my other early importation, Emmrill Buck's Peppie mated to Emmrill Roxiana, also by Red Rocket.

Another of the early champions was Ch. Adella of Bendorwyn. Adella and her equally pretty sister Annita of Bendorwyn, owned by Mrs K. Clark, born 18th February 1954, were regular winners. Also in Scotland, Mrs Mooney of the Winterlea prefix had imported La Oro Esquela who left America in whelp to Scott's Si-Si Boy, an American champion. Unfortunately, this poor little bitch whelped on the journey and a little red and white dog that was named Cisco Kid of Winterlea survived. His career was a very exciting one and well repaid the anxiety his arrival may have caused for he was to become Ch. Cisco Kid of Winterlea in record time.

Mrs Jean Rawson was winning well at this time and made up her Ch. Brownridge Jofos Paloma (known as Dove to her friends). Jean was able to replace Brandman's Modelo by another son of American Ch. Wolf's Dustin, Brownridge Brandman's Modelo's Memory and his litter sister Brandman's Brownridge Chatito II. When Modelo's Memory was mated to Ch. Brownridge Jofos Paloma the resulting litter made international history for it contained Brownridge Birthday Toy who was exported to Mr Erik Abild in Sweden and became famous in the Scandinavian show circuit as Int. Ch. Aku Aku Brownridge Birthday Toy. Jean Rawson and I attended the International Show at Gothenburg in 1958 and were present when she won further laurels. I took with me, for Erik Abild, a tiny son of Red Rocket and Emmrill Mielacita, Emmrill Sky Rocket. He was doing well at the shows but, unfortunately, was dropped by a visiting child and broke both front legs. He too made history as he was the smallest dog the veterinary surgeons in Sweden have ever operated on. They made him a sort of frame of wheels and he was able to get around while his poor little legs mended.

Another early breeder was Miss Betty Smith who held the prefix of Yotmas and bred Yotmas Angel Kiss, who was acquired by Mr and Mrs J. Currie.

Mrs Joan Forster won well with Jofos Sadie and her home-bred Jofos Trino who won the dog C.C. at the Three Counties in 1954.

Mrs Fearfield's Bowerhinton Isabela was the first bitch champion. She was bred by Mrs Horner by Denger's Don Carlos out of Denger's Dona Maria. Another Denger's to make history was Mrs Wells's Denger's Don Armando who became the second dog to become a Chihuahua champion.

Mrs Fearfield had another success with Ch. Bowerhinton Ollala who was bred by Ch. Rozavel Francisco out of Bowerhinton Carmencita. Francisco was a half-brother of Ch. Rozavel Diaz having been born in quarantine by Salender's Darro Pharche out of Rozavel Irra Pettina. Ch. Rozavel Francisco was most noted perhaps as the sire of the record-breaking Ch. Rowley Perrito of Sektuny who with Ch. Rowley Umberto, son of Ch. Rowley Emmrill Lolita by Ch. Rozavel Humo, another son of Ch. Rozavel Francisco, founded the famous Rowley Kennel of long coats for Mrs Margaret Rider whose recent death robbed the breed of one of its staunchest supporters and a most successful exhibitor, breeder and judge. 'Auntie Peg' Rider, as she was lovingly known by her many friends in the breed, was a character that is too rare, showing her dogs up to the end of a very long life and winning both C.C.s and Best of Breed at her last show when illness could easily have kept a lesser spirit at home. Many of today's breeders owe their start in the breed to her and I can look back on a long association when some of the most amusing and interesting episodes I ever experienced when showing dogs were spent in her company.

It was with Peg Rider and Mrs Eileen Hubberstey, another early breeder who included Red Rocket in the breeding programme of her Rosaree Chihuahuas, that I travelled up to Manchester to help organise the first show put on by the British Chihuahua Club— an Open Show at the Astoria Ballroom lent to the Club by Mrs Kay Stuart, owner of the Kaitonia's Chihuahuas. Despite a lot of gloomy predictions as to the wisdom of holding a show in those early days, there was an entry of 123 Chihuahuas for Mrs Thelma Gray to judge on the 18th April, 1958. Mrs Gray made Don Silver of Wytchend, owned by Messrs. Hutchinson and Cady and bred by Mrs Anne Ellis-Hughes, Best in Show and Ch. Bowerhinton Ollala was Best Opposite Sex. Six months later the British

Chihuahua Club held another show, this time in London at the Marylebone Youth Centre, and Mr D. Cady was the judge. His choice for Best of Breed went to Mrs Thelma Gray's Ch. Rozavel Uvalda Jemima, bred by Mrs M. Payne, and Best Opposite Sex was the long coat Ch. Cholderton Little Skampy of Teeny Wee, imported by Mrs Mary Bedford and to which further reference will be made in the chapter devoted to long coats. The entry at the second show was 131. Mrs M. Fearfield judged the third Open Show in Manchester with an entry of 104. Her Best in Show was Int. Ch. Seggieden Tiny Mite, a very small son of Ch. Seggieden Jupiter and Faye of Bendorwyn, and the Best Bitch was Mabelle Carlita. At the summer show that year Mrs J. Forster judged the entry of 124 and she made Ch. Rozavel Bienvenida Best of Breed and Ch. Cholderton Little Skampy of Teeny Wee was again Best Male.

It took until April 1960 before the Kennel Club allotted the British Chihuahua Club their first sets of Challenge Certificates. Mr Leslie Perrins, the Chairman of the Club at that time, was the judge and again Ch. Rozavel Bienvenida was Best of Breed and Int. Ch. Seggieden Tiny Mite was Best Male.

Another historical date to be noted in the affairs of the Chihuahua was the very important event at Cruft's Dog Show in 1965 when two sets of certificates were on offer, one for smooth coats and one for long coats. Thus the Kennel Club recognised the two distinct varieties in the breed. At the first show where two sets were on offer, Mr Bill Siggers, the noted all-rounder, gave the smooth-coat tickets to Int. Ch. Seggieden Mighty Dime, and Tinkerbell of Glenjoy owned by Mr Turner and Miss Massey; the long-coat tickets went to Olijon Teeny Roddy, and Int. Ch. Aztec Ita Stardust owned by Col. and Mrs Harmar who had just imported her from the Son-ko's Kennels of Mrs Dorothy Baesel.

I was desolated to lose Emmrill Son-ko's Red Rocket at the Blackpool Show in 1958; he was then only three and a half years old. It was a day when he was not being exhibited and he and his tiny daughter Emmrill Zara were put in a Perspex travelling box and left in Mrs Gray's car while I helped her in with her beagles. I returned quite soon to find that the two little dogs were overcome with the heat from the back window which must have cooked them under the Perspex which does not insulate like fibreglass. We got them out and poured cold water on their heads; I

called for a vet for hours but there wasn't one on duty so I carried
them in my arms to the nearest vet. He would not let me stay but
told me to come back at about five o'clock. I went back at four.
Zara had recovered but Rocky breathed his last as I rang the bell.
I had asked the vet to do anything to save them whatever the
expense, but my bill was only for 7s 6d. When I asked him to sign
a certificate giving cause of death for the insurance company the
vet asked me why I hadn't told him that they were valuable dogs.
I'm glad I never had to see that vet again.

I should have contacted Mrs Baesel for another little stud dog
but I was so upset at losing Rocky who was far more than just a
dog to me. He was my constant companion and went literally
everywhere with me. The only time I left him was when I went
into hospital to have my youngest son; Rocky was so upset that
he had to be smuggled in so that he could make sure I was still
about.

CHAPTER 6

The Long-Coat Chihuahua

The first Chihuahua to be taken back to the United States from Mexico by Owen Wister and Charles Stewart was Carenza who was reputed to be a 'long coat'. He was the foundation sire behind the Meron strain and it has been proved that intensive in-breeding in this line can produce long coats. I can vouch for this fact myself, for I mated a dog from Meron blood with his own daughter and produced my first long coat in Emmrill Candy.

Also in America was a strain of long-coated Chihuahuas that had originated in Brazil, and Cuba also made claim to similar specimens.

When the Chihuahua was re-introduced into this country soon after World War II there were no long coats to be found. None of the earlier mentions of the breed say anything about long hair and there does not seem to be any record of long coats in Malta where several strains of smooth coats have been found in recent years.

The eminent dog judge and television personality, Macdonald Daly, wrote an article in *Our Dogs* in which he mentioned being fascinated by the appearance of a long-coated Chihuahua, the illustration for which was captioned 'Nellistar Schaeffer's Taffy Boy—Will he be the "Adam" of this variety in England?'

Mrs Kay Erskine was certainly very enterprising; she had also imported some bitches and is easily the first breeder of long coats in this country. Taffy soon made his presence felt and was in the cards under Mr W. S. Hunt at the Ladies' Kennel Club Show in 1955 and won the Res. C.C. under Mr Cady at Birmingham the following month. Taffy was bright red with a beautiful coat that made him look on the large side, but nobody could deny his soundness. He soon had a lot of admirers who wanted the extra glamour of the longer coat with its attractive feathering. The Russell-Allens imported a whole lot, mostly blues, as Miss Geraldine Russell-Allen liked them so much. Mrs Mary Bedford of the Cholderton prefix asked me to try and find her a long-coated dog, so I wrote to my friend Mrs Dorothy Baesel who put us in touch with Mrs K. Lacher. Mrs Lacher agreed to send from America her Little Skampy of Teeny Wee (by Little Meron out of Lacher's White Fluff) who was born on the 24th February, 1957. All the arrangements were made and the money sent, and the quarantine kennel were to let us know when he arrived there safely. However, just when I was expecting a call from Mary Bedford to tell me all was in order, I got a frantic message to say that the travelling box had arrived on the plane but there was no dog in it. It seems the little dog had been sent in a sort of cardboard box and for something to do on the long journey had amused himself by chewing his way out. Mary lived outside Salisbury and I in Hampshire so I offered to go up to the airport and try to find him. An airport is a very dangerous place for a dog to be on the loose, and I was worried in case he had bolted away, frightened by the noise of the planes, and ended up under a car, or worse. However, before I left the house I received a message to say that he had been found and was on his way to the quarantine kennel. Ch. Little Skampy, as he soon became, proved a little 'gold-mine' and bred some super long coats. He is behind many lines of excellent type as he had an outstanding head, beautiful body and abundant coat. It would be easy to imagine that Mary Bedford would be too nervous to attempt to import any more stock after the terrible fright she had had, but she soon got another dog—a blue and gold—but he was much too big for show and went to live with a friend. She bred a steady flow of good long coats and Skampy lived for a very long time. When the Long-Coat Chihuahua Club was formed, Mrs Bedford became the first president.

Mrs Beryl Mason was one of the breeders who fell for the charms of the long coats and she mated her smooth coat Jofos bitch to Schaeffer's Taffy Boy. The result of this was a litter of two long coats and two smooth coats born in December 1956. The smooth-coat and long-coat bitches were mated back to their father and the result was all long-coat puppies. Mrs Mason then added a long-coat dog and a bitch from Mrs Bedford's Cholderton strain and soon her Rediviva long coats were making their appearance in the show ring.

Mrs Olga Frei-Denver, of the stage act 'The Flying Denvers', had owned and bred long-coat Chihuahuas when she was living in America. She first became interested in Chihuahuas when she woke up in hosptial and found two on her bed that had been put there by Abbie Lane who was then the wife of Xavier Cugat, the band-leader who always conducted with a Chihuahua under his arm. In her act, Mrs Frei-Denver was on the receiving end of an axe-throwing turn and, unfortunately, the axe had cut her head open. Abbie Lane was also in the show and had given Olga the dogs to make her take an interest in life again. Needless to say, they did just that and Olga has never been without them since, winning Best of Breed at Cruft's in 1965 with Pequeno Little Caesare bred by Mr and Mrs F. Griffiths.

The first bitches Olga Frei-Denver brought over were mated to Taffy Boy and her strain soon became established over here.

Mrs Beryl Mason and Mrs Olga Frei-Denver were the pioneers of the Long-Coat Chihuahua Club which came into being in 1964 and is now able to hold championship shows with its own C.C.s. As the years have gone by, the two varieties achieved equal status and there are as many long coats—in fact sometimes more long coats—entered at championship shows. The reason that the long coats have been able to make such swift progress in numbers is due to the genetic factor of dominant and recessive genes. That smooth coat is dominant to long coat is proved by the fact that two long coats mated together will only produce long coats, whereas two smooths, if they carry long-coat blood in one or more of their ancestors, will produce long coats, but two long coats mated together will never produce smooth coats. It is said that because the smooth coat can hide the fact that it is carrying long-coat genes then the smooth coat is dominant and the long coat 'recessive' or 'hidden'.

It is possible to apply Mendel's theory by taking a pure long coat and mating it to a pure smooth coat. If the litter product is four puppies the result will be that there could be a pure long coat, a pure smooth coat, and two that carry equal mixtures of smooth and long coat. These 'mixtures' are the niggers in the wood-pile for if breeders wish to keep their strains pure to smooth coat the recessive long coat will keep appearing. This can go on for generations and generations and at the present time a pure strain of smooth-coat Chihuahua is a real rarity.

Although the Kennel Club wished breeders to breed only to one coat, until recently it had not laid down any hard and fast rules or forbidden the practice. The result of this was that while breeders knew the Kennel Club intended to stop the interbreeding, they continued to cross the two coats, so that it became harder and harder to protect the smooth coat. In my capacity as vice-chairman of the Long-Coat Chihuahua Club some years back, I tried to persuade members to discontinue mating to smooth coats, only to be laughed out of court and told that some of their best long-coat champions were out of smooth-coat bitches or from smooth-coat stud dogs. However, in the *Kennel Club Gazette* 12/75 the Kennel Club had this to say about the division of the breeds: 'By 1978 breeders will have had to get their houses in order because they have got until 31st December 1978 to do so. After that date they will not be allowed to register the progeny of the interbreeding of the two coats.'

Emmrill Son-ko's Red Rocket carried a gene for long coats, for when I mated him to his smooth-coat daughter from all smooth breeding the result was a smooth-coat dog, Emmrill Ric-a-Roc, and a long-coat bitch, Emmrill Candy, the dam of my champion Emmrill Fudge from a mating to Ch. Rowley Umberto, a long-coat son of Ch. Emmrill Lolita, a smooth coat mated to Ch. Rozavel Humo, also a smooth coat. Ch. Rowley Emmrill Lolita, whom I gave to Mrs Rider, was a litter sister to Emmrill Honora who was mated back to Red Rocket to produce Candy, a beautiful, typical long coat. When she was mated to Ch. Cholderton Little Skampy of Teeny Wee she produced the well-known winner, Emmrill Gold Dust, and when she was mated to her own son, Ch. Emmrill Fudge, she produced a fine litter of three, one of which, Emmrill Praline, was mated to Ch. Kaitonia's Canberra Billabong, a grandson of Fudge, and this produced Emmrill Booster who has proved a real asset in the breed as he was prepotent for heads, type, good coats, marvellous outgoing temperaments and great soundness. On paper, this pedigree is very in-bred but, because of the high quality of the individuals, it has worked.

Mrs Thelma Gray's Rozavel strain has also produced a great many good long coats without any effort. Two lines of Ch. Rozavel Francisco in a pedigree produced Ch. Rowley Perrito of Sektuny who was acquired by Mrs Peggy Rider, and with Ch. Rowley Umberto, who was also a grandson of Francisco, she founded one of the leading strains of long coats.

Mrs Gray mated her Rozavel Rowley Polka Dot to my Red

Rocket and produced her first long coat, Rozavel Querissima. Querissima in turn was mated to Ch. Rozavel Humo and a son of this mating, Rozavel Big Bad Wolf, was mated to Ch. Rozavel Bienvenida and produced Ch. Rozavel Wolf Cub, a long coat, and Ch. Large as Life, a smooth coat.

When Querissima was mated to Ch. Rozavel Francisco she produced Rozavel My Fur Lady and when she in turn was mated to Ch. Rozavel Humo, a smooth coat, she produced Ch. Rozavel Fine Feathers. I have reason to be grateful to My Fur Lady as she once reared an orphan litter of toy poodles for me when she came into milk through a false pregnancy.

Ch. Rozavel Wolf Cub sired long-coat champions in Ch. Rozavel Mermaid, Ch. Rozavel Alphonso Zapangu, bred by Mr Brian Mitchell, and Ch. Winterlea Lone Wolf bred by Mrs Mooney, but perhaps his most important legacy to the breed was his smooth-coat son Ch. Rozavel Chief Scout who, born in 1964, has had a most tremendous effect on the breed—in both coats—affecting colour, from his blue-bred dam, and size, from Wolf Cub. His progeny are too numerous to mention. I used him on a smooth-coat Fudge daughter to try to breed a smooth-coat stud but the result was a single dog puppy, Emmrill Humfri, a very small, wolf-sable coloured long coat of extremely good quality and soundness who won two C.C.s and two Res. C.C.s but never got made up. Mated to my best Ch. Fudge daughter, Emmrill Tu Tu, I got Emmrill Hubert, perhaps the most perfect-headed Chihuahua I have had since Rocky. Tu Tu was a beautiful red sable like her sire Fudge. She won extensively at championship shows including Cruft's but never got a C.C. because the judges all thought she was too small to breed from. She produced Hubert without any bother in the most natural way but by that time she had lost some teeth so I never tried to show her again.

Mrs Mollie Moorhouse of the Molimor Chihuahuas had Wolf Cub and Chief Scout stock in her foundation stud dogs, and her kennel is now one of the leading ones for champions and show winners.

Mr and Mrs G. Grevett used Chief Scout and Ch. Pedro of Yevot in their early breeding and they achieved some of the highest recompense when the little long-coat bitch they bred and sold to Mrs Gray went Reserve Best in Show at Cruft's. Ch. Rozavel Tarina Song (Squirrel, to those who know her well) has gone higher than any other Chihuahua to date and her name will be in the hall of fame for all time. A most gratifying result of a very careful breeding programme. Tarina Song was by Rozavel Pirate Flag out of Tarina Melody, a grand-daughter of Ch. Rozavel Wolf Cub.

Miss E. Boyt from Haverfordwest in Wales has used Rozavel lines in breeding her long-coat champions. Mr and Mrs Motherwell used a concentration of Rowley blood and have produced some very fine champions.

Mrs Dorothy Garlick and Mrs E. F. Nicholl have bred numerous long-coat champions. I gave Mrs Garlick's Ch. Chitinas Nixtrix Prince Charming Best of Breed when I judged long coats at Cruft's in 1969 and I gave the bitch ticket to Ch. Rozavel Tarina Song. Mrs Nicholl of the Nixtrix prefix bred Prince Charming and has since bred many more long-coat champions.

Mrs Edna King has several champions made up in her Raygistaan line of long coats. Mrs King has an artist's eye and is a stickler for perfection. She recently designed a new badge for the Long-Coat Chihuahua Club in place of one that had always annoyed lovers of the breed as it was all wrong in make and shape. Mrs King's new model is a great improvement.

Mr John Parker of the Delarchi Chihuahuas used Rowley, Emmrill, Rozavel and Winterlea in his foundation lines. In the early days he was unfortunate enough to lose a bitch while whelping and he travelled all the way from Malvern to Reading with the puppies on a hot pad. I met him at Reading Station and took the little orphans home and reared them on a poodle bitch. They were called Goldfinger and Pussy Galore, so it is easy to guess at what period of time it happened. Pussy grew up to be a regular show winner and I naturally took an immense interest in her progress because she was also a Ch. Emmrill Fudge daughter.

Mr and Mrs Taylor of the Taydor prefix obtained some of their breeding stock from Mrs Jean Gagen's Lilycroft strain. Mrs Sylvia Borthwick made some important contributions to the breed and bred many winners and owned Ch. Deodar Winterlea Wolf Whistle, a son of Ch. Winterlea Lone Wolf by Ch. Rozavel Wolf Cub.

Mrs Olga Harbottle bred my lovely little champion bitch, Ch. Emmrill Meringue of Aes, by Ch. Emmrill Fudge out of Xepherine of Aes, and Mrs Horton-Hall bred Ch. Montezuma Mr Chips by Pancho of Dapplemere by Ch. Rowley Perito of Sektuny. Mrs

Pat Jennings also showed Ch. Wingreen Aphrodite, another grand-daughter of Ch. Perito and line bred to Parrussell St. Erme Pinto bred by Mr Pack at one time vice-chairman of the British Chihuahua Club. Another vice-chairman from the very early days was Mrs Daisy Colbern-Hart who bred the Canberra Chihuahuas and whose breeding lies behind many of the present-day champions. She left England to join her daughter in Australia after serving the club for the greater part of its existence.

Mrs E. I. Foster bred Ch. Venico Momento who went Best of Breed at Cruft's under Mrs Thelma Gray in 1968. Mrs Steinmetz made up Ch. Dekobras Danny Boy, a dark red, and Mrs M. Kempson brought out Ch. Ranji's Carmencita by Ch. Emmrill Fudge. Ch. Taydors Gitana and Ch. Rozavel Fine Feathers were 1968 champions and Mrs Rider was showing Rowley Petticoat Line, perhaps the prettiest of all her champions.

Mrs Burt bred Ch. Duniver's Angel's Ace and Mrs Hollows bred Ch. Dorrow Small Fry from Duniver lines. Mrs Friedeberg showed Stretrose Perio Caractacus and Mrs M. Spurrell, who bred Caracterus, showed Perio Pandy's Boy by Ch. Perito out of Perio Pandora. Ch. Hayclose Harrison was shown by Mr J. Stott bred by Ch. Duniver Angel's Ace ex Parabar Rosaleta. Mrs Frei-Denver had Pequeno Meeney, Miney and Mo and she made Miney a champion in 1965. At this time, Mrs Lily Busson was showing the lovely Simchalas Heavenly Mink, and Mrs Lansdale was winning with Ch. Lansdahlia Talaloc Twinkle, bred by Mrs Eileen Good-child. Mrs Peg Rider was winning with Rowley Limmerlease Fantasia, bred by Mrs Lorna Cleeve by my Emmrill Gold Dust out of Limmerlease Emmrill Butterscotch, litter sister to Ch. Emmrill Fudge. Mrs Rider also bought Emmrill Peppermint Cream, an all-white long coat and litter brother to Ch. Emmrill Fudge. The next year, Mrs V. Riley made up Ch. Johara Romeo, a pretty little peach-fawn son of Rediviva Diminuto (Ch. Skampy of Teeny Wee) out of Johara Princess Salome by Nellistar's Schaeffer's Taffy Boy.

Mrs Frei-Denver made up Ch. Pequeno Maria next and Mrs Gray brought out the very beautiful Ch. Rozavel Mermaid. I showed Emmrill Tu Tu to her Junior Warrant and she won right through the classes at the first long-coat classification at the British Chihuahua Club's show where long coats were shown without tickets and were judged by Mrs Jean Rawson. There were so many entries that the show went on too long and we ended up in the laundry room of the Seymour Hall, London, as the hall we had hired for the show was needed for an evening entertainment.

A long list of show winners can get boring, but this is just to show how many good-quality long coats there were in the early days and how keen their owners were to get them in the show ring.

The early long coats that were bred from smooth-coat Chihuahuas had, as a rule, good typical heads, but, unfortunately, a lot of people wanted to get on the wagon as soon as possible and made short cuts by crossing Chihuahuas with Papillons and other long-coated toy breeds. I once had a Pekinese cross and a Yorkshire Terrier cross shown under me. The unfortunate owners had bought them in good faith. On several occasions, in my capacity as a Kennel Club championship show judge, I was asked to give an opinion on doubtful ones and I could not state that all of them were typical long-coat Chihuahuas. The breeders who had sold these specimens denied that they were not true-bred, but in one case the breeder had a vigorous little Pekinese stud running about her premises and it is more than likely that an accidental mating must have taken place. The breeder involved, however, denied that it could have happened and refused to give her poor customer any redress. Some very typical specimens have been bred from some of these early mis-matings as study of the Long-Coat Chihuahua Club's pedigrees of champions will show. Of course there is a lot of waste in cross-bred litters and even if some unscrupulous people attempt to breed long coats this seemingly easy way, a large percentage would have to be sold off without papers for a very meagre price. The time gained would therefore have been off-set by the number of generations it would take for the strain to come into line, and as bad faults can crop up after many, many generations of good breeding, it makes one wonder how long before the other breed used will stop making its presence felt.

There was a tendency for the early long coats to be rather larger than the smooths, not only because of the heavy coats which some of them carried and which would, of course, make them look larger, but also they had heavier bones and larger frames than their smooth litter mates. The American Chihuahua Club recognised this and at one time allowed a weight limit of eight pounds for their long coats, but this practice was voted against and so they now have the same limit as the smooths, namely, six pounds.

Some exhibitors feel that the long coat is there to hide a multitude of sins and that long coats do not need to be as sound as the smooths. To a certain extent this is true, because the smooth coats reveal any faults they have for all to see. However, an experienced judge will soon spot an 'out at elbow' front and poor hind action, which are all the longer hair can hope to hide.

With a breed so small yet so large in numbers there is no reason why faulty stock should be bred from. If only the best bitches are used for breeding and if they are only mated to champion or top stud dogs there must be an improvement in soundness. The breed is so popular with the pet-buying public that there are always more people wanting to buy than pet puppies to offer them.

The long-coat Chihuahua is a delightful breed and nowadays is often superior in numbers at championship shows, which is the usual way of assessing its popularity with exhibitors.

It is now a separate breed on its own and the Kennel Club expect to discourage the crossing of the two varieties by not allowing the offspring to be registered.

CHAPTER 7

Judging the Chihuahua

Judging the Chihuahua is a comparatively straightforward matter as long as you have an eye for conformation and soundness. The smooth coats are easier to judge than the long coats, for the smooths display their faults for all to see, but the feathering on the long coats should not be so heavy that it hides the front legs or obscures the hind action. If it does, it is not a correct coat.

The most important feature of the Chihuahua is the head. In the days when exhibits were judged by awarding marks for each feature, the head could warrant as many as 25 points out of a possible total of 100.

Body and condition warranted 15 points, and level back and hindquarters were also important. The correct, large, luminous eyes were a feature that scored heavily, as did a short nose, deep stop and apple dome.

Nowadays, the points system of judging has fallen out of use. Instead, we are given a blue-print of the breed (in the form of a breed standard) and can choose to allocate points or not. But if six exhibits all gained the same number of points yet were completely different in appearance, the judge would still have to make a decision as to which was best. He must, therefore, be able to judge according to the Standard of the Breed.

The head should be round and high domed. There should be an angle of near 90° from the bridge of the nose to the dome of the forehead—the angle to be at the stop, i.e. the indentation between the eyes. The Chihuahua is the only breed that has a molera in adult life. Some people would breed this feature out altogether, but it is a sign of purity and the correct high dome of the real 'apple' head is protection enough for the brain. The head should be carried high on a well-arched neck which should slope at a wide angle into the shoulders to give correct front movement.

The ears should be set on at an angle of 45°. They should start at the side of the head and be as far apart as possible. A good guide would be for the bottom of the ear to be level with the corner of the eye. When in the ring, the dog should carry his ears at the alert.

The eyes should be round and luminous, and there should be a wide space between them. They should be quite large but must not protrude.

The teeth are considered more important in the Chihuahua than in other toy breeds and many judges expect perfect bite, complete dentition and no missing teeth. It goes without saying that judges expect clean teeth and are quite right to be severe in this respect.

The muzzle should be about one-third of the length of the whole head and slightly pointed; broad, flat noses are not correct. A long, pointed nose gives a terrier appearance and is not acceptable.

A feature of the breed is its flat, badger-like tail which should be furry in the smooth coats and well plumed in the long coats. It should join the body at an acute angle and be carried high with an upward curve. It may be carried out behind or up, but should not twist or touch the back.

The body should be round at the ribs and the back level and parallel to the ground. The length of back should be only very slightly longer than the height at the withers (top of shoulder-blades). The breed must look elegant and dainty and this is impossible if the legs are short and the back is long. There should be no resemblance to the dachshund at all. The dog should stand almost four-square with the front legs under the rib-cage and the hind legs correctly curved from the hip-bone to the stifle joint and then perfectly straight from the hock to the ground. The back legs should stand away from the body when the dog is standing but move out behind him when he walks correctly. The two front legs should be parallel to each other, and the front action should carry straight, i.e. it should not be bowed in any way or out at elbow, or weave or cross in front, or paddle, as in the case of being wide at the elbows, or be stiff like a 'goose-step'. The action must be swift-moving and brisk. All movement should be smooth and well co-ordinated.

The very ugly movement where the hind-quarters move from side to side on their own is caused by there being too long a space from the first rib to the hip-bone. A Chihuahua shaped thus will often roach its back, which is another extremely ugly fault.

The texture of the coat is something that can give a judge a lot of problems. The ideal is a soft, silky coat that lies sleekly on the body. Any tendency for it to feel wiry should be penalised, as should a woolly, wavy coat. Some smooths have patches which are almost bald and the edges of the ears are sometimes serrated or coated with a scabby substance. This is a sign of the owner's lack of attention to important details. Any Chihuahua with these faults should not receive a prize card.

Any colour or mixture of colours is permissible. Litters can sometimes be of so many colours that they look like 'Liquorice All-sorts'. Noses and eye-rims can be self coloured or pink. It is quite in order to show an albino dog, i.e. one without any colour pigment at all, but I should think it would be rather ugly. Some judges have prejudices about putting up dogs with pink noses and eye-rims, especially if they themselves keep a breed where these points have to be black, but they are very wrong to refuse to place a dog which has these features.

A Chihuahua with too long nails won't be able to walk properly and may be placed low even if it is an otherwise good specimen.

When judging this breed it is advisable to place a non-slip mat on the judging table. Some of the more untrained dogs can wriggle a lot, so the owner should be advised to hold the parts you are not judging. Owners should also be asked to open the mouth for you if there is any reluctance on the dog's part to allow this.

The weight limit for the Chihuahua is six pounds and it is wrong for a show exhibit to be either too thin or too fat. Although bones should be fine and dainty, the Chihuahua should be firm to handle. The good ones have surprisingly solid little bodies for their size.

A dog that bites should be disqualified, and one that appears very nervous should be heavily penalised.

The most important thing to remember when judging the Chihuahua is that he belongs to the smallest breed in the world and must be appreciated for his tiny size. All other points being equal, the smaller exhibits should always have preference over their larger opponents.

STANDARD OF THE BREED
CHIHUAHUA (LONG COAT)

The Standard of the Chihuahua (Long Coat) is the same as the Standard of the Chihuahua (Smooth Coat) with the exception of the following:

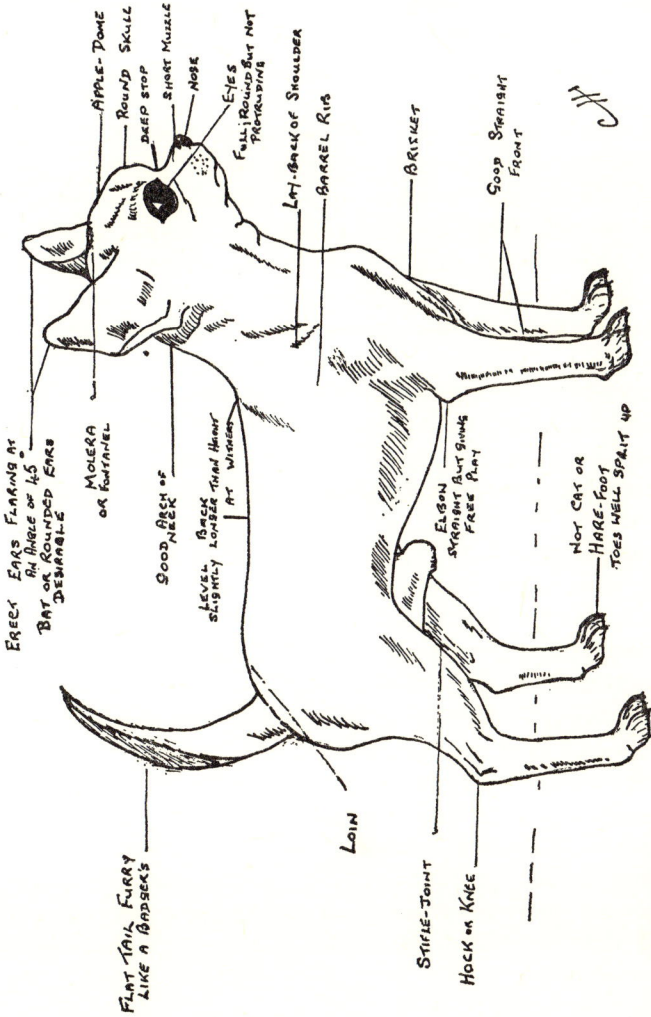

Fig. 2   The Chihuahua Standard as illustrated by Caroline and Mona Huxham

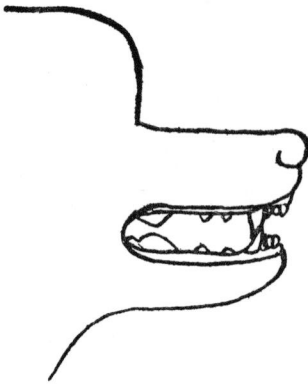

CORRECT SCISSOR BITE   OVERSHOT BITE

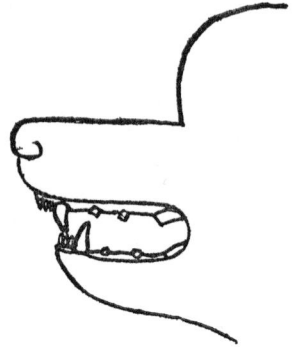

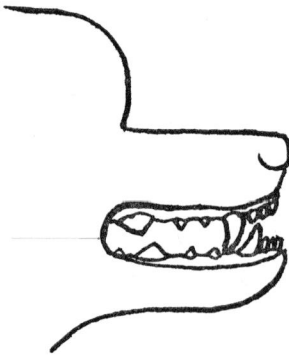

UNDERSHOT BITE

Fig. 3 Correct and incorrect mouths.

Coat—Long, of soft texture (never coarse or harsh to the touch) either flat or slightly wavy. No tight curly coat. There should be feathering on the feet and legs, pants on the hind legs, a large ruff on the neck is desired and preferred, the tail should be long and full as a plume.

CHIHUAHUA (SMOOTH COAT)

Characteristics—An alert and swift moving little dog with a saucy expression.

General Appearance—Small, dainty and compact with a brisk forceful action.

Head and Skull—A well rounded 'Apple Dome' skull with or without Molera, cheeks and jaws lean, nose moderately short, slightly pointed. Definite stop.

Eyes—Full, round but not protruding, set well apart, dark or ruby. (Light eyes in light colours permissible.)

Ears—Large, set on at an angle of about 45 degrees; this gives breadth between the ears.

Mouth—Level, scissor bite.

Neck—Slightly arched, of medium length.

Forequarters—Shoulders should be well up, lean, sloping into a slightly broadening support above straight forelegs that are set well under, giving free play at the elbows.

Body—Level back, slightly longer than the height at shoulder. Well sprung ribs with deep brisket.

Hindquarters—Muscular with hocks well apart, neither out nor in, well let down.

Feet—Small with toes well split up, but not spread, pads cushioned. Fine pasterns (neither 'Hare' nor 'Cat' foot). A dainty foot with nails moderately long.

Tail—Medium length carried up or over the back. Preferred furry, flattish in appearance, broadening slightly in the centre and tapering to a point.

Coat—Smooth, of soft texture, close and glossy.

Colour—Any colour or mixture of colours.

Weight—Up to six pounds, with two to four pounds preferable. If two dogs are equally good in type, the more diminutive preferred.

Faults—Cropped tail, brokendown ears.

CHAPTER 8

How to Choose a Chihuahua Puppy

The above title is something of a misnomer for, on the whole, anyone who has had much to do with Chihuahuas would tell you that it is usually the Chihuahua who chooses its owner-to-be.

Chihuahua mums too are very active when it comes to choosing new owners for their precious offspring. In many cases, she has had a lot of trouble producing her young and her reaction to anyone who comes near her puppies is inclined to be tense. I have learned over the years that, if a Chihuahua mother shows active resentment about the prospective buyers of her puppies, it is far better to make an excuse and let the people go without buying than to put up with the aftermath of resentment and worry that will ensue if she thinks her family have gone to unsuitable people. If my bitches accepted the customer that had just bought one of their pups, they would stay in the house with me when the people left. If, however, the buyer was not acceptable, they would chase the car up the drive and come back and sit whimpering. It took me some years and quite a few bitches before I caught on to the significance of all this. I thought, at first, quite wrongly as it turned out, that they were more fond of some of their puppies and grieved for the favourites yet were quite pleased to see some of the not so favoured ones go away.

Finding the right homes for puppies is one of the most important responsibilities of the Chihuahua breeder. Most puppies of other breeds soon settle where they have the individual attention of a single household and thrive under the love and attention they receive. The Chihuahua puppy, however, is far more particular about his own needs and it is essential that his needs are considered rather than the desires of a prospective owner or, rather, a buyer who has the temerity to wish to be owned by a Chihuahua. For that in effect is what happens. Chihuahuas like plenty of affection but they can be quite happy without it. What they really want is a group of people who are prepared to spend all their time waiting on them and pandering to their wishes. That is the life their ancestors were given in the old days of the Maya and Aztec eras. Then Chihuahuas were looked on as vital elements in the after-life of humans, for without the aid and guidance of the dogs their souls would never reach the seventh heaven of their desires. This attitude has been carried on over the centuries and it is strange how it can be applied to modern living. Rather like a cat, the Chihuahua is absorbed with his creature comforts. For instance, on a cold day the Chihuahua will sit as close to the fire as possible. If I am working at my desk, the other side of the room from the fire, the poodles will all sit round my feet as their only idea of comfort is to be as close to me as possible—even if they nearly freeze to death. The Chihuahuas, on the other hand, will all sit on the hearth as near the fire as they can get and, if there is a fur slipper or a cushion that they can pull down for added comfort, they will not hesitate to make themselves as snug as they possibly can. It is the same out-of-doors. If ever the Chihuahuas were found sitting in the middle of the lawn you could be sure that the day was very warm, without the slightest sign of a breeze, and the sun would be shining down on to their backs. On the other hand, if it was a bit windy, even just a bit draughty, and the day was sunny, they would lie against the south wall of the house, out of the breeze but in the best place to catch the warmth of the sun. On those days when it was dull, a bit cold or threatening to rain, they would refuse to go farther than the porch. My lot found a huge old bay tree outside the front door and they would, if pressed, run under that to perform their toilets and make a dash back almost before I had shut the door. However well trained in the matter of house manners Chihuahuas are, they will never give themselves the discomfort of getting wet or cold in order to preserve the niceties. After all, what is a mere human for except to clean up behind them? Many people would not wish to become a vassal to a tiny imperious little dog, and quite rightly so, but prospective owners should be warned of what will be expected of them, then, if they do decide to take on the job, they have only themselves to blame. Not for them then will be the glorious welcome of the poodle and suchlike whose one idea of happiness is the company of their beloved master or mistress. The Chihuahua will greet you with a wag of the tail and a joyous bark but it will be rather in the nature of 'Oh goody, now we may get some food down us and a walk in the park.'

Contrary to some thought, the Chihuahua is not a lap-dog par excellence. They do need to be exercised and the farther the better. Nobody will tire a fit and active little Chihuahua just by walking it. My daughter once took her pony out for its daily exercise and when she had gone several miles she was amazed to find two little five-month-old Chihuahuas trotting at her heels. She hadn't noticed them in the long grass she had been riding through, but when she came to an open heath she heard them barking merrily behind her. She carried them home on her saddle but when she put them down they started playing ball and raced about the whole of the evening. There is a feeling that Chihuahuas only need to run about in the house to give themselves plenty of exercise. My study of the breed disproves all this and I insist that mine get adequate regular daily exercise. I start putting the lead on before ten weeks of age and I find that they accept it better then than at any other time; older ones sometimes reject the lead completely and refuse to have anything to do with it. The reason some owners always carry their dogs is because they refuse to walk for them. Although the Chihuahua has a strong will he will only respect someone who has a stronger one. Very much patience is called for as the slightest trace of annoyance in the voice will cause the Chi puppy to sit down and refuse to budge.

Perhaps the Chihuahua should best be described as a dog for connoisseurs, those who would prize it as a rare item, but love it too, so that they can put up with its idiosyncrasies better. Not the dog for the pet-buying public who need something to keep the kids happy, rid the garden of the neighbour's cats, walk down to the local and back, and to take on picnics at week-ends. It is not good as a status-symbol dog either because if owners wish to keep up with the 'Joneses' the Chihuahua will soon ferret out the local 'Jones' and move in with them if they have more comfortable arrangements to offer, in the same way as cats will. No comfortable patio chair in any neighbour's garden is safe if there is nothing more than two-inch chain link fencing round it. Most Chihuahuas, unless they are very fat, can get anywhere where their head can go and they are so appealing that there are very few neighbours who can resist them. All these factors have to be taken into consideration when deciding to share your life with a Chihuahua.

The Chihuahua would seem an ideal pet for a flat-dweller. They are so tiny that they can just be popped out on the balcony at intervals or allowed to relieve themselves on paper in the bathroom. There are hundreds of tiny toy breeds all over the world that live in this way, and there are a few Chihuahuas that have never known any better, but by and large, they enjoy a much more varied existence and can bark for hours on end if they think it is time for them to go out for a walk, or shopping to the butcher's, or riding in the car (which they all love above all other forms of transportation).

They like very comfortable beds—not the wooden or plastic boxes that are sold for other breeds, and they don't like baskets either unless they are lined with blankets and cushions. Cushions, however, must only be used in the Chihuahua's bed. No more will they be safe on chairs or settees, as the Chihuahua is apt to hide underneath them. There have been gruesome tales, sadly all too true, when tiny Chihuahuas have made themselves comfortable under a cushion and someone has come and sat on the cushion and squashed the little dog to death. Chihuahuas like to burrow and hide themselves away to sleep. There was a worrying but true story of how one made himself a comfy bed in the pile of dirty household washing just as his owner was making out the laundry list. She closed the lid down and tied up the box without seeing the little dog hidden under the sheets. The laundryman called, took the box away in his van and the woman went on with her morning chores. When she was eating her biscuits with her morning coffee she missed the Chihuahua, as he was apt to help her eat them. When calling him did not bring him to the coffee table she made a thorough search and realised that he must have been taken away in the laundry box. Not being a car driver, she ran out into the road and found a greengrocer making his rounds. Jumping into his van in her house-slippers and apron, she told him of her fears and he broke all records in getting her to the laundry, as they did not know how soon after arrival the clothes were put into the hot water. She was relieved to be told that the particular van had not yet arrived and when it did she found her little dog not much the worse for his worrying experience.

Another Chihuahua who also liked to wrap himself in the laundry got himself into the tumble-drier and that had a much worse effect as he was given to fits afterwards.

So here we have what makes a suitable home for a Chihuahua :
   Plenty of time to get him regular meals.
   Energy to exercise him.
   Very comfortable bed.

One pampered Chihuahua I knew of had a bed consisting of a large, square biscuit box lined with quilting and fitted with a cushion. It had lots of little blankets embroidered with the Chihuahua's name and then an eiderdown on top. It took quite a time to settle the Chihuahua down; he would not stay in his box a minute until he got a goodnight kiss on the top of his head. This was his signal and he then lay down and went to sleep till morning.

Chihuahuas are good, heavy sleepers and usually sleep the whole night through. Perhaps it is true to say that they are little creatures of habit who can be trained by regular routine to accept a definite sleeping pattern which will be very difficult to break. If they are used to sleeping from 12 o'clock until 8 a.m. they will keep to this and it will be difficult to change them to another time schedule. In the same way, they like their meals at regular intervals and they will always look for the same pattern. It will take about a week for this pattern to be changed without causing the puppy quite a mental upset, so it is best done over as long a period as possible.

Having studied the type of home and family that is most suited to the Chihuahua, and being quite certain that this little gem is the only breed that can satisfy your need, then the sooner one is acquired the better, for the only thing that is really better than living with a Chihuahua is living with two Chihuahuas. If the expense this would entail would be the only thing that would stop you, it may be a good idea to buy a bitch in the first instance with a view to letting her have at least one litter in order to give you a second puppy. I do not mean to suggest that this would be the cheaper method—in fact, breeding and rearing Chihuahuas can be quite an expensive way of acquiring another puppy, but it will be a very satisfying one.

This will alter the requirements of the first purchase in that a bitch could be as desirable as a male, which in many breeds is far from the case. Actually, being so tiny there is no difficulty about keeping a little lady safe from harm while she is in her twice annual heat period. Carrying her to and from the house will keep all followers away and bitches can be given pills especially manufactured for the purpose of making them unattractive to males. The substances that used to be sold for this purpose were often most offensive in their smell, so the more modern methods are to be recommended.

A household that contains young children, or has young children as regular visitors, must be careful in its choice of Chihuahua puppy. They do not all like being handled and may get quite stroppy if continually picked up by children who they fear might drop them. Another type of unsuitable owner is the loud-voiced person who screams at his puppy. This makes the Chi, who has very sensitive hearing, cringe and in most cases bark back in a most aggravating way. The least change in usual household sounds will be followed by the most hideous shrieking barks from the Chihuahua, and, as they usually like to get in the last word, you are soon in serious trouble with the rest of the neighbours, not to speak of any unfortunates living in your own house.

Chihuahuas can be quiet, well-behaved little dogs and it is well worth spending a bit of time and trouble in the early stages in order to make them this way. Once a habit like incessant barking has been allowed to interfere with the harmony of the home, it will be very hard to break.

When buying a Chihuahua, it is better to start with a puppy of eight to ten weeks of age as they are over their early dependence on their mothers, ready to try new food and quite independent in their attitude to new horizons. They are probably more ready than most breeds at this age as they mature far more quickly than bigger breeds. They can be started on weaning at a month, or earlier if need arises, and they are up and scampering about quite soon after this. Their eyes seem to open earlier and I am sure they can hear a lot sooner than other breeds.

It will be seen that the acquiring of a Chihuahua puppy is going to entail a lot of time-consuming activities that may never have been attempted before, but it can be said that these will be more than repaid in the joy of owning a tiny little creature that can be taken everywhere and that can be allowed the most improbable liberties without any adverse results. One little dog was even taken to a diplomatic dinner, and another on a conducted tour of the House of Commons, hidden in his owner's muff or stole. I took my dogs to church, to the theatre and to eat at exclusive restaurants where the head waiter would have had a fit had he known of the presence of Red Rocket or tiny Zara lying quite squat under my table napkin. Both these little charmers enjoyed the joke and I only had to say, 'Here's the waiter coming', and they would lie quite 'doggo' on my lap until told, 'He's gone now.'

A six- to eight-pound Chihuahua, though rather big to expect show awards, would make a fantastic family pet—more intelligent than most other breeds, able to romp and play without fear of irreparable damage to wind and limb, and small enough to tuck in out of the way on journeys and expeditions, so that he is far more a part of the family than almost any other pet could possibly be. There is a danger here, however, that should be pointed out. As they are so much a part of the family, they can be very jealous if they feel that they are not getting the attention they expect. This was evidenced when my last baby was born. Rocky, who up to then had been the centre of our daily life, suddenly found this strange bundle getting even more attention than he was and this made him furious. He was not bad-tempered about it in the ordinary way but showed his displeasure by not showing well at dog shows. He must have sensed, although I never said as much, that I was disappointed when he didn't win so he tried not to win by sitting down, refusing to walk properly and looking abjectly miserable all the time. He had beaten all the reigning champions at some time or other, but for the first year of my new baby's life he played us up like anything. Eventually he decided in his own little mind that the new acquisition meant some added comforts, in the way of comfy rides in the pram, extra outings and a lot of very interesting items in his diet from eating up what the baby left, and a change gradually took place. At Cruft's that year he showed well and won third in the Open Class, only to die soon afterwards without ever really reaching his potential in the show ring. He was worth far more than just a show-dog to me, and I shall always be grateful for the time I did have him, for in a lifetime of owning dogs as pets and giving my heart to them in no small way, Rocky still stands far above the others as the star in the firmament.

Not everybody will be as lucky as I was, but it is fair to say that once you have shared your life with a Chihuahua, you will never wish it to be any other way again and the loss of one will only be consoled by getting another as quickly as possible.

The best way to find a Chihuahua puppy is to attend shows or get in touch direct with someone who breeds them. If there is any difficulty about finding a breeder, the Kennel Club will send you

a list of the ones nearest to you. Make an appointment to visit the
kennel as it is not always convenient for the owners to entertain
visitors, and it will pay you dividends to get the breeders in an
expansive mood so that they will give you plenty of time and tell
you as much as possible about the stock they have. Don't expect
to see dozens of puppies; not many people breed them on those
lines. Most people keep a couple of bitches in the house and the
litter may be in the bathroom, kitchen or utility room. These are
not the most hygienic places, maybe, but that is how the little
Chihuahua mother prefers it. Tu Tu liked to have her puppies in
her own bed on top of the dresser. That way she could attend to
her motherly duties and not miss anything that went on below her.
She was missing out on the puppy den on the floor where we
wanted her to be. Her puppy became one of the family at once and
we would never have sold him. By the time he was six weeks old he
was joining in everything and was particular well adjusted.

A lot of reasons behind a dog's behaviour can be traced to his
beginnings and his upbringing, so it is wise to shop around and
find not only well-bred and well-reared puppies but ones that have
been subjected to human companionship, which can never be the
lot of puppies born and brought up in outside kennels.

At two months, the puppy's temperament is largely fashioned
and will be influenced by the things that happen to him in early
life and also by his mother's temperament. Where there is a
temperamental characteristic that can be related to a heredity
basis, then the sire can also have an influence on temperament.

Having found a suitable puppy from a suitable environment,
what qualities should be taken into account?

First look for a well-rounded firm little body, a sleek shiny
coat, bright eyes and a naughty, happy outgoing disposition. The
naughty puppies usually turn out to be the most intelligent. Skin
should be loose to the touch, supple and soft. Any hard places on
the ears or elbows are suspect. The eyes should be particularly
bright and shining and free from discharge or staining underneath.
There should not be a red rash on the skin or dandruff in the coat;
the stools should be firm and dark and should not smell offensively.
Any bad smell to the urine will be evidence that all is not well with
the kidneys or the pup has been kept in unclean conditions. It is
important to see that the mother and any other older puppies are
of a happy, friendly disposition. Watch the back legs for any sign

of stifle trouble, which can be evidenced by a tendency to favour
a leg. Suspicion that all is not well can be proved one way or the
other by handling the back leg very gently and, if there is any
sign of a 'click', forget it. If there is any reluctance to show the
mother, go to another breeder who may not be so reticent. If
all is well, breeders are usually only too eager to show off their
stock, and any reluctance can only be taken for desire to hide
something.

Collect your new puppy when you are going to have plenty of
time to stay with him until he has got over the distress of leaving
his mother and his brothers and sisters. It is his most traumatic
experience and the little puppy will need all the help he can get
to recover from this upheaval as quickly as possible. The answer
is to make a fuss of him and give him such a comfortable place to
live in with so many things to do that he won't have time to miss
his first home. He will also need patience and much understanding
the first night away from the warm nest of his birth and early days.
Don't shut him up in a room and expect him to settle down to a
peaceful night without any signs of how much he is missing his
family. Give him a warm hot-water bottle or heated pad, and a
ticking clock wrapped up in an old sweater will mimic the noise of
puppies' heartbeats with which he has always gone to sleep hearing.
He will wake before the family and probably howl from sheer
loneliness, but it is better not to accede to his lament by taking
him up to bed with you because this will only prolong the agony.
If his cries keep you awake, stuff cotton wool in your ears and try
not to listen until he calls at a reasonable hour. When you get up,
let him outside before anything else as he won't be able to control
himself for many months. It is quite a good idea to let him sleep
in a sort of play-pen with a comfy bed in it and to provide a tin
tray or newspaper for him to use through the night until such
time as he can learn to wait. Baby puppies cannot hold themselves any better than babies and don't have the advantage of
napkins.

A big, meaty bone and some toys will keep him occupied if he
wakes in the night. It is better not to leave water down otherwise
he will drink far too much out of sheer boredom and then be quite
unable to wait until the family arise. By keeping him in his play-
pen there will be less likelihood of the dramas that so often accompany the arrival of new puppies in homes, when they get into all

sorts of danger and mischief and generally make themselves unpopular with the first person to get down in the morning.

Good house manners can be instilled at this stage, so the puppy should be placed outside and left to perform. If he is at all slow to cotton on, it may be as well to put him outside in the play-pen he has slept in, but put it in a place where the effect of his urine will not spoil any plants.

All puppies should be put outside as soon as they wake, immediately after eating or drinking and at regular intervals during the day.

If the puppy has had good house manners instilled in him in the nest by giving him paper to be clean on, he will leave his bed and use the paper from a very early age. A clean mother, too, will teach her puppies but, as is often the case, the pups leave her before she has completed the lesson. If the little one has no idea of where to be clean, and the new owner is too kind-hearted to scold or at least be firm with so tiny a baby, then the amazing thing is that if he is allowed to get away with it just once he will try it on again. Poodles learn by their aim to please their owners and this can be utilised by using a particularly pleased tone of voice when praising him and a very cross voice when he has failed to please. The poodle may react to this but the Chihuahua won't. He isn't really bothered about pleasing anybody else and would much rather please himself, so if it is cold or wet he won't want to go out whatever the consequences in displeasing his owner. Perseverance and making him go outside in all weathers is the only way to achieve results. Insist that he goes outside, even if it means putting a cover over the play-pen and popping him in that until he performs. Rocky spent six months in quarantine and was over a year old before he came to live with me, but I taught him in a week and he never let me down, although he was a regular stud dog. Fudge was also famous as a stud dog but his mother, Candy, brought him up most strictly and he would always ask to go outside. I never saw him lift a leg in the house until the day when he was Best of Breed at Cruft's. He arrived back from the show after having appeared on television and been interviewed by several celebrities. He walked into the living-room and lifted his leg at every chair- and table-leg there. As we had never had to scold him we can only think that the defiance he was showing was against his mother—showing her who was the big boss then. After Cruft's he got a lot of publicity locally and when the local photographer came to take a picture of him with a big cup he had won, we sat him on a little silk cushion to encourage him to sit still. Ever afterwards that cushion remained his. He would always sit on it to wait for the bitches that were being brought to stud for him. He knew that if he was bathed and allowed to run about afterwards he was going to get a bitch and he would sit on his special cushion in the drawing-room to wait for her arrival. Chihuahuas evidence so much intelligence in their daily life that new owners need to be warned that Chihuahuas never do anything because they don't know any better. Once they have been shown, they know!

The first thing a new owner must know is the correct way to handle tiny puppies. They should be gripped very tightly as they don't know they are tiny dogs and they get quite annoyed when they are picked up and take the first opportunity of jumping down to the ground again. Never pick one up by the scruff of the neck even if his mother carried him this way. Never pick him up by the front legs as they can so easily be dislocated. The best way is to hold the body with one hand and support him under the bottom with the other. It is very bad to force a hand between the front legs as this can push the shoulders out, and it is very uncomfortable for the puppy if you only hold the top and let the rest of him hang down unsupported.

When nursing a Chihuahua puppy, one hand should hold its bottom and the other hand should be placed round the shoulders, holding them in. In this way no harm will come to the bodily construction of your puppy.

All the above affects both the pet puppy and the one chosen to be a show or breeding proposition. Buyers should explain to the breeder their reasons for buying or much time will otherwise be wasted being shown pups that are too expensive for the buyer's needs. Where children are concerned they are just as likely to lose their hearts to the most expensive as to the cheapest.

Where Chihuahuas are concerned even the pet puppies are expensive, so the money asked for top-class specimens can be very high indeed, even if out of the same litter. It takes a lot of experience to be able to differentiate between Chihuahuas in the litter stage, but by three months or so the ones that are not going to make it show-wise begin to make their presence felt. One of the easiest faults to spot is that the ears are never going to stand erect in the correct position. Sellers can tell you that they will go up all right and that they have always been up until your visit. Be that as it may, some dogs have ears that are very large, wide, of a 'heavy appearance' and hang right down, and no amount of massaging the back of them will make any difference. These ears are wrong and won't ever go up. This will not affect the love and companionship this little puppy can give and should not spoil a pet sale, but if there is a chance that you will want to show or breed from your pet this will alter the matter completely. I would rather not buy a puppy from a litter that had a drop-eared one in it. 'Soft' ears are a hereditary failing and, even if taping is performed on them, the fact that there is a gene present for poor ears would stop me from buying that puppy and would be a wise policy for newcomers to make note of.

The first thing a prospective buyer for show and breeding stock should do is obtain a copy of the Chihuahua Breed Standard—the blue-print on the breed which can be bought from the Kennel Club or from any of the breed clubs that cater for the Chihuahua. This should be studied thoroughly and as many shows visited as possible, making sure that the breed is to be featured beforehand. The dog press and the Kennel Club are the best sources of information on the times and venues for dog shows, and the more time you spend looking at as many winning dogs as possible the sooner you may achieve 'the eye', which in this case is not a wink but a mind-picture of what a good specimen should look like. Buyers who pick out a pretty puppy just as a pet and make it into a champion at their first try are very rare indeed. It has happened, it is true, because any litters by champions must contain some of the genes that made the parent champions stand out. The chances that they will all descend to one pup and the breeder won't nab it for herself immediately is even more unlikely. Every pup in the litter will have some of his parents' good points as well as some bad, but they even out and almost disperse over a large litter so that the good points are so minimal that they won't help much in the show ring.

Even an almost fully-grown top-class specimen can change a good first set of teeth for faulty ones—either over-shot or under-shot—and this is a serious disadvantage for breeding and showing. Ideally, no Chihuahua with a faulty mouth should be used for breeding, so that, in time, the mouths will improve and litters may be born with sound mouths. It would be a very good thing if a breed council could be formed to try to put such ideas across. There is plenty of good, sound stock available so breeders don't need to use the dog out of a faulty bitch. I would go so far as to have a dog with a very imperfect mouth castrated, even if I would hesitate to spay a bitch in case she died under the anaesthetic, as can happen. I would like to see such bitches given a Kennel Club registration certificate with 'Not to be used for breeding' written across it.

It is a very wise policy to buy a Chihuahua for show and breeding purposes only if it is accompanied by a vet's certificate stating that it is constructionally sound—free from slipped patellas, hip-dysplasia and hereditary eye and ear faults which do occur in the breed. This will cost a few pounds but will be well worth the disappointment a crippled Chihuahua will cause you. The Kennel Club have schemes whereby dogs who are free from certain hereditary fault conditions are given a certificate to this effect and yet, there are foolish people about who pay out vast sums in stud fees to use dogs that do not carry this obvious guarantee. Lists of these valuable dogs can be obtained from the Kennel Club. The veterinary profession, by and large, is not very concerned with hereditary problems in tiny dogs—they are far more worried about the conditions of the larger breeds. Chihuahua breeders, however, are very aware of which strains have tendencies to carry through the wrong traits, and a wise newcomer would do well to question them on these subjects.

Another fact that the breeder for show will have to decide is which coat he is going to prefer. If he chooses the long-coated variety his task will be light indeed, but if he decides to devote himself to the breeding of smooth coats only and be sorry if he gets long coats in his litters, he will have to search very hard indeed to find strains of Chihuahuas which are potent for the smooth coat. Since the Smooth-Coat Chihuahua Club has been formed for the sole purpose of promoting the smooth-coat Chihuahua, there is a hope that breeders of like persuasion will aim to keep their strains free from any mixture with long coat.

CHAPTER 9

Breeding from the Chihuahua

Breeding Chihuahuas is an absorbing though costly hobby and if the only reason my reader is interested in the breed is to try to make money, then my advice would be to get himself an Alsatian and he will soon be in profit or, if that breed is too large, to choose a toy poodle or a Yorkshire Terrier both of which are popular sellers, command fair return for the outlay and are fairly easy to cope with.

Chihuahua bitches are anything but easy and the better-headed ones have a harder time whelping than the narrow-headed ones. You should use the best-headed stud dog you can find in order to produce the best type of puppy, but the broad head holds up the labour considerably and, more often than not, help with drugs and even a Caesarean section are necessary to save the bitch, let alone the puppies. Most Chihuahua bitches are too small for forceps to be a useful aid and I found that I had to learn some obstetrics in order to save my little bitches from some of the more usual hazards. At the slightest suspicion of anything abnormal I never hesitate to call for veterinary help. If an operation has to be performed, there is a danger of the bitch not wanting her pups or being too weak from her recent complications to be able to do much about them. Trying to feed new-born Chihuahua babies from birth is possible but I would never claim that it is the easiest way of making a living. After about a week of night-and-day duty one gets so 'bomb-happy' that the second and third weeks go by almost unnoticed, but by the end of the fourth or fifth week the strain is considerable and I am never surprised to learn that a Chihuahua breeder's husband has left home.

If, after all these words of warning, the bitch owner is still of a mind to mate his little charge, then the matter must be put in hand without delay as the best stud dogs get booked up early and a great many bitches come into season in the spring and autumn. It is very disappointing not to get the dog of your choice after much studying of form and pedigree. Second best is never quite as good.

THE STUD DOG

There is a lot to be said for keeping Chihuahua stud dogs for profit; they are the cheapest to feed and house, easiest to exercise and keep healthy, and the amount of grooming they need is minimal. Each dog would be very costly in time, for it would have to be shown up and down the country and would also have to win a championship and conform to the standard of not having any hereditary failings. Once a dog has won his way up, he needs to be advertised and his pedigree printed on cards which have to be sent out to the owners of prospective bitches. There is grave responsibility on the part of the owner of a stud dog to be very particular about the quality of the bitches that are brought to be mated. If they carry serious faults the offspring are almost sure to possess some of these, and even if they do not show in the first litter, several of the offspring will carry the faults as hidden recessives. Stud dog owners need to be particularly careful that the bitches they accept are healthy, soundly made and well bred enough not to produce anything for which their dog could be held responsible. The peculiar thing is that although it takes a dog and bitch to produce a litter, the stud dog alone will be blamed for any faults that may appear in the puppies.

An unacceptable yet understandable attitude of the stud dog owner is to accept all-comers on the basis that if he doesn't accept their money some other stud dog owner will. It needs a lot of forbearance to be a successful stud dog owner. Another important matter is the number of bitches a stud dog should mate in a week and whether he may be allowed to mate one bitch more than once —the stud fee is for the stud service only and not for the proposed litter, so before any transaction is completed the bitch's owner should ascertain that a repeat 'free' mating is available if the one paid for proves ineffective; this should be stated on the stud receipt and the dog owner's signature should accompany it.

No stud dog should be expected to mate two bitches in one day. Most male dogs need up to forty-eight hours to be ready again. Continued mating can put a strain on a tiny dog's heart and it is most important that he does not get too plump as this will make it a greater strain too.

The stud dog will not develop properly for mating until he is nearly a year old. It is a sensible policy to let him try to mate an old experienced matron when he is about a year old and then let him rest a few months before putting him to stud properly. Used sparingly at first and handled gently and carefully, he can last as a potent stud for many years. If he starts to miss bitches, then is the time to get a younger dog to take his place.

The temperament of many a young dog improves a great deal after he has mated his first bitch. Very often, young untried dogs get very thin and worried after bitches and get right out of condition for show. They need careful handling and training to be successful stud dogs and I would advise a novice owner to restrict himself to bitches to start with as they are easier to manage than stud dogs. It nearly always happens that the bitch is taller than the dog and, even if he wants to mate her, he cannot possibly reach her. Making him higher by standing him on a step or something will only frighten him and much patience is required. I let my first stud dogs be handled professionally as I did not want to spoil them by my inexperience. It took many months before they were very accomplished and even then they were always nervous of big bitches. Nowadays, I like the dogs to do the mating on a table and this often frightens novice studs as they are afraid of falling. However, once they have mated a bitch successfully they are more amenable to being handled, and although it may take several months for them to achieve complete confidence that I won't let them fall, I find the trouble worth it. In the old days I would get down on my knees so that the dogs would not be afraid of falling. I had a special block fashioned with slots to stand the bitch's back legs in and it was made of very thick solid wood so that it did not rock about. 'The raping block', as it came to be called, did away with the height discrepancy and it was solid enough underfoot to give the dogs plenty of confidence about slipping off. Gradually, they came to accept my help and would even stand on my hand to reach an awkward bitch.

One danger to tiny stud dogs is the chance of a robust bitch struggling and damaging him when he is mating her. It is important that the bitch be held firmly by someone well used to the practice and not by her owner, who will not want to be too firm with her. Any harm done to the stud dog will stick in his mind and make him reluctant to try again, so ideally someone he knows well and trusts should hold the bitch firmly by her shoulders in such a way that she cannot turn her head and give him a sharp nip in the middle of the proceedings. Although it is nice for them to have time to play beforehand, Chihuahua bitches are usually so spoilt that even when Nature tells them they are ready for mating, they themselves refuse to admit it and they can be very rough with the unlucky stud dog. Even in play they can be over boisterous. I have formed the habit of getting the mating over and letting the dogs get acquainted afterwards as champion stud dogs are hard to replace and the stroppy little bitches are more amenable after mating. Every time I took Candy down to mate to Mrs Bedford's Ch. Scampy of Teeny Wee she would fly at him in a rage and yet she would have been tailing eagerly to my stud dogs at home. She was the sweetest tempered and mildest bitch I knew and yet she made a terrible fuss about being mated to him but not about being mated to any other dog. She had several litters of beautiful puppies by him, but she didn't approve of him at all as a husband.

When mating Chihuahuas it is wiser not to let the dog 'turn' as he can get into difficulties through being so much shorter than the bitch. I usually hold him on the bitch during the 'tie' and take him off when the bitch releases him.

The mechanics of mating are that the dog forces his penis into the bitch's vagina and after working spasmodically will become erect; he will then work his back legs much more vigorously and start to eject spermatozoa inside the bitch. The bulbous part at the base of the penis will then swell up and, when it comes in contact with the bitch's vagina, a sort of violent reflex takes place and the penis becomes engorged with trapped blood because a valve cuts off the normal blood flow. The bulbous part then gets very hard and this causes the 'tie', which results in the dog and bitch being unable to release one another for some considerable time. This is Nature's way of ensuring that as many ova (or eggs) as possible can be properly fertilised.

It is possible, of course, for conception to take place without the actual 'tie' but it is a good way of making the pair stay together. Even with a 'tie' of up to an hour, bitches don't always get in whelp but it means that there is some reason for this not happening and advice may be needed as to the best time in the season. Mating too soon or too late in the season, even though a 'tie' is effected, is a most usual reason for no puppies being produced.

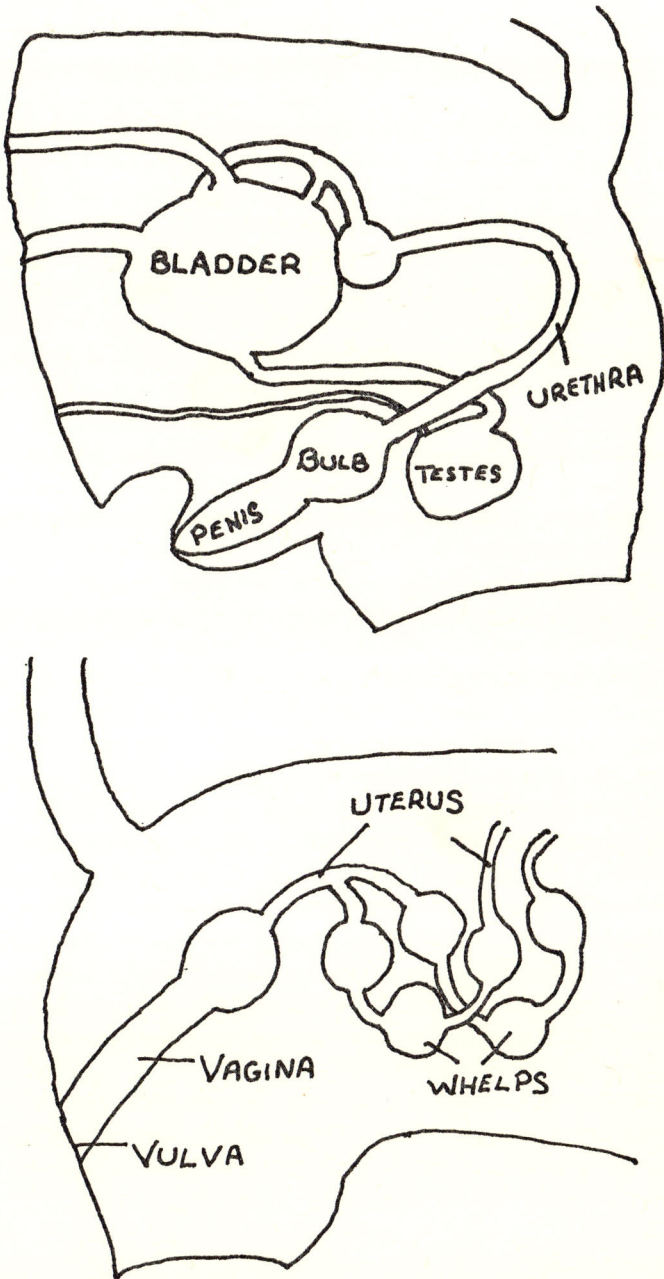

Fig. 4 Diagram of sexual organs of dog and bitch.

After the mating, the pair should rest. For a few days after a mating the stud dog does best if fed on raw meat with a raw egg added.

Mating is best in the middle of the bitch's heat of twenty-one days. About the tenth to fourteenth day is safest although some bitches go against all rules and only take on about the third day, and some even as late as the twenty-second day. The only criterion is experience, for what goes for one bitch will not do at all for her litter sister.

THE BROOD BITCH

Bitches can only be mated during the biannual 'heat' or season. This shows itself as a blood-red discharge which, over a period of about ten days, pales out in colour so that when the bitch is really ready for mating there is no colour left in the discharge. The vulva will swell up and look very pronounced. The bitch will become very affectionate with the other animals in the house and, when her tail or back part is touched with something cold, she will turn her tail up and to the side and make the motions of being mated. At this time she is very attractive to any dog roving about and so she must be guarded very thoroughly. Even about ten days after her mating she is still capable of attracting a very different dog than the one she has just had.

Most bitches are much better off if they are not mated at the first, or even second heat. They need time to develop and a maiden bitch can be terribly distressed by the mating and the consequent whelping.

Some people tell me that their vet has advised mating in the first season, as then the bitch's bones are supposed to be pliable and she will whelp much easier. I have never gone along with this theory as I am convinced that bones are as set at ten months as they will ever be. I questioned my own vet on the subject of first-season matings and he said that what a lot of breeders say to him is: 'It will be all right for me to mate my maiden bitch at her first season, won't it? She will be well over twelve months when she whelps.' He agrees that it probably will be all right but if they have any difficulty to get in touch with him. In this way, he covers himself, but he does not agree with first-season matings either.

It is easy to see why people are anxious to breed puppies of their own and why it is hard to wait another six months. The results of waiting, however, will be far superior in quality and quantity for, even if a very young bitch does get pregnant and produces a large litter, the chances are that the whelps will be weakly and small and very difficult to rear. This is because the bitch still needs calcium and other nutrients to make up her own body and, if robbed before she has finished, she may always be a poor whelper and her pups weakly and inferior. Waiting another six months will pay off in a healthy bitch who, by then, will be old enough to be sensible and much more settled in her nature. She will have a placid labour, produce fine, husky puppies which will be a credit to her, and be able to rear them without too drastic a drain on her own constitution.

All females of the species are meant to be able to have young. Chihuahua bitches are no different but you may find that some bitches are better able to bear litters than others. Not all the tiny bitches are to be avoided though, because some of them are born with much wider and roomier pelvises than others. A clever breeder would measure the distance between the pelvic bones by seeing how many fingers can be put between them. Some tiny bitches are roomy in this respect yet other quite large bitches droop away to nothing and then they could be in trouble. If there is any doubt your veterinary surgeon will soon give you an opinion and, having paid for his advice, it is necessary that it be taken notice of.

If a bitch is wanted for breeding, only choose one that is well shaped, with good round ribs for plenty of heart room, wide pelvic bones and a well-muscled body. Size should be in the five to seven pound region, which would not make for a good show size but she could breed quite tiny pups if mated to a fairly small male with small size prominent in his immediate background. It is wise to spend some time studying pedigrees and looking over different studs in order to find the best one. As a rule, 'like to like' is a good guide. The farther apart in type the breeding pair are, the less likely they will be to produce even-type litters. There is a wide divergence of type in the breed and this lack of uniformity is not good.

If there is any doubt in the prospective breeder's mind, it is best not to part with any money to buy a bitch until advice is obtained. There are members of breed clubs that advertise themselves as willing to help novices, and it may save a lot of time and money if their help is sought early on in the negotiations.

Having obtained the bitch, she should be fed properly in order to get her in the best condition to bear and rear a strong, healthy litter without turning into a physical wreck herself. Many products are available to modern-day breeders and some foods are advertised as containing everything a breeder needs to keep his stock in the right condition. However, I once investigated one of the most famous and well-advertised brands of dried food and was amazed to find that it did not contain a vestige of Vitamin E. As this is a vital requirement for both dogs and bitches when breeding, I strongly queried its lack. I was told that it was very expensive to add and most breeders had not noticed it was missing from the formula. Once I had complained, however, it was added, so I suppose this food could be called adequate. Myself, I prefer to add the vitamins and minerals that are going to be needed, when and how they are required. Over a long period I have used SA 37 successfully. On its label is listed every known requirement that a dog needs as a daily nutritive in order to maintain good health and they are all mixed in the formula. Most of the minerals are trace elements but without them serious deficiencies can be experienced. For a dog of the size of a Chihuahua, a tiny pinch daily is all that is needed for a normal diet. At times of stress however, such as pregnancy, whelping and lactation, at least a saltspoonful is necessary. A daily dose, right through these danger periods and for about three months afterwards, will keep your little bitch in splendid form and it will not be necessary to add anything else. Most of the products on the market contain Vit. D and A but no Vit. B. Yeast products are rich in all B Vitamins but lack A, C, D, E and so on. SA 37 can be obtained in some chemists but, in case of any difficulty, your vet can always obtain it for you. It is manufactured by the Bristol Co., Reading, Berkshire, and I have had excellent results with it and have used it solely for a good many years.

Most of the prophylactics that we used to give in order to avoid eclampsia—e.g., Sterogyl or Collo Cal. D—are now difficult to obtain and some of them are no longer produced. Some of the products that are given in tablet form are in too large a dose to be given to a Chihuahua; it is difficult to judge the correct amount and this could lead to serious over-dosing.

Chihuahuas require at least four ounces of meat and meal daily. With such a small quantity it is important that a high quality is maintained—good quality muscle meat from beef or lamb, enough offal, such as liver, to give iron, and eggs and milk to add some of the other important nutrients. A lot of Chihuahuas are vegetarians in their likes and they will need greens in the form of parsley, water-cress, spinach and various seaweeds. A comprehensive list of dog herbal products can be obtained from Denes, and they will gladly send a brochure which gives correct doses for tiny dogs. Most of their products are made in toy-sized doses as well as in larger doses for bigger breeds. We in the dog world owe Buster Lloyd-Jones, the man responsible for marketing the wonderful Denes Products, a tremendous debt of gratitude for all he has done to educate us in the needs of a dog's diet in illness and in health, and I can thoroughly recommend his books which have earned him world-wide fame.

The best time of year to mate your bitch is wholly a matter of choice. Some large breeds have to be housed in outdoor kennels and it is obvious that spring and summer litters are much less costly to keep warm. This hardly applies to the Chihuahua, so the time to have the first litter is entirely when it would suit the person who is going to look after them. Exhibitors prefer winter litters so that they are free to go to shows in the summer when they may be away from home for several days at a time. It is important that a heat of about 80°F (26°C) is kept up for the first few days but with a tiny Chihuahua pup this can be obtained with an infra-red lamp overhead or a heated pad underneath the bedding. In these days of intermittent fuel cuts, other means of heating must be available for the first few days and it can be reduced to 70°F (21°C) or so if necessary. It should be borne in mind that if the whelping is intended to be an annual event, this time every year will be taken up with looking after a litter, so long-term planning is necessary. One litter every other season is a sensible rule for a breeding bitch. Those greedy people who must have a litter every six months would do better to have two bitches and let them breed alternately. If a Chihuahua bitch is bred from every season, it will weaken her drastically. She will have poorer quality puppies and will get in such poor shape herself that much money will be needed for vets' bills or tonics and her breeding life will be severely cur-tailed. I have found that if I breed from a Chi bitch once a year she will go on breeding successfully for quite a long time. I retire mine anyway at six or seven but I know of quite a few that have gone on producing healthy litters until they were ten and more. If a bitch only rears one or two puppies at a time, it is in order to mate her again in six months' time and then to rest her for a year after that. A Chihuahua bitch is doing very well if she rears four puppies a year—more than this is a bonus.

Care of the Bitch during Pregnancy

The nomal gestation period of a bitch is sixty-three days—nine weeks from the day of mating until the puppies are born. The majority of Chihuahua bitches go the full time but, as so often in Nature, there are always the few that are different and whelp quite a normal litter about a week early. When the bitch has been mated more than once, it is very difficult to know if she is going to take to the first or last mating, so this makes it even harder to judge when the pups will arrive. It is sensible to have everything ready a good week before the due date and make her acquainted with the place where she will be whelping. Like most females at this time, your bitch will be very contrary and will probably have already made up her mind that she will whelp on your best eiderdown or on the feather cushions in the lounge. Telling her otherwise is not going to make a jot of difference and the only way out will be to put her in a pen with a lid on it so that she can't get out. Her cries will be pitiful and it will take a hard heart to keep her there but, unless you don't mind where she has them, in case of accidents she should be put to bed at night in her whelping quarters, in a warm place, and left to get used to it.

There is no need to make many changes in the bitch's diet immediately after mating, but as she increases in size her meals can be made much smaller and more numerous. By the sixth or seventh week she should be getting three or four small meals of very nourishing food. All-Bran or Bemax can be substituted for biscuit meal—just a teaspoonful—and this will replace the bulky biscuit meal of her normal diet. Give meat, fish, and half a beaten egg daily, with SA 37 given in one dose or sprinkled over every meal, whichever is most convenient. She should have as much exercise as she will take. Chihuahuas can be notoriously lazy about this and should be encouraged to walk at a good steady pace for ten minutes at a time, at regular intervals through the day, especially last thing at night. The more elastic her muscles, the easier time she will have when actually whelping. Little bitches, who are so full of puppies that their loving owners are too kind to make them walk, are the ones whose muscles fail them at the vital moment; they go into complete inertia and simply cannot give birth. This won't happen to a well-muscled bitch, but she must be exercised even if her puppies are almost dragging on the ground. Walking on the grass will be softer for her tummy and, as long as it is a slow and steady movement and at regular intervals throughout the day, she can only benefit.

While it seems that all puppies are born with worms, it is good policy to worm the pregnant bitch with a mild vermifuge about three weeks after mating. Chihuahuas are so small that there really isn't room for worms *and* babies and they are better off without such parasites. My vet gives Coopane for this and my bitches have never had any ill-effects. A week later the dose must be repeated to get rid of the worm eggs that may hatch in that period. If the owner is nervous of dosing with worm medicines, a double dose of liquid paraffin may do all that is necessary to expel the worms, but it is not a certain cure like Coopane.

If the little bitch has the energy, she should be discouraged from jumping up on the furniture or into cars, etc. Jumping down will do even more harm as the jerking may dislodge the puppies from their position in the uterus and kill them. The ones farther up the uterus may not be harmed because they have more protection, but a puppy that is dead will decay and infect the others. By the time the puppies are born they could all be dead or so weak that they will die from the very shock of coming into the world. If they do manage to survive, the chances are that their health will be so seriously impaired that they will be weaklings all their lives. Care of the bitch in whelp is essential and her life must be managed so that she won't be exposed to any of the dangers mentioned above. Fighting, if such a thing occurs, is equally harmful and must be avoided even if you have to send any likely sparring partners away for the time being.

Benger's Food, Sanatogen, Farex, Complan or Casilan are good substances to fortify the milk intake so that there will be no drain on the bitch's system when making milk for her puppies. If you learn that her own mother or grandmother ever suffered from a shortage of milk to feed their pups, or if they produced no milk at all, there will be no need for this to repeat itself if the bitch is given Lactogen—cotton seed cake—which is used even on women to encourage a good milk flow. On the whole, this is quite a rare condition in bitches, but Chihuahuas are usually rather spoilt and shortage of milk and refusal to feed are largely psychosomatic.

During the last three weeks of pregnancy, the hair should be clipped from the nipples of the long-haired bitch, not forgetting the ones at the very top which, although they may seem to be 'blind', get very congealed at times and can cause mastitis. The smooth bitch is probably free from hair underneath but she will benefit from a wash with pure, white Windsor soap and warm water. A gentle massage with warm olive oil will help to keep the udder soft and pliable. At the same time, the back parts of the bitch and under the tail require attention. Warm water and the same soap with a tiny drop of Cetavlon added will keep away germs, a very great danger at this time. This treatment should be continued daily for the next few weeks, finishing off by drying with a very soft towel or muslin napkin. Paper towels are good for this and a roll amongst the whelping kit will fit lots of needs.

The whelping box needs to be no more than two feet square and can be custom-made of wood or plastic (most hygienic) or be a strong cardboard box obtained from the grocer, but not one that has contained soap powder as this causes sneezing. It must be strong enough to withstand the violent scratching and tearing up that the bitch will soon be doing. If a square is cut out at one side it will make it easier for her to climb in and out. The box should be placed in a warm place, out of all draughts and away from the normal hurly-burly of the household. The other day my dustman handed me an extra black plastic bag as he thought I had more rubbish than my bins would hold. The bag went straight into the next whelping box, folded in two as a liner in the bottom. On top of this I put a generous stack of newspaper—a few copies of *The Times* are very adequate. On top of this I put my bitch's favourite blanket in order to encourage her to use the box. When she starts to whelp I remove the blanket and replace it with more newspaper. I let her tear it up herself as this gives her the feeling that she is making a nest and the exercise is good for her. A big juicy bone will keep her from getting bored, and when she loses interest in the bone completely it shows that her time is getting near. About twenty-four hours before whelping starts she may lose any wish for food and drink and this is quite normal. One or two bitches will eat a hearty meal just before producing a litter, but they are in the minority.

When the bitch refuses all food and declines to go outside, or if she rushes back to her bed eagerly after going outside, she should have her temperature taken. If it has dropped below the normal of 101.5°F (38.6°C) she is now within hours of whelping and it is better to arrange to sit near her where her every movement can be seen. Now is a sensible time to inform your vet that she is likely to whelp in a matter of hours. This will enable him to line up any staff he may need in case a Caesarean section becomes necessary, and he can check up that his equipment is sterilised and ready, and that he has the best anaesthetic in stock. It is no wonder things go wrong if the first warning a vet gets that he has to perform a serious operation is when you tap on his door in the early hours of the morning or ring him out of a deep sleep to give him the grim details. He may not have an assistant at hand to administer the anaesthetic or to watch the little bitch all the time while he is occupied on the actual cutting. Having been present at such an operation and realising how very occupied the vet and his assistant are with the bitch herself, I do not know how they could have given the puppies the resuscitation that I was able to give while they were too busy. This may be why there is such a serious loss of puppies from Caesarean section. Another cause is that the bitch is taken to the vet too late to save the litter and sometimes too late to save herself.

For this reason a careful check on the time must be kept—a pencil and pad are better than trusting to memory where the life of your bitch is concerned.

Having informed your vet, the next thing is to check over your equipment and put everything you are going to need where you can get at it quickly.

Useful Equipment For Use During Whelping

1. A deep basket or cardboard box containing a hot-water bottle wrapped in a blanket, or, if available, a blanket or old woollen sweater folded envelope shape to hold new-born pups, or an electrically-heated pad kept at a constant heat, ready and waiting before pups start to arrive.

2. Scissors for cutting cord and thread to tie it up. Iodine to seal the end of the cord.
3. Roll of cotton wool.
4. A few J-cloths, pieces of sterilised muslin or butcher's cloth ready to help pups to be born.
5. Hydrogen peroxide, 10 vol. strength.
6. Surgical clamps to hold cord until afterbirth arrives. Their use will prevent the end of the cord disappearing back inside the bitch.
7. Brandy or whisky to use as a stimulant when needed. For the bitch, mix one part of brandy with two parts of warm water and add some sugar.
8. Thermos flask of tea or coffee in case there isn't time to make yourself a drink. It is essential that the helper keeps awake and does not leave the bitch by herself.
9. Pack of cards or some knitting in case you have a long wait.
10. Clock or watch, and pencil and paper to note down times when labour pains start, length of time between puppies and any discrepancy of afterbirths, etc. Time when whelping finishes should also be noted.
11. Pail with a lid to hold soiled bedding and afterbirths, etc.
12. Bowl of water, bottle of Dettol or other disinfectant, and soap and towel for washing hands.
13. Plastic sheet and an old towel to stand bitch on to be examined. They should be put on a table under a strong light.
14. Jar of Vaseline to lubricate the bitch.
15. Plentiful supply of newspapers to keep the bitch's bed replenished.
16. Fresh cardboard box warmly lined and filled with several thicknesses of screwed-up newspaper which has been flattened to give the necessary comfort for when the pups are sucking. This box will replace the one the bitch has soiled when whelping. The old box can be burned and she can start fresh in clean bedding.
17. Check there is plenty of fuel to see you through the night and plenty of water to refill the electric kettle.
18. Have the vet's telephone number handy and a coin for the phone if you have to use a public call-box.

Once this equipment has been checked you will feel much more relaxed and a cup of tea, or a meal if this is due, will make you feel better. The chances are that a first whelping will be a protracted affair, so you will need to be able to cope without extra fatigue and stress from missing meals and drinks. A calm, quiet helper is what the little bitch will need and she will react to nerves and fears by being nervous herself. A quarter of a calcium lactate tablet put down her throat will act as a sedative if she appears very distressed. I have found that a dosing of raspberry leaf—Denes tablet form—is helpful in easing whelping in Chihuahuas. Give one tablet per week after mating and one tablet per day during the last three weeks. In the last week they can have a treble dose safely and after the whelping this dose will help clear away anything harmful (e.g. afterbirths) that may not have come away at the time.

You will know the labour pains have started when the bitch tears and scratches madly at her bedding, making it fly in all directions. The harder she works the easier her pains. Weak, hardly noticeable pains are the first sign of inertia. The digging will go on until she seems exhausted. After a time she will lie down quietly and this is when you must leave everything else and watch her constantly. When you see her stiffen her tail and arch it away from her body she is trying to bring a puppy into the world. You may see a little bladder protruding from her vagina. If it is clear, that will be the water-bladder, but if it is hard to the touch it will have the puppy inside it.

A normal whelping will have the head of the puppy coming first. If the feet come first this is called a breech birth and is not so simple as the pup may get stuck at the shoulders. The head is the widest part at birth and if that can get through the rest of the body can too. There is no time to wait for help if a breech birth is already presented, so the helper should get a piece of thin muslin or J-cloth, grasp what is protruding and hold on firmly, hoping that gentle tugging will get the whole of the body away. If you have help available, get another person to hold the bitch firmly round the body—on the table is the best place and under a strong light—while you grab the part of the puppy already born and, after putting plenty of Vaseline round the vulva and as far in as possible, hold the bitch's tail in one hand and with the other try to ease the puppy out. If stuck at the shoulders, use both hands on the puppy—hold with the left hand, and with the right hand get a finger as far inside the bitch as possible and try to move it round the part that is stuck, gently pulling the rest of the body towards you. It is surprising how strong a pull will be needed, but gently and firmly go on easing out and pulling, twisting the body slightly as you do so. If the bitch is willing to bear down as well, try to time your pulls with her efforts as this will add momentum.

Don't give up now even if you think all is too tightly wedged to move. A continued pressure from you and the bitch is bound to have some effect. Nature means this puppy to be born and you are only helping Nature. Go on trying with your finger, working round the wedged part and keep the other hand pulling and twisting. When you feel that all is lost you will suddenly feel it move and 'Hey presto' there you are with a live puppy. After taking such a long time to be born, you must quickly wipe the pup's head and shake him upside down to drain all the moisture that is in its lungs. Hold the puppy firmly, being careful to support the little head, and swing it in a downward direction. Keep this action going until the puppy cries, then you know you are winning. Hold the pup upside-down and wait while the moisture drips away, gently wiping the nose and mouth all the time. A strong gasp will be your reward and then rub the pup gently all over to get the circulation going before handing it to the mother for her expert attention. You must clear its lungs after a breech birth or any other time when the puppy does not respond and breathe at once. Prompt attention in this way has saved numerous otherwise still-born puppies.

If the birth is normal and the puppy comes head first with its afterbirth attached to it on a long cord, the bitch may be left to attend to this and she will bite through the cord and eat the afterbirth. One is all right but too many can upset her, so when the next puppy comes either sever the cord with your finger and thumb nails, which is a good way to seal up any loss of blood, or cut it quickly and cleanly with a pair of sterilised scissors, leaving a good two inches of cord on the puppy. If the bitch severs this cord too close to the puppy and makes it bleed the puppy will soon die, so the cord must be tied tightly with some thread. If there is not enough cord to tie, the bleeding must be stopped with iodine, friar's balsam, peroxide or potash crystals. Watch must be kept that the bleeding does not start again.

After the first puppy is delivered the bitch may wait some

considerable time before she starts again. Note must be kept of what time the pup was born, so that if the bitch goes on a dangerously long time before the next the vet can be informed. In easy whelpings, which occur surprisingly often, the next puppy could start to come as soon as the first is cleaned up. The first puppy is safer if placed in a warm little box with a hot-water bottle so as not to catch a chill. It has just come from a very warm place and will lose body heat at a dangerous rate. It won't cry if covered over warmly and you can then give all your attention to helping the bitch with her next puppy. An older Chihuahua bitch who may have lost her teeth quite young will need the cord cut and then she will manage the rest. I find it is better to cut the cord than risk the bitch pulling it too roughly and causing an umbilical hernia which, although it may be harmless, is very unsightly. Afterbirth and messy bedding should be removed at once to a pail put there for the purpose and clean bedding introduced in its place. When the bitch starts digging up again watch for the stiffening of the tail which will indicate the next puppy arriving. With luck that will be a normal birth, but if another breech carry on as before. A woman is gentler than a man and less likely to injure the pup in pulling out a breech puppy. I once had a vet who stood the bitch tail towards him, grasped the protruding body between the knuckles of his first and second fingers and pulled straight towards him. The result was a pup with a neck about a foot long and the poor little mother's legs were crippled for the rest of her life.

This same bitch had had an unfortunate beginning because she was born by Caesarean section and the same vet cut a long gash in her head. She came home with about four stitches in her head, the marks of which never left her.

It is important that there is an afterbirth for every puppy. Make sure that they correspond, otherwise if one or more are left behind they will set up a very serious infection and you could easily lose the bitch and have a litter of orphan pups to rear. If there is the slightest suspicion that one has been left inside or if the bitch runs a very high temperature the next day or so, then this is likely the cause and she must be rushed to the vet without delay and given a course of antibiotics.

It is difficult for quite experienced breeders to know when a bitch has finished whelping. Sometimes you can feel another puppy inside her but sometimes what seems to be a puppy is only one of her organs. Her attitude is of some help and if she is willing to go outside to relieve herself and if she looks in her bowl and accepts food or milk this can be taken as an indication that she has had them all. Only close observation will tell you the truth and it is better to sit up with a whelping bitch in case she has another than to go to bed and leave her to it, which could result in a dead pup because the bitch delayed too long. I have known Chihuahua bitches take two days to finish producing a litter but, as a rule, twelve hours would be the maximum. If there is any hold up like this, the vet must be informed at once and allowed to decide what to do. It is always a dilemma to know when to call the vet and when you are merely being over-anxious. After a time, you get a sort of instinct that tells you all is not well but it needs a lot of experience of difficult whelpings before instinct is a reliable agent. It is better to call your vet out if you have the least sign that all may not be well. He would rather have the bitch in the early stages of labour if he has to operate than at the bitter end of a long, exhausting labour or hours of soul-destroying inertia. All Chihuahua breeders need to get the help and support of the vet, and if they feel the vet is not understanding or willing to have a look at a bitch in the hands of a novice breeder, then it is better to change the vet and try to find one that is more understanding and knowledgable.

After a few experiences of the wrong sort I changed my own vet and now have one who has attended my dogs for a great number of years and I have every confidence in both him and his partner. My previous vets were horse and cattle vets and my present ones have a special interest in small animals and this is what Chihuahua breeders require.

Once all the puppies are delivered and the bitch has been outside and had a drink, etc., she can be left quietly as long as she is warm and safe from any outside interference. She must lie down contentedly with her puppies in order for them to suckle. If she is continually sitting up on her haunches they won't be able to feed and she will get nervous. A thick blanket round her pen will not only give extra warmth but will give her the privacy she must have. If left under an infra-red lamp it should be tested for heat by holding your own hand underneath it for some time. If there is a burning sensation the height should be adjusted.

The best time to allow visitors is a matter for the bitch's own temperament. It is wiser to keep her to herself for a few days to let the puppy proudness wear off a bit as she could damage her pups by springing up to snarl at visitors who she thinks may harm her little charges.

The bitch will need unlimited liquids and a very nourishing diet while she is feeding her litter. If there is a single or only two pups a few days on honey and water in very small regular quantities will help her balance out the extra milk she will have made and save her suffering from a most uncomfortable and painful congestion of the milk glands.

Many bitches refuse to eat away from their nests so it is best to feed them in their beds while they are so fussy. If her bed is in a wire pen, the hanging feeding dishes, such as those used in parrot cages, will answer very well and prevent her spilling food and drink on her pups—it takes very little to quite soak a tiny Chihuahua baby.

If, after a few days, one or more of the puppies does not seem as warm and round-feeling as the others he may be a fading pup and could die. Sometimes the bitch will pick on one and continually throw it away from her, or she may sit with it in her mouth all the time. She knows, of course, that all is not well with this one and it is best to take it away and try to rear it yourself. Sometimes, it has not been strong enough to suck and so has been pushed away from its food and gradually got weaker. If this is all that is wrong a few feeds from a kitten's bottle, eye-dropper or tube feeder may get it back to normal. Puppies can live for up to seventy-two hours on the nourishment left in their bloodstreams which is derived through the umbilical cord from the placenta. After this has been utilised the puppies must be nourished regularly or they will die. If you handle them often you will detect one that is not doing as well as the others early enough to be able to supplement the food he has been getting from the dam. Sometimes the milk does not suit a particular puppy and bottle feeding must be resorted to, but this is a very rare occurrence. A crying pup can often be comforted by a tiny dose of magnesia or gripe water. He needs to be 'burped' like a baby and will then settle down having got rid of the 'wind'. A crying puppy making a squeaking kind of noise is a bad sign; it may have a cleft palate or hare-lip. Close examination of the roof of its mouth will show if this is the case. If there is a triangular hole at the back then the pup won't be able to suck. Vets have a way of closing the gap, so help must be obtained without delay. I have never had a Chihuahua with this condition but quite a lot of griffons have it.

The Chihuahua bitch is a splendid and devoted little mother and, unless she has had a Caesarean and come out of the anaesthetic before her puppies have been put to her, she will nurse her puppies for as long as she is required. In fact, so diligent are my bitches that they have to be taken right away from their pups for several hours a day when I need to wean them, otherwise they keep getting back in to feed them when they should be relinquishing their duties.

The secret of getting a bitch to feed her litter if she has been Caesared is to be sure that they are sucking strongly before she comes round. For this you will need to get the co-operation of your vet, then she will come home with her puppies round her instead of in separate boxes, as is usually the case. The reason for this, of course, is simple—the bitch has just been under anaesthetic and the fumes of it are still hanging about her and may affect the whelps. If she can be put in an open-topped box or a wire cage, like I use, then this will mean that the pups will come to no harm by being with her. Never leave a dog in an enclosed space after anaesthetic or he may never come out of it.

At first, the mother won't want to leave her litter for long but after the first week she should be taken for short walks on a lead. This will help her regain the strength in her muscles so that everything will be pulled back into place again and you won't be left with a female who has lost her figure completely by having heavy teats hanging between her legs for the rest of her life. The aim is for her to leave her litter in as good shape or better than when she was first mated.

If she rears her puppies till weaning time and leaves them with a plump body, sleek coat, sparkling eyes and a good tight shape underneath, then you have done all you can to become a good 'breeder' and you will be able to look forward to your next litter instead of dreading it.

For the first month at least, the bitch will do everything necessary for the puppies in the way of cleaning up after them. All you will need to do is to keep her bedding clean and sweet, feed her and provide constant clean water and daily SA 37.

If the puppies' nails are kept nice and short it will save the mother a lot of discomfort from a scratched undercarriage. The nails should be cut where they start to curl over, using tiny nail scissors. Puppies' nails should receive weekly attention in this way so that when they go to their new owners they won't become unpopular right away by ruining nylon tights and furniture, and scratching children's bare legs and so on. If started young, they won't fight against it, but I once had a tiny bitch that so hated her nails being cut that she would go berserk and we could never hold her steady enough to dare cut her claws. In the end I gave up trying and the vet cut them when she was under anaesthetic having a Caesarean.

REARING THE LITTER AND WEANING

When the puppies start putting their heads in their mother's food, they are getting ready to be weaned. If the litter is over four in number, weaning should be started at three to four weeks whether the pups are looking for it or not. Weaning can start with a milky feed of thin Farex or Complan mixture, very sweet and warmed to blood heat. If the pups are hungry they will get right in and start lapping it up. If they are a bit reluctant they can be encouraged by holding their noses just over the food and putting a spot on their noses. Some people stick the noses right into the liquid but this can be dangerous to a Chihuahua. It is better to wait until their tongues come out to investigate, then put some more on the tongue with a finger. After a time, the puppy's head can be guided over the dish, and if it is shallow enough he will be able to reach it all right. Once he gets the idea he will never look back and the next time a dish of food is offered to him he will know just what to do.

The substitute feed should be offered at the same time every day for a week and then the bitch can be taken away for a couple of hours and some scraped beef offered to the pups. Take a large slice of beef and scrape it with a sharp knife blade until you have a few teaspoonsful of a sort of paste. A little should be placed in the mouth of each puppy and the puppy held until he has swallowed it. If any runs out of the side of its mouth, retrieve it and try again. This is a most important time, for once the pup has accepted and learned to cope with raw meat and milk he is nearly ready to face the world on his own. The mother will not want to clean up after him for long once he is eating solid foods, so a regular cleaning up of the pups will have to be performed.

In the third week the puppies can have two meat feeds and the mother be kept away most of the day but allowed back with them at night. Feed them well before she returns so that they won't empty her out and cause her to produce more milk. The idea is to let her reduce her milk supply gradually. When the pups are seven weeks old they should be on four good feeds a day—two of milk and cereal mixture and two of raw meat, one with SA 37 on. They can then be given drinks of water through the day to make up for the loss of their mother's milk, a good percentage of which is water, and if they can be given a long milky drink before retiring, the mother can be taken away at night as well. Let her stay around the nest for an evening or two, and if she insists on getting in with the pups let her. When she leaves them now take her right away and keep the pups in another part of the house so she can begin to forget them. It may take a week for her milk to go completely and she should have a meagre diet for a few days and no water left down other than a small drink with her food. If her teats get congested, they may be rubbed with camphorated oil.

Worming Baby Puppies
From three to five weeks of age is the best time to worm the puppies against roundworm, or ascarids as they are known scientifically. These are worms that abound in the intestinal and digestive tract of the dog and may be present even before the puppy is born, despite the fact that the dam may have been dosed for worms while she was carrying. They can be from one to eight inches in length and are often expelled twisted up in coils. They are hatched from eggs that are laid on the inside of the intestines. When these eggs are passed out in the faeces of the animal, they can be picked up and swallowed by another dog and in twelve days are almost fully developed. If puppies are wormed with a safe worm dose at three weeks they will be saved from having a nasty drain on their systems. If the dose is repeated in twelve days it will get rid of any worms that may have developed in that time. All bedding and excreta should be burned and the puppies watched carefully in case one of them vomits the dose. Coopane is very safe for the deworming and the dose is one tablet for ten pounds of body

weight. Scrubbing all equipment, etc., with very hot salty water and drying it in strong sunlight is about all that can be done to discourage the eggs. If the puppies get reinfested in twelve days they are back to square one again. The whole thing can be a vicious circle, so regular attention and dosing are the only answers to roundworms.

Tapeworms rarely attack puppies but the mother must be dosed against them before she is mated and again a few weeks after mating. It is not advisable to treat her near her time as the dose

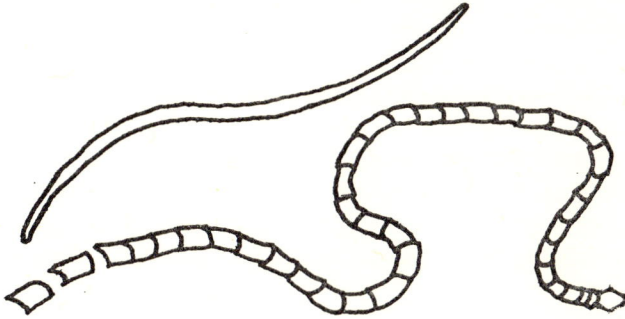

Fig. 5   Tapeworms are segmented; roundworms are excreted whole.

required to destroy a tapeworm is very severe. The tapeworm is evidenced by the appearance of dried segments of the worm on the anus and though these in themselves are harmless they are a sign that a large tapeworm is present in the dog. The tapeworm needs a host, such as a flea or blood-sucking louse, so that when the flea lays its eggs, the head segment of the worm, which is the dangerous part, grows in the lung section of the tiny flea. When the flea bites a dog's skin, the dog will feel the irritation and nibble the area. If the dog swallows the flea, then the tapeworm head will pass into the dog's stomach. It makes good sense to try very hard to prevent your Chihuahua from ever picking up fleas and lice as there is no knowing what they are being hosts to at the time. A tapeworm can be several yards long and as thick as rope, but only the head is vital for its growth. This has to be removed in order to expel the worm and the drug that acts on this is very severe, for even though the head is pin-head size it is very difficult to detach from the dog's inside. Raw rabbit or other wild animal meat can be infected with tapeworm and if the dog eats this then he could soon become badly infected. Fleas are the more common carriers, so regular anti-flea treatment is essential. Some owners of tiny dogs are nervous of using strong insecticides on them, so a bath is indicated. With an in-whelp bitch it will be necessary to go through

Fig. 6   Enlarged drawing of flea (*left*) and louse (*right*).

her coat with a flea-comb or a very fine-toothed steel comb. This must be done on paper which can be sprinkled with a strong flea-powder so that as the fleas are combed out this will immobilise them until they and the paper can be burnt.

Feeding the Chihuahua Puppy

A dog's digestive system requires a largely protein diet with some carbohydrates for warmth and energy and some sort of roughage to give bulk and aid elimination. Dogs fed on an all-meat diet will not receive this necessary roughage and the result will be an infected anal gland. Very young puppies cannot digest strong fibrous food so it must be fined down. It is possible to use full grain cereal and, by boiling it and rubbing through a jelly bag or sieve, come up with a suitable substance, but, in these days of time shortage and inflated wages, there are not enough hours in the day to play around like this. Most of the baby-food manufacturers make excellent, cereal-based fortified foods and it is possible to experiment and even mix them up, e.g., one that contains eggs can be mixed with another that contains meat.

Bitch's milk is much richer and more concentrated than the cow's milk used for dried baby milk. Many animal-food producers make a substitute for bitch's milk and this is the best one to use for early weaning. If cow's milk is used it must be fortified with margarine, and dried milk needs to be mixed at double strength.

Backward puppies, orphaned ones, and those that are in the least sickly, will readily take honey off a finger. Nestlé's sweetened tinned milk can be used as it is to get the little mites interested in food; it can then be watered down a little to stop any fear of dehydration, a condition which will soon kill a puppy.

Once the tiny stomachs of a Chihuahua litter have adjusted to mixed feeding, the puppies will soon make headway, for they are greedy little feeders as a rule and have to be watched carefully to stop them over-eating. In fact, they don't seem to know when they have had enough and fill themselves to bursting point which can also kill them. Another danger is that over-feeding can make the body too heavy for the little legs to carry. The legs may bend in order to compensate and the result could be bandy fronts, pot-bellies and cow-hocked rears. A small amount of nourishing food is always better than a large amount of stodgy food when feeding a Chihuahua of any age.

The following is a useful diet that will see them through baby-hood and can be handed to new owners and easily followed in later life :

FEEDING CHART FOR PUPPIES UP TO 8 WEEKS

For cereal food, mix two packets of Farex or Farlene, one packet of Casilan, and half a packet of Glucodin. Mix together well and, if stored in a dark jar, the goodness will be retained.

BREAKFAST Take sufficient of the above mixture to give all the puppies in the litter enough. Mix with warm milk and allow about a tablespoonful each to start with, increasing as the puppies grow. Feel each puppy after feeding. The stomach should be nicely full, but not hard like a tennis ball. After a few feeds the right amount will soon be found.

LUNCH   Scraped or finely-minced raw beef or lamb (chicken is too dry at this stage). Feed to capacity as meat, providing it is raw, is the easiest of all food for the dog to digest. Sprinkle a pinch of SA 37 on each pup's feed. A drink of clean water, with the chill taken off, can be given at this time.

TEATIME   As Breakfast while very young, but when teeth are coming through the puppy will need some hard biscuits, such as Lactol Milk Biscuits, or hard-baked rusks to help cut his teeth and introduce him to hard food. A drink of milky tea or milk and water in the ratio 50:50.

SUPPER   Minced meat with one teaspoonful of cooked mashed liver and a very small quantity of Atora suet as a puppy's diet should consist of about seven per cent fat. If no suet is given, a tiny drop of mixed fish oil (cod-liver oil and halibut oil) should be given instead as the skin needs it to prevent dryness. Any scurf on the skin may be due to lack of fat or through taking cow's milk whole, giving a too acid condition.

OR

Fish cooked in its own water with margarine added and a drop of milk to cool it down.

OR

A few fresh herrings cooked in a pressure cooker, mashed (whole heads, bones and all) and mixed with some brown bread crumbs. This is excellent for putting weight on a lean dog and is most nourishing.

Clean water should be available in the day but not at night.

Puppies of eight to twelve weeks old should be fed four or five meals a day. From twelve weeks old they should have three meals a day, omitting the teatime feed and late drink, and from six to nine months feed twice daily, keeping a milk feed until all teething is complete. Adult dogs can have one or two feeds daily, whichever is preferred by owner and dog.

When a puppy goes to a new home, big, meaty, raw bones are an essential item for keeping gums and teeth clean and healthy. Chihuahuas are notorious for losing their teeth very early in life but if you allow them to chew bones they seem to keep their teeth healthy for as long as other breeds. As they are so aggressive over bones they must be left alone and allowed to enjoy them in peace. If the meat on the bones is objected to, the bone can be cooked in a pressure cooker until it is thoroughly sterilised. A dog should be allowed to take a bone on long car journeys or left with one when the family go out without him or when he has to spend much time alone. It is the best way of keeping his teeth out of other people's valuables. Even a tiny Chihuahua can do his share of damage to shoes, curtains and furnishings, but if he has his own toys from the very beginning he won't look for anything else. Boredom is the main reason why puppies get into so much mischief. No one would wish to deny a baby puppy his fair share of fun and games and naughty pranks—indeed that is one of the reasons why puppies are so popular—but destructive mischief will make him unpopular, and eating things like coal and coke and packets of poisonous substances can be downright dangerous.

To help him settle in his new home, the Chihuahua puppy may be given a warm drink last thing at night. My Chihuahuas like to drink half milk half water instead of plain water and I let them have it as the extra nourishment must be good for them.

Teeth

A puppy has only twenty teeth in the first set of milk teeth, which come through when he is four or five weeks old. The permanent set of forty-two don't start coming until after sixteen weeks or even later in the case of small Chihuahuas and this is quite normal. A lot of Chihuahuas have correct mouths in the first set but get undershot jaws when the permanent teeth arrive. This cannot be rectified and will go against a Chihuahua being shown, although it makes little difference to a pet dog unless it is so bad that the bottom jaw sticks out enough to show the bottom teeth when the mouth is closed. The opposite condition, when the top teeth stick out over the bottom teeth, is called 'overshot', but this is not so common in Chihuahuas. It gives the dogs a horrid 'rat-faced' appearance and is to be avoided.

A lot of Chihuahuas get two sets of teeth in their mouths at once. This is because the second set comes through before the baby teeth have dropped out. In most breeds, the first teeth disappear of their own accord, but Chihuahuas may need help in this respect. If the first teeth are allowed to remain with the second ones they will start to damage the enamel of the second teeth. They will also cause the mouth and jaw to grow wrong as there is not enough room in the tiny mouths for so many teeth. It may need several visits to the vet in order to have the baby teeth removed, but careful watch must be kept and the extra teeth extracted without delay. The eye teeth, or canines, are usually the worst offenders and often they are embedded in the gum by a good half an inch, so a general anaesthetic will be needed before the vet can get them out. There is danger here: the tiny Chihuahua is not a good subject for anaesthetic so the smallest dose possible should be given.

General Management

As soon as the puppies leave their mother they will want room to play, proper places to sleep and to keep themselves clean. A play-pen, something on the lines of a real baby's play-pen but with fine wire mesh for its walls, is admirable as the puppies are able to see out and take in the happenings around them. It has been found that pups who are allowed to grow up behind solid walls tend to be nervous when they meet new people or new places.

Care should be taken to find a pen with the uprights on the outside of the wire, not inside it. I once had two very young pups who were playing a furious game of rushing round the pen and one of them banged his head on the edge of a corner support. In no time I was rushing his unconscious little form to the vet, but all in vain, for his tiny skull had cracked from ear to ear like an egg-shell. Round pens would be best of all and a cover will stop any monkey-business like climbing up the sides and falling out.

Ponds and swimming pools are best kept out of bounds when a Chihuahua puppy is growing up. You have to try to foresee trouble and forestall it, although sometimes this is very difficult. I once had a tiny little long-coat bitch who got into so much mischief that I didn't think I would ever get her safely through her puppyhood. One day, when my daughter was washing the kitchen floor, Merry, as this little imp was called, kept on tugging at the other end of the cloth, making the proceedings very difficult, to say the least. The telephone called my daughter away and she put the cloth in the bucket of water before she went to answer it. On her return she missed Merry who seemed to have disappeared and, thinking she would get the floor finished in good time with Merry out of the way, she reached for the cloth in the bucket and caught hold of a struggling little body instead. There was Merry swimming round in about two gallons of water. She had obviously gone in after her cloth—her plaything. None the worse, she went under the hair dryer and the number of times she did so must have had a good effect on her coat for she grew up to be very beautiful and became Champion Emmrill Meringue of Aes.

Selling the Puppies
When the pups are old enough to assess, it is wise to get an experienced eye to run over them and tell you which to keep for show or for breeding and which to sell as pets. It is doubtful that there will be more than one good one in a first and trial litter and you won't wish to miss the best one. Get the litter looked over before you offer any of them for sale so you will know what you have to offer when enquiries arrive. Surplus pups are best offered locally so that you can watch them progress and also make friends with their owners. This is the best way to make friends, for there is nothing as strong as the friendship of people who have received a loving and healthy pet from your hands. An advertisement in the dog press will get you more money but you will not see or hear of your puppy again; it may even get sold to someone who will sell it again and you may not approve of its final destination.

Ask a fair price, bearing in mind the amount of time and trouble you have taken over rearing the litter and the cost of it if you charged your time on an hourly basis. When determining how much to ask, remember to allow for the food and heating, the stud fee and the price you paid for the mother. You could also ask advice of other breeders and enquire how much is being asked for similarly bred puppies. Don't expect to get as much as breeders who have made a big name in the breed on their show wins and the wins of the stock they have sold. Such a reputation takes a lot of time and money to achieve and such breeders have earned the extra money their stock can command.

When answering enquiries, beware of the buyer who asks for more than one puppy or offers to buy the whole litter. This will be for resale and as you will wish to get to know your customers this is not the way to do it. Tiny baby puppies who leave a hygienic background and are exposed to the mixed bag of pups often found in pet shops are very vulnerable to disease. It is wise not to let them mix with outside dogs until at least two weeks after inoculation against hardpad and distemper, which dreaded diseases are best avoided even if the vaccination is a costly one.

If you have a puppy that must face the danger of mixing before he is fully protected, a dose of measles vaccine at any time in his young life will give complete immunity for six months or at least until such time as the permanent shot of distemper vaccine can be given. If this is given too young—under ten weeks or so—it will have to contend with the natural immunity the puppy has already received in his mother's milk—the first milk, or colostrum—which contains all the antibodies the mother has built up in her own system and which will fully protect the puppy while it is feeding from her. When she stops feeding it, it will take a couple of weeks for the antibodies to become ineffective and so make it safe to inoculate permanently.

Distemper is such a dreaded disease not only for the severity of the illness itself but also for the terrible after-effects which usually ruin the dog's chances of ever being completely healthy and normal again, and the resultant discoloration of the teeth will make a show career impossible.

When you sell one of your puppies, make a note of the full address of the buyer so that you can send on any Kennel Club Registration Certificates that may be outstanding. A register of all your customers makes an interesting document and one which you will wish to refer to when you have bred lots more puppies. A simple ledger is all that is necessary or, if you intend going in for breeding in a big way or making it a regular event to sell puppies, it may be a good idea to apply for a registered prefix with the Kennel Club and to have printed receipts and pedigree forms with your prefix on the heading. Some insurance companies who specialise in dog breeding will supply you with printed receipts and cover notes with your own name and address. They can even make you an agent, issuing cover notes and collecting fees for the first month's insurance from new puppy owners. The price paid for Chihuahua puppies makes this a very feasible proposition. The counterfoils in the book are then a true record of all your transactions and make for easy reference.

CHAPTER 10

Training the Chihuahua Puppy

AS A PET

If the Chihuahua goes to a new home and is to be a household pet, the first thing to do is to teach him to be clean in the house. If his breeder has paper-trained him or his mother has taken him outside and shown him how to behave, then there will be little trouble, but if he has been allowed to mess in his bed or soil the floor wherever he pleases then the new owner has quite a problem on his or her hands.

Persistence and never ignoring a mistake is the only way to achieve results. Put the puppy outside immediately he wakes up and straight after eating or drinking, and for the rest of the time 'on the hour, every hour' is not a bad motto and should be continued even though the weather is foul, in which case you can put him outside in a play-pen with a waterproof cover. Letting him out last thing at night is very important. Don't leave any water down for him at night because he will drink it out of boredom and then won't be able to hold himself until he is let out in the morning. Prevention is better than cure in this matter. If he persists in wetting in the house, soak some of it up with paper and put this paper under a brick where you wish him to perform outside. When he smells the paper he should get the connection and wet it again, eventually forming the habit. There are preparations on the market which are designed to do the same thing, but the puppy's own urine is easier for him to recognise and doesn't cost anything.

Until the puppy is reliable in the house he should only be allowed in rooms where the floor can be thoroughly washed. If he wets on a carpet the smell will linger however much you wash it, so it is better not to give the puppy a chance to misbehave in the wrong place. A lot of scolding and shouting when he does wrong is apt to confuse him and it is no good at all scolding him ten

139

minutes after he has disgraced himself because he will not see any connection between his wrong doing and the punishment you mete out to him. If you scold him a lot and rub his nose in his mess he will be frightened and afraid to mess at all, or he may hide away and do it under chairs or cookers or somewhere that he can't be found out, which will also be somewhere that will be very difficult to get at to clean. An easy-going attitude is the only one to take and the knowledge that once he has learnt what is expected of him he is so intelligent that he will learn the lesson thoroughly and never forget it; even when he gets too old or too ill he will try his best to get to the door.

The next important lesson is walking on a lead. These days, even the amount of traffic on the quieter roads is frightening, and no dog should be allowed near a road without a lead on, even if he has been trained to walk to heel.

The Chihuahua is about the most difficult breed to train to walk on a lead. It is the only breed that has a large number of owners who have given up trying to get them to walk on their own and have to carry them instead. This is all wrong, of course, as dog and owner would benefit from regular walking, and once the stubborn little creature has discovered that walking is feasible he gets a lot of pleasure from it. He knows, however, that he looks so very fragile that any rough tugging could harm him and, when he sticks his feet in the ground and refuses to move, there is nothing to do but pick him up, especially if there are other people about who might report you to the Royal Society for the Prevention of Cruelty to Animals for your unkindness.

You must give him the early lessons in lead walking in the confines of your own home—either in the house or garden—where strangers, who don't realise what a difficult task you are trying to perform, cannot see what is going on. It is a good idea to start by tying a little piece of soft ribbon round the puppy's neck with a long end attached and just let him play about with it for a few days until he forgets it is there. When he is ignoring it completely, pick up the end quietly, without him noticing, and let him walk you about all over the place. The busier he is, the better and if he runs you must run with him. If he sees you pick up the ribbon and he keeps his tail up and runs about with you then you can continue, but if he sees you and puts his tail down and stops in his tracks, let go of the ribbon at once and try again the next day.

If and when he sees you hold the end and he walks along with you, take him as far away from the house as you can and when he begins to pull, turn sharply round and walk smartly back to the house. After this take the ribbon off completely—that is enough for one day. Part of the trouble with training baby Chihuahuas is that they get bored with a game and want to change, and when they are forced to go a way they don't wish to they get very peeved, and then they get stubborn and refuse to co-operate. If forced even more, they will take a positive dislike to the idea of walking on a lead and go and hide whenever they see a lead being produced, so what you have to try to do is make them so pleased to see the lead that they welcome it eagerly.

During the training, feed the puppy at the same time and place every day. Then one day, let him see that his meal is put ready for him but, instead of letting him eat it, carry him away from his dinner but so that he can still see it. The collar and lead should be put on at this point and he should be placed on the ground and allowed to walk to his dinner. The collar and lead should be left on while he is eating and removed when he has finished. Then allow him to run about in perfect freedom. This policy must be followed every day until it is firmly fixed in his mind that collar and lead mean dinner and afterwards 'playtime'. How long this will take will vary with individual dogs, but if carried on over a long period there will be no more fighting when the collar and lead are put on.

The daily walk will not start in earnest much before the puppy reaches six months of age and by this time he should be quite at ease on the lead. Baiting him with titbits of liver or cheese is acceptable for the show ring where you only have a short time to show off his prowess, and reluctance to walk will go against him. In the street you can hardly go along proffering bait in this way, so it is worth giving lead training a lot of importance in the puppy's daily routine.

Chihuahuas have very sharp hearing and make noisy, alert little house-dogs. They should be trained to recognise regular callers and not to bark at the postman and milkman. My first Chihuahua, Driada, had a strong dislike of the postman and barked at him most ferociously although she was normally a very sweet-tempered little thing. Her great-great-grand-daughter, Roguey, who was not nearly so sweet tempered, hence her name, must have inherited this trait for she had an absolute hatred of the postman and so great was her feeling that she would hide in the uncomfortable lobby at night so that she would be able to attack him when he brought the mail in the morning. He always opened the back door and put the post on top of the fridge out of the way of the dogs, and if Roguey happened to be in the lobby she would fly at him —and one day she tore a button off his jacket. (She must have jumped quite high to do this.) The postmaster sent us the button with a piece of cloth she had torn with it and we had to apologise and offer restitution. Till the end of her long life she hated postmen even though some of them were extremely nice and good tempered about her. It made no difference to Roguey until, one day, my eldest daughter did a post-round to get pocket money over Christmas and Roguey wagged her tail and welcomed her with delight despite the postbag. Not at all stupid. Training Chihuahuas out of these bad habits is well nigh impossible and it is better not to let them start giving vent to their aggression in this way. They don't realise they are such tiny dogs and think they are big enough to tackle anything because their spirits are so large.

Many Chihuahua males will fight fiercely and some kennels find they cannot mix them. Mine, on the other hand, got on well enough once they had sorted out who was to be the 'boss'.

Chihuahuas seem to love car travel and don't seem to suffer from the movement which makes so many larger dogs miserable. A cushion on the floor or even a travelling-crate is the safest way for a Chihuahua to travel in a car. Sudden braking can cause such a tiny dog to fly off the seat and get hurled against all manner of dangerous objects, and it makes for a very nervous driver if he is afraid for the Chihuahua's safety. I have never seen a safety harness small enough to anchor a tiny Chihuahua.

It won't take much time to instil good car behaviour and will be well worth while. I once had a tiny Chi bitch who used to travel inside a jerkin with an elasticated waist. I had to wear this jacket all the time so that Zara could ride in comfort. I did not, however, let any of the others try this mode of travel.

Once a few basic lessons have been grasped it will be no time at all before the Chihuahua will be one of the most popular members of the household. Once he is accepted and allowed freedom to expand a bit he will soon be joining in every activity and will be such a delightful companion that you will soon wonder how you ever got along without him. He is rarely a one-person dog and accords everyone their due for what they do for him. He likes the one who lets him out first thing, the one that feeds him, and the one that plays with him. If a Chihuahua ever singles you out for his undivided attention and affection you are blessed indeed, for his loyalty and devotion, when they are given, are supreme.

TRAINING FOR THE SHOW RING

It is possible to attend classes for the purpose of training dogs and owners to make the most of themselves in the show ring. The teachers are properly trained and they have to be what is known as 'good with dogs' in order to be successful.

I have never lived in a district where such classes were held so I have always had to train my dogs myself and I have found enormous enjoyment in it.

The first requisites for the trainer are a great deal of patience and a very real affection for the little pupil. When there is this rapport the young pupil will know that you mean him no harm and, if the things you are trying to teach are quite incomprehensible for him, at least there will be a certain harmony and enjoyment in one another's company, which will mean that sooner or later the desired result will be achieved. Many of the Chihuahuas that I have trained for the ring have known better than I what was expected of them and they would dance about on a lead with their tails up, eagerly awaiting the bait that they knew would soon be given to them. It is impossible to train a Chihuahua to show without encouraging him with bait of some kind.

When I tried to show Red Rocket I did not know the value of 'bait' and so he did not show to his best advantage at all. Zara, his very beautiful tiny daughter, was a most reluctant shower and one day in the show ring she slipped her lead, which she always hated, and dived under someone's chair and refused to come out. I found myself lying full-length on my stomach trying to coax her out without any joy. The lady sitting on the chair above me was eating her lunch and she kindly gave me a bit of sausage to tempt her. It acted like a charm and Zara came out far enough for me to put her show lead back on her. She ignored this and pranced along looking for the remains of the sausage and I had the sense to ration her with it until after she had finished showing. The change in her attitude was amazing and she won her class hands down to the delighted applause of the people around the ring who knew what trouble I had had in trying to get her to show off her many charms. After that I always took a piece of sausage and Zara showed a treat.

The knowledge that Chihuahuas needed baiting in order to get them to show to advantage was a turning point in my show career in the breed. Afterwards, I always took something to tempt them. At first, I took anything that happened to be handy, but Fudge, who became a champion at Cruft's in 1965, showed best for chicken livers until he got to like the ring so much that he would show off like mad just for the sake of the applause. He thoroughly enjoyed his moment of glory, walking down the red carpet to the judging dais at Cruft's with all eyes on him and the spotlight picking him out. He got quite a taste for the limelight and never needed baiting again. He never lost his taste for the ring and was still winning veteran classes in his ninth year.

His grandson, Emmrill Humfri, was a different type completely and showed beautifully if he was given chicken. One day, I took roast lamb instead and he refused to walk an inch. When the class was over and he had failed to win, a friend offered him some chicken in consolation. The difference in his attitude had to be seen to be believed. I learnt my lesson and never took him anything but chicken again.

My latest show puppy has decided that he is going to show for cheese only—best English cheddar, of course. This is an improvement on many others and much cleaner to handle. Plastic bags or boxes are useful containers for 'bait' so that the recipient can see what he is getting. It is no good just showing him though, he has to taste it at regular intervals. If you think this is a silly idea I should advise you to get another breed to show that is not so determined as the Chihuahua to get things his own way.

The Chihuahua should show on a loose lead and walk with his head and tail carried up proudly. It is also better if he keeps his ears erect as well when he is actually moving for the judge. If his ears tend to droop when the judge is looking at him, a sharp click with the nail will make him prick up his ears to listen, and if this fails, a dropped handkerchief will attract his attention and make him prick up his ears in interest just long enough to show the judge how he can look. It is the job of the handler to persuade the small exhibit to show off the breed's essential points and the dog's own attributes to the best advantage. The longer an exhibit can be persuaded to hold a pose when all the dogs are being examined in a bunch, the more likely he will be to catch the judge's eye and make him call your exhibit to the centre for a prize.

CHAPTER 11

The Character of the Chihuahua

People who have Chihuahuas as house pets are always amazed at the unusually high intelligence of these tiny dogs. It may be that the Chihuahua's sense of self-preservation makes him more alert than others. Over and over again one hears stories of their clever, almost uncanny behaviour. For instance, one lady always wore a hat when she went out. If she went upstairs and got her hat, her Chihuahua would always be waiting at the front door with his lead in his mouth. If she came down without a hat on, he would be waiting at the bottom of the stairs. She used to demonstrate this to many of her friends and visitors and they were all amazed at the extraordinary power this little dog possessed of being able to foretell whether his mistress was going to come downstairs with her hat on, even though he could not see her. It was a long time before his secret was revealed. His mistress kept all her hats in a big drawer of a chest on the landing. When she wanted a hat she would open the drawer, select a hat and go to her bedroom mirror to put it on. The little Chihuahua would hear her bang the heavy drawer and while she was putting on the hat he would run and get his lead and be waiting at the front door when she came down. If he didn't hear the drawer bang he would wait at the bottom of the stairs to join her when she came down.

When my youngest son was at boarding school, his own little pet Chihuahua knew that he would come home for a day every other Sunday. On the days he was coming home she would be in the garage ready to jump in the car to go and meet him, but on the alternate Sundays when he was not coming home she would lie in her favourite position by the Aga cooker and not move all morning. We could never fathom out how she knew the right days. She was devoted to my son as he was to her. When he was very young he gave me a penny for her, so we called her Emmrill Pennyworth. To the family, however, she was simply known as Bunny.

Bunny joined in all his games when they were both very young. She came along when I took him to and from kindergarten and missed him almost as much as I did when he went off to prep school. By the time he had gone on to public school she had got it all worked out and when the holidays came round she was in her seventh heaven. I let her have the odd litter to keep her occupied when he was away, but her litters were few and far between as she wasn't really a brood bitch and I dreaded anything happening to her. She was a Fudge daughter out of Roguey, the postman killer, but her nature was of the sunniest and she got on well with dogs and humans alike. She once had a daughter called Halfpenny who was an absolute poppet and so very pretty that I was offered a lot of money for her. Bunny taught her to be devoted to my son, just like she was, so she couldn't be sold and became one of the family too.

Fudge's mother, Candy, was a real 'family favourite' and started on a show career as soon as she was six months old. Once, she jumped over a fence and broke her front leg in two places and my vet thought she would never use it again. I had seen a film in Sweden of a broken bone being mended with a silver pin being inserted through the marrow and asked my vet if he could perform such an operation on my very valuable show bitch. He said the only vet who might be able to perform such a new and delicate operation would be Mr Brian Singleton, so we made arrangements and took Candy up to his London surgery. He knew about the operation and had actually done a successful one on a bull terrier but nothing so small as a Chihuahua. Candy was long haired and, when Mr Singleton had finished the operation, the place where the stitches were put in never grew any hair so I never showed her, but the operation was a hundred per cent successful and Candy walked without any limp and never suffered any trouble for the rest of a long life. She stayed with Mr Singleton, who was to become President of the Veterinary College of Surgeons, and she completely won him over. He told me she was one of the nicest little dogs he had ever known. When she gave me Fudge she more than repaid me for all the time and expense her operation had cost. She was a real pet and full of fun, and she joined in all the family happenings. She played Cowboys and Indians with the children and when they pointed a gun at her and said 'Bang, bang', she would lie down and 'die'. In fact, in the end, you could point at her from the window and wherever she was she would lie down and 'die for the Queen'. Her one drawback was her mania for sweets. She would almost sell her soul for a chocolate and could look so woebegone that nobody could resist her and would give her sweets galore. In the end, she got so fat that she had to go on a rigorous slimming diet and we had to harden our hearts to her constant appeals for sweets.

Her son Fudge was our house pet for over nine years. His mother ran a high fever when he was a few weeks old and so the litter had to be fed by hand and I became very attached to the baby Fudge. It was a bonus that he was so good looking for he was destined for a pet before all else. He quickly assumed command of the house and none of the other dogs were allowed to put a paw over the front-door step—this honour he reserved for himself. The poodles and Yorkies and all the other Chihuahuas had to use the back door. Even after he had been dead for several years, the poodles would still refuse to come in by the front door, so firmly had he laid down the law.

His favourite place was in a bed against the Aga oven which was alight day and night, year in and year out. When a new litter was born, the puppies' bed was put against the Aga and if it was where Fudge liked to lie he would get into the bed with the new-born pups. However much the mother objected, he took no notice and remained in the puppies' bed until it was moved to one side and his own bed reinstated. After a time, the mothers got quite used to Fudge's little ways and would let him take over their litters when they went outside to be clean. He would lick the pups and nuzzle them quite gently, but the horrified expression in his eyes when one of them tried to suckle was very comical.

Like his mother, Fudge loved sweets and if I ever went away he would wheedle extra sweets out of one of the people left in charge, on the grounds that he was a poor deserted wee creature who needed consoling. The result was that he developed a tricky heart condition for which he had to be given a tiny red pill every day. The only way we could get him to take this pill was in a piece of fried bacon. As I cooked bacon every morning, this was no great problem and he would take his pill eagerly. If I was ever in a hurry to catch a train or meet someone, or if there was any urgency about my journey, I would give Fudge his pill before I started off. If I was in too great a hurry so that Fudge felt rushed, or if

I showed any impatience to be off, he would sit on the door step and as I bent to pat his head in farewell he would deposit his pill without the bacon, at my feet. He knew this would stop me in my tracks and I would start afresh and give him his pill all over again. He had a special smirk he kept for these occasions, and my daughters learnt to recognise when he was going to play his trick by the wicked gleam in his eye. He had a great affection for his mother and for Topsy, one of his wives. Topsy was very mischievous and when an important photographer came to take pictures of all our dogs, she stole a handkerchief out of the photographer's pocket and, in the background of nearly all the serious pictures of my show dogs posing, she can be seen having a lot of fun 'killing the hanky'.

Fudge and Topsy had a beautiful little daughter, Tu Tu, who liked her comfort very much. One day, one of the staff wore a fur hat on her way to work and put it in her shopping basket when she took it off. When she put her hand into the basket to get her hat out to go home in, she was shocked to feel a sharp bite. Tu Tu had found a very comfortable bed and was furious to be disturbed and have it taken away.

Chihuahuas must be hardier than they would appear from the way they shiver at the slightest excuse. This is more to get noticed and to be put in the warmest place than because they feel the cold. I once knew a little black and tan smooth coat called Peeps who stayed with me while his family were abroad for the Monte Carlo Rally, which is always held in the coldest part of the year—January. He would shiver so much that his owner had knitted him a set of little rolled-top sweaters. In fact, she brought a clean one for every day he was staying. Peeps ran about all over our house and would follow me all the time when I was there. I would open the french doors and he would go out and bark when he wanted 'in' and he never gave me the slightest trouble. But one Sunday, I had to go away for the day to attend a christening so I left him with my daughter, whom he knew very well. In the afternoon, some young visitors arrived so my daughter put him outside the door so that they wouldn't see him and want to pick him up. They stayed longer than expected and when she went to call him in he had disappeared. Despite her frantic calls and hurried searching, there was no sign of him. I came home to find that his owner had returned too, and when she came to collect him and found him missing she threatened to kill me.

We both searched all over the farm with powerful lanterns and car headlights which we took over as many fields as possible. The ploughed fields were too wet to search and by the time we returned to the house the owner had calmed down enough to send out notices of an enormous reward for his return. Nobody went to work in our village, they were all scouring the countryside for Peeps. About ten days of the most foul weather held up the search and the days were very short, but I still spent most of them calling his name round all the field boundaries. As our land was surrounded by a river, which he would meet whichever way he went, we made up our minds that he must have been drowned. There were plenty of rabbits on our land and my husband always took his gun when he was walking over the fields. Late one afternoon, two weeks after Peeps went missing, my husband fired at a rabbit, and when he bent down to pick up the quarry, a warm excited little body in a tiny red sweater jumped into his hand and gave him a most joyous welcome. Peeps was apparently no worse for his adventure, even though he had never been outside in the slightest chill air and was always cuddled inside a fur coat or in a big woolly scarf. Anyway, all three pounds of him were delighted to be back in the house with us. The vet found he had food inside him and was in no way harmed by his two weeks' exposure.

Another of our survivors was Real Happiness, who lived up to her name by grinning broadly at everyone with a smile from ear to ear. All the dogs and humans loved her except our old Yorkie bitch, Charm, who hated the sight of her. We kept them apart as much as we could but whenever they got together there would be a furious set-to and poor little Happy would be knocked unconscious. The vet would attend her and after a lot of nursing she would recover. One day, they had a fight and Happiness got covered in mud. My daughter had to put her under the yard tap to find out where she was injured. As soon as the cold water touched her head she came round completely, so afterwards we gave her the 'cold water treatment' and she would become conscious at once and go off again to finish her fight. We thought about getting her some sort of 'skid-lid' for protection as she seemed to be very vulnerable to blows on the head.

Brought up with farm stock, most of my Chihuahuas gave the

cattle and horses a wide berth but some got a lot of enjoyment out of chasing the geese. One little long coat called Twiggy (because she was so fat) liked to join in the fun but wasn't very agile, and one day she forgot herself enough to chase our house-cow, who promptly kicked her in the mouth, smashing her jaw. We took her body to the vet expecting him to put her to sleep but to our relief he said that her heart was quite strong and she could stand an anaesthetic. He wired up her jaw and she made a complete recovery from her injuries—and from cattle chasing!

Early in the nineteen-hundreds, Miss Rosina Caselli had a large troupe of performing Chihuahuas that she used to take round the music halls. It was a very successful act and much in demand. Nowadays, Mrs Olga Fred-Denver has a troupe of Chihuahuas that are known on the stage in Britain and Eire. Training such small and individual dogs to perform correctly and obey commands is no small achievement. Chihuahuas are not usually to be found taking part in obedience trials in this country, although I have seen quite a number of them put up a very good show indeed and some have even obtained a degree of CD (Companion Dog) and even CDX (Companion Dog Excellent).

CHAPTER 12

The Chihuahua in Old Age

The unfortunate thing about dogs is that they cannot live as long as we humans would wish them to. A year in a dog's life is equal to seven of human life so that when a dog is ten years old he is about seventy human years, and like a human, whose physical make-up he resembles in quite a number of ways, he will be starting to lose his hair and his pigmentation and showing signs of nearing senility.

Obesity is one problem that affects the older dog. Too much fat round the heart makes it difficult for the dog to breathe, resulting in shortness of breath, and heart weakness can occur through carrying too much surplus flesh. A Chihuahua's little legs will find it difficult to support the weight of a very fat body and can collapse.

The dog is much too fat if it has a large fold of fat just above its tail. A much reduced diet and even a special slimming diet must be given and strictly adhered to if the fat dog is to be able to live his full complement of years.

Urinary problems, kidney trouble and weakness of the bladder are all conditions that are found in old Chihuahuas and they require a bland diet, plenty of barley water and white meat, rabbit or fish. With care, many dogs with such chronic diseases are enabled to live quite comfortably into old age. Chihuahuas are particularly fond of home comforts and make the most of everything offered; they are content just lying on a soft bed in a warm place with all the household at their beck and call.

There has been quite a lot of diabetes found in dogs recently and when insulin has to be given in tablet form it is no problem. If it has to be given intravenously—injected into a vein with a hypodermic needle—then I can see a good many owners, who may not be able to afford daily visits to or from the vet, agreeing to have the sufferer put to sleep to save it getting the very distressing complications this horrid condition is capable of causing.

Modern knowledge and medical technology has extended the life cycle of the human by about ten years and the same can be done for the dog. Chihuahuas have been known to live over twenty years before this, so given the loving care that they usually receive, it is to be expected that their lives will be longer.

The oldest dog I ever heard of in the breed reached twenty-five years, and he was killed by a car!

I have never had an old Chihuahua go blind or hard of hearing as happens in some other breeds; in fact, they seem to stay remarkably alert right up to the end. The hair loss and baldness can be helped by rubbing in the same hair tonics that humans use. Bay rum, rosemary and coconut oil, and various trade-marked remedies are all useful and the Vit. B complex, in tablet or powder form, helps their skin to keep healthy. Daily brushing and a rub over with a piece of silk or velvet, which are excellent grooming aids for Chihuahuas of all ages, do just as much for the old ones. Dandruff cures or sulphur and lard will get rid of scurfy skin and so make them look more attractive.

Loss of teeth is the first sign of age but, unfortunately, in the Chihuahua this can happen at only two years and missing teeth and the consequent gaps are usual in many otherwise top-class Chihuahuas. Experiments have been performed with antibiotic tablets dissolved in warm water. At regular intervals the solution is sponged on to the gums and held there for five minutes. The tablets are obtained in Sweden but I am trying to find out if they can be made over here. My experience has been very satisfactory and I found Swedish exhibits all with beautiful strong teeth at over five years of age.

Some male Chihuahuas get very stuffy and short-necked-looking as they get older which prevents them being shown. This applies especially to some stud dogs. The reason is that they are of a stockier type; the more slender type retain their elegance right into old age. Ch. Rowley Perito of Sektuny, who was shown when he was eleven, and my own Fudge were examples of males that retained their figures and elegant style into old age. Perito was used at stud probably more than any other male of his time but he never coarsened or lost his zest for life. It is character as much as good looks that makes a great dog truly great, and old age cannot affect it.

CHAPTER 13

Grooming and Preparation for Show

The first thing to do when starting to groom a tiny Chihuahua is to get him used to standing on your lap or a high table. If started as soon as he can stand on his own feet, and if his favourite treats and plenty of petting are forthcoming, he will make up his mind that the table is the place where pleasant things happen. A table top can be a very long way from the ground for such a tiny creature, so part of the training must be in getting him over his fear of the height. Make very sure that he never falls off a table and that nothing frightening, like a loud noise or the table shaking suddenly, makes him nervous of the table in the beginning. Of course, a Chihuahua is so tiny that he can be accommodated on your lap quite easily but it is not nearly as convenient to groom a dog if you have to use one hand to hold him on your lap. The table is better because you can see what you are doing, have plenty of light, and freedom to use both hands.

Put a fairly large rubber mat on the table so that the puppy cannot slip on the surface, and make sure the table legs are rigid. When the puppy is standing in a relaxed way on the mat, play with him and give him a titbit, then open his mouth and pop another sweetmeat in. When you open his mouth again, he will think you are going to give him something nice and let you do it. His teeth must be examined and any surplus ones removed by the vet.

Having got his mouth in order, his teeth should be kept clean with a tiny bit of smoker's tooth powder on a dampened cotton-wool bud. If you don't have the powder handy, a mixture of hydrogen of peroxide and milk, on a 50/50 basis, will make the teeth sparkle and remove any tartar. He will appreciate his mouth being rinsed clean, with warm plain water on a piece of cotton wool, and wiped dry. His eyes will need attention now. Wipe them over with warm water or weak tea on a swab of cotton wool— always use a clean piece for each eye. If there is any sign of inflammation—running eyes, redness on the whites of the eyes, or screwing up the eyes away from light—he may need some ophthalmic ointment which should be obtained from your vet who will know a suitable one for use on a young puppy. Corto caps are better than antibiotics if there is no infection in the eye. Stains from the eye can be dealt with by using a special lotion according to the instructions on the bottle, or a very mild solution of peroxide. Salt water is also useful for these stains—one teaspoonful to half a pint of water.

Attend to his mouth and eyes regularly, and get someone else to open his mouth and handle his head at times so that he won't mind the judge doing it when you show him. Don't fight or struggle with him if he objects; leave it until another time or he could become neurotic about the table.

One of the most important points is the coat, but your puppy won't grow a good coat unless the skin underneath it is healthy, free from scurf and, most important, free from parasites. Most insecticidal powders are very strong and can give the dog and person handling him a very bad allergy. Bathing with one of the proprietary brands of shampoos is safer, much more pleasant to use and, because the shampoo is rubbed in all over the coat, is less likely to miss any part of the skin, as so often happens when powdering. So far, sprays have proved dangerous and I cannot recommend one.

Kurmange is a cheap and effective shampoo for skin irritations and will kill many insects. Many sulphur treatments can be recommended but the essential fact to remember is that the treatment does not end with one bath. It must be repeated three times, at least, so that any eggs that have hatched or any females that emerge from underneath the skin and escape the first dressing can be dealt with in the next. In ten days' time the dose should be repeated, and if any more signs are found the whole three or four treatments must be started all over again. It all depends on the life-cycle of the mite being dealt with and this can best be observed by trial and error.

Once the skin is clear and healthy then the daily grooming can start. Because of the clean state of the skin, the coat will soon flourish and, if a long coat, the feathering will start to reveal itself.

Smooth coats may seem to need a lot less grooming but there is a stage when they can be completely denuded of hair on their heads and throats, so the same treatments must be put into action so that healthy skin can have the desired effect. A brush down, using a soft baby brush dipped in warm olive or almond oil, and then a rub all over with a piece of silk or velvet will give the hair of the smooth coat the gleam of good health that will show the judge that the dog is in the peak of condition. This, of course, can only really come from within, so good bodily condition is the pre-runner to a healthy skin and coat.

The edge of the ear often gets chapped and sore, with the skin becoming hard and scaly. Vaseline, coconut oil, warm olive oil or liquid paraffin are all good remedies for this and there are a lot of products on the market that are said to cure it. Keeping the skin on the ears free from chaps and under-the-skin mites will effect a cure and the hair will grow again. Long coats suffer the same way and the same treatment goes, but, of course, it will take longer for the long hair to grow enough to go into the show ring. Regular attention to the ears will prevent this unsightly condition.

Any canker inside the ears should be treated with a dry canker dressing and if used regularly it will keep the ears sweet and clean.

The long coat must have a longer-bristled brush than the smooth coat. It is as well to comb through the coat with a fairly fine steel comb to remove all foreign matter, such as dead grass, twigs and cleavers, etc. This will also remove any snarls if done well enough and the hair won't break as easily as if they are brushed out.

The brush should be a good quality bristle and if dipped in coat tonic it will stimulate the skin as well as groom the coat. A softer brush dipped in almond oil can be used for finishing off, except when going to a show when this may make it look too greasy, but its action is to stop the ends of the coat splitting so that the coat will grow luxuriant and long. Too heavy feathering is not good but what your dog has must be long and silky looking. The tail and ears must be covered with a lot of hair for best results, and a full ruff around the neck is also desirable and likely to attract the judges. Colour is of no consequence but the black- and dark-coloured dogs have their beauty enhanced if their coats are shown shiny and glossy so that highlights are seen. A good conditioning cream used as a rinse will help, also rinsing with lemon juice or vinegar added to the last rinsing water. Brush, brush and brush again and this will give the desired result.

No dog can walk properly if his nails are too long. Many

exhibitors, who have their Chihuahuas' coats in gleaming good condition, fail to trim the nails so that their dogs can walk comfortably. There was once a school of thought that deplored the cutting of Chihuahuas' nails because of their affinity with climbing trees and digging in the desert. Our Chis don't have to do any of these things and they look and walk better with short nails. Care must be taken not to cut below the quick, which is difficult to see on dark nails. If a little is cut at a time and safety clippers used, the result will be satisfactory. If the nails bleed it is terribly painful for the dog and it is doubtful if you will ever be allowed near its claws again.

When showing a Chihuahua who has spent hours in a crate on the way to the show, it is a kindness if he is taken for a walk to stretch himself and allowed to relieve himself before entering the show ring. It is pathetic to see a little dog, whose needs have been neglected, forced to relieve himself in the ring in front of everybody. They know very well what is happening and it often affects their showing. Some dogs, of course, don't mind a bit but it is not very polite to the other exhibitors. Chis can be quite fussy in these respects. We once had a bitch who so hated getting her hind legs wet by long grass when she went out to relieve herself that she learned to do it standing on her front legs with her back legs in the air. She never seemed to mind what happened to her front legs, which not only got wet in the grass but also quite profusely by her own efforts.

CHAPTER 14

The Chihuahua Abroad

The Chihuahua is a native of the American continent so when he is in Britain and Europe he is really abroad. He is an excellent traveller and will settle down most happily in any environment or climate as long as his immediate comforts are taken care of. Some of mine have gone to the tropics and are extremely happy in that rather trying climate. A few went to Finland and the colder north of Scandinavia and the cold hasn't worried them. They have, in fact, grown thicker and closer coats to offset the colder climes. In a warm climate, they would probably shed a lot of coat to make themselves more comfortable.

It is a comparatively short time since the breed was universally recognised yet in that time it has made tremendous strides in a lot of very different countries. Those people who have taken them up are, without any exception, delighted with this unique little dog, and the new clubs, which are constantly being formulated to extol his virtues and introduce him to even more people, give an idea of how popular the breed has become.

In the U.S.A., where he has been the most popular pet dog for several decades, the show ring gives no indication of his great popularity for the entries are small compared with the vast number of specimens in private homes. In Britain the reverse seems to apply; the show ring is well patronised but the pet-buying public have a craving for large and unsuitable house pets like Alsatians, Afghans and enormous St Bernards and such. If they could only see the wisdom of sharing their rather tiny homes with a little dog, who would fit in and leave them plenty of room in car and garden, they would be far more comfortable, and because a Chihuahua can play and enjoy himself in the smallest space, they would add an amusement to their homes such as they had never dreamed of. One day they may realise these truths and then regret the time they wasted when they didn't have a Chihuahua.

The Scandinavian countries, France, Germany, Austria, Holland,

Belgium, Spain, Italy and Portugal all have Chihuahuas continuing my breeding line. Switzerland has a few Chihuahuas but not any that I know about. There has been a German Bundessigeren (Best Bitch in Show) on several occasions when Mrs Port showed her German Champion Emmrill Perfecta. Emmrill Perfecta was not only the best bitch in Germany for several years but produced a litter a year as well. The German Kennel Club (Verband für das Deutsche Hundewesen—VDH for short) of Schwanenstrasse 30, Dortmund, which is the only German dog club recognised by our Kennel Club, have to give their permission for each dog and bitch to be mated. Before mating, both dogs are given the most thorough examination by experts and have to comply with a very high standard of soundness and conform to all points of the Standard before the mating is allowed. When the litter arrives it too is subjected to the same stringent inspection and any whelp that does not meet with approval is taken away and destroyed. Unsound mouths in adults would prevent them being mated at all. Other points that are taken into account are coat type and colour, inherited physical disabilities, and weaknesses in body and make-up. No weaklings are reared under these conditions. German breeders have to breed to a very high standard and before they can do this they must start with the best quality stock available. If British breeders feel they would like to export their Chihuahuas to Germany they must make sure that only the very best and soundest stock is sent over. Poor quality stock will soon meet with a sticky end and it is very costly for the German breeder who must face up to a lot of expense in such matters.

The French Government curtails the importing of dogs by inflicting very high import fees—sometimes 75 per cent. In these circumstances, French breeders won't want to waste their money on inferior stock and although their kennel club is not as strict as that in Germany, the Federation Cynologique International, to which all the Clubs under its jurisdiction have to conform, has the making and breaking of champions and instructs the judges of its shows what standard they require. For instance, an English champion if exhibited in France could not win if she was seriously short of teeth—forty-two are expected and only one missing is allowed on toy dogs. I have even seen top English imports relegated to the lowest rank because they have failed to come up to the standard required by the Continental judges.

Holland uses a lot of German dogs in her breeding so her stock too must meet a high standard, and teeth are most important. Hind dew claws are a sign of degeneracy in Holland and Dutch breeders would not be allowed to breed from Chihuahuas with hind dew claws. Even if these claws have been removed completely, the scar will still disqualify.

Belgian breeders are able to study dogs in France and Germany and have several quite important shows themselves which are attended by both their neighbours. The Belgian pet-buyers are attracted mostly to the tiniest of the species. They place a lot of emphasis on size, so once a show pup is selected the rest of the litter is usually put on the pet market. I have met Belgian, French and German judges who have been to America to judge, so they know how the breed can look and some of the Belgian breeders are regular attenders at shows over here and know our dogs thoroughly.

Sweden has very beautiful Chihuahuas and Mrs Carolina Robson, who is in partnership with her daughter Mrs Marguerita Dahl, at present living in England, has some of the best I have ever seen and I am very glad to know that there are a few Emmrills in the pedigree somewhere. Both long and smooth coats are of extremely high quality in the show ring in Sweden. Had it not been for the quarantine laws I might have brought one home. Fees in quarantine kennels are enormous these days compared with the time when I had mine in the kennels.

There are quite a lot of Chihuahua Clubs in Australia and New Zealand and many tremendously keen supporters of the breed travel great distances to attend shows and social gatherings. They write to me asking for the standard to be clarified regarding nose colour which is often penalised in Australia and New Zealand if it is not black. Tails twisting over the back worry some of their judges too, and they have a strain of monorchids that keeps cropping up. It is difficult for breeders so far away to follow form over here but so great is the interest that they often get together and spend a lot of time looking at movie films of Cruft's and the various Chihuahua shows. Many of them belong to parent clubs at home and read all the literature avidly. At one time, dogs could only be shipped to Australia in crates on board one of the liners carrying passengers. They were in the charge of the ship's butcher and they usually had to travel with five weeks' supply of food. (One of ours once travelled on the bridge with the captain and had a lovely time.) After arrival they had a short spell in quarantine. Nowadays, the Australian government allows dogs to be sent by air and although there is a long spell in quarantine at the other end, it solves the problem of the dogs spending five weeks crated-up as cargo, which is a great relief. This will open up the export market to a lot more English breeders who earlier refused to send their dogs by boat for such a long tedious voyage.

Brazil likes long-coated Chihuahuas and there is a very good strain to be found there. Dogs exported to Brazil need consular stamps over all the papers and a lot of documentation. Argentina is also very particular that the vets who sign the certificates are genuine and authentic. They require the college stamp on top of the signatures and a Foreign Office confirmation that the Royal College of Veterinarians is an authentic body. If a dog arrives there at the week-end he will be locked up and not released until the following Monday unless a large sum is available to bail him out.

The airline offices and the Ministry of Agriculture are the best sources of information if any dogs are to be exported. The Ministry will issue a certificate to the effect that the dog you are sending was born in this country and has never left it; they will also indicate for how long the country has been free of rabies. All this is free but must be applied for well in advance to allow for delays in the post.

All airlines have firm requirements about the kind of kennel that a dog should travel in. It is wise to follow their instructions to the letter otherwise they may refuse to handle your dog when you take it to them. Livestock has special priority all over the world and you can safely leave the airport staff to deal with your little dog. They will put his box in a warm office where the tropical birds and fish are kept in transit and they will give food and water if instructions are put on the box. Freight planes carry specially-trained staff to look after the animals but they are not pressurised so it is better to send your Chihuahua by passenger plane.

Instructions must be given to the airport office staff about how the dog is to be met, and the telephone number of the consignee is required so that on the way he can be radioed that the dog will arrive on a certain flight and given the approximate landing time. If the consignee is late, the dog will be put into a special office to await collection and his home telephoned. Everything is done to make travelling easy for dogs and Chihuahuas won't mind being crated if they have received a few meals and been allowed to play in the crate beforehand. Shredded newspaper in a thick nest will make a good and hygienic bedding for the journey. It will keep the dog warm, cushion him against bumps and will prevent him standing in any mess as, if it is made very deep, he will be able to bury his toilet and keep clean and dry on top.

The size of the crate is important. There is a minimum freight rate which will enable you to send a tiny Chihuahua in a far bigger box than he would need for the same price as sending him in the smallest one made. If the journey is a very long one the box should be larger but stuffed with a lot more shredded paper to act as protection as the dog could roll about all over the place in an almost empty one. Ideally, the crate needs to be high enough for him to stand on his hind legs without hitting the top and wide enough to let him stand upright but not fall over if the box is jerked about. Some firms make their travelling kennels with food and water containers that can be removed from outside the box for easy filling which saves having to open the door. These are admirable and should be ordered if the dog has to be fed on the journey.

Before travelling, a heavy meal is to be avoided. A drink of milk and glucose at the last moment before leaving him will be very acceptable and he can be safely left with some hide chews or a large safe bone to stop him feeling bored. Young puppies don't turn a hair while travelling but older dogs might be alarmed at all the strange faces and noises. If his pet name is printed in big letters on his box passers-by can speak to him by name and this is very reassuring for him. It will also help his new owner to communicate with him immediately, which cannot happen if he does not know what to call him.

At the moment of writing, breeders in Rhodesia are still importing dogs from Britain and English judges are continuing to attend their dog shows and visit their country. South Africa regularly imports dogs and British judges find that they have quite large circuits to cover when judging out there. I have met many Chihuahua owners who find that Chihuahuas settle in well and don't seem so troubled as some breeds by the ticks and other parasites that attack dogs out there. The only complaint I have heard is that a lot of Chihuahuas start growing again when they get out there and get leggy and untypical. I have heard this about other breeds as well as Chihuahuas so there must be some explanation. The stockier, shorter-legged subjects would seem to be the best kind to send but the buyers' requirements are the most important criteria.

The South African authorities require a statement signed by a commissioner of oaths that the dog being exported is the property of the consigner and that it was born in Britain and has never been away from Britain. This, of course, is because Britain is a safer bet against rabies than other countries.

Speaking of rabies, Italy insists that dogs imported there are vaccinated against rabies. If they are not done before they arrive they get the injection at once. Austria and Switzerland insist that dogs are vaccinated twice, at two monthly intervals.

Sweden is very concerned that the disease leptospiral canicola is kept away from their country which up to now has been free from it. It is a rat-borne disease and we get our puppies vaccinated against it in two doses.

Before leaving for Sweden a dog has to have a blood test which must prove negative for leptospirosis. They are blood-tested again when they arrive there and if the test proves positive the dog is destroyed. Taking blood from a tiny Chihuahua's vein is very difficult and the vein is prone to collapse if too coarse a needle is used.

CHAPTER 15

Ailments and Accidents

It must be stated here that any serious illness or accident is best left to a veterinary surgeon and professional advice obtained at the first opportunity. The following ailments and remedies are only for those who cannot obtain a vet or who have to cope with conditions that are of such an urgent nature that the dog may die before veterinary help can be obtained. The best way to cope with broken bones, shock, poisons, bites and fits are explained so that the best and quickest first aid can be tried and the promptness may save a life. Snake bites and poisons will still need to be treated by a vet but the sooner some remedy is forthcoming there is a faint chance that death can be warded off, and at least some relief from frantic pain given.

ANAL GLAND INFECTION: The anal glands are like marbles on each side of the anus and when faeces are firm they can squeeze them clean as they pass through, but if the diet is lacking in fibrous material it will result in the faeces being too soft for the glands to do their work and a secretion accumulates in the glands making them very painful and obnoxious smelling. It is very dangerous to try to empty the glands of a tiny Chihuahua yourself, so it is necessary for the vet to do it as he will know where to put pressure and how to expel the offensive matter. A change in the diet will make a marked improvement; mix All-Bran or Bemax with the meat and give brown bread instead of white biscuits.

ANAEMIA: A shortage of red corpuscles in the blood is the cause and plenty of iron-rich foods, in the form of partly-cooked liver, parsley, spinach and cress, are missing from the diet. Vit. B12 and iron injections will cure the condition and Parrish's Food or Benbow's Conditioner are old and tried remedies.

ANAESTHETICS : Chihuahuas are very bad subjects for anaesthetics and they should be used as little as possible. A mixture of morphine and air, given continually with an oxygen mask, is sometimes used and some vets use a spinal injection. It is dangerous to give a Chihuahua bitch an anaesthetic after she has been given an injection of Ergot or Pituitrin. The action of these drugs is so violent that not only is the pain induced more than a tiny bitch should be called on to bear, but also the strain on the heart is so great from the violence of the muscular spasms they cause that the little heart will give out at the first whiff of an anaesthetic. It is far safer to do a Caesarean section at the first sign of complications and the chances are it will be entirely successful.

ARTIFICIAL RESPIRATION : Place the hands on either side of the rib cage, press down and allow the chest to expand in time with your own breathing. Cover the dog's nose and using mouth-to-mouth blowing try and get him to breathe. Be careful not to blow too hard. In the case of drowning, all the water must be drained out of the lungs by holding the dog upside-down.

BAD BREATH : A common and unpleasant complaint with tiny toy dogs. Caused by mouth infections, tooth decay, dirty teeth and a disordered stomach. Magnesia will help the stomach and veterinary treatment will cure the mouth problems. Chlorophyll tablets will cover up the smell until treatment is complete.

BALANITIS : Inflammation of the sheath, often found in older dogs. A creamy discharge is seen at the end of the dog's penis. Antibiotic injections and a mild antisepic douche given in a clean jam jar will clear up the trouble.

BALDNESS : Sometimes caused through a nervous state called alopecia and can be helped with injections and the Vit. B complex and Vit. E. Seaweed meal sprinkled over the food has a beneficial effect, and massaging the head and bald patches with eau-de-cologne, bay rum and oil of rosemary may be all that is necessary. In old dogs suspect a hormone deficiency which may need a hormone treatment to get things right.

BRONCHITIS AND TRACHEO-BRONCHITIS : Also known as Kennel Cough. The condition should respond to a course of antibiotics and the cough can be soothed with linctus. If the cough persists after treatment it may be due to a worm in the throat and a dose for worms is necessary.

CHOKING : If a Chihuahua chokes on something, as he is so small he can be held head down and shaken to dislodge the foreign object. The tongue should be pulled forward and the little finger hooked down the throat to ease the object out. Give artificial respiration if necessary.

COLIC : A serious condition. The violent stomach spasms may be caused by a stomach chill (from eating frozen food not defrosted), or by eating infected or poisonous substances. Chlorodyne in minute doses in water, or brandy and warm water, is a fine remedy. Pain is intense so the chloroform, cocaine, morphia and opium which make up Dr. Collis Browne's Chlorodyne is more than justified although it could become habit-forming.

CONCUSSION : A very frequent occurrence with some Chihuahuas as they have a soft spot or molera in the head and their skulls are particularly vulnerable. Call the vet, place the victim in the warm—a hot-water bottle would help—and put a cold compress on the head. The tongue should be pulled well forward so as not to cut off the supply of air to the lungs. Any form of unconsciousness could mean damage to the brain, so the sooner veterinary care is available the better.

CONJUNCTIVITIS : Chihuahuas are very prone to have their eyebrows grow very long and these constantly rub against the eyeballs, causing inflammation. Treatment consists of trimming off the eyebrows, bathing with eye lotion and applying Golden Eye Ointment or one of the antibiotic eye ointments, and keeping the patient away from winds and dust. Never let a Chihuahua travel by car with his head out of a window—it is asking for trouble.

CONSTIPATION : Active little dogs, given the correct diet, should never suffer in this way, but the over-fat lap-dog that gets little exercise and eats too bland food lacking the normal roughage will need dosing with Rhubarb Tablets or Milk of Magnesia. Liquid paraffin is not a good remedy, nor is castor oil, as both of these have unpleasant after-effects.

COUGHS AND COLDS : All the dust from the ground and the draughts from under doors join to make the Chihuahua cough and sneeze. His bed should be raised out of the draughts and away from cold floors. To help matters, his bed could have a hooded cover and be lined with a warm blanket. Although high heat in the house is not necessary, the temperature should not be below 60°F 15°C) in winter and 55°F (14°C) in summer.

DANDRUFF : Can be the result of an attack of mange, eczema, a too acid diet (full milk) or a lack of fat in the diet. If the cause is dietary, change from cow's milk to dried milk and add cod-liver and halibut oil to the diet; linseed oil and olive oil are also good, so too is sunflower oil and ordinary margarine. When the diet improves, the condition should clear up. It can be helped by rubbing the dry skin with sulphur and lard or bathing the dog in one of the patent dandruff cures, taking care to comply with the instructions. Wash all brushes and combs in disinfectant and burn all old bedding in case the cause is contagious or due to a living mite under the skin. Stergene with one part T.C.P. is a home-made remedy that is effective in curing some conditions of scurfy skin and can be tried if the other remedies fail.

DIABETES : If, when tested, sugar is found in the urine the cause is almost sure to be diabetes, and a craving for water and sweet sickly smell on the breath will confirm it. Daily insulin will be as effective with dogs as it is with humans and your vet will have to stabilise the patient to ascertain how much his daily dose will need to be. This treatment must be continued as long as the dog lives.

DIARRHOEA : This is often a symptom of some other trouble rather than an illness in itself. It can easily kill a tiny dog like a Chihuahua as, if prolonged, it will result in extreme weakness as everything that is eaten is expelled before it can provide any nourishment. Kaolin mixed with morphine is a quick and efficient first-aid treatment but the cause of the infection should be discovered and some antibiotic taken to drive the infection from the stomach. Neo-Sulphentrin is very effective and is potent against all known stomach germs. Clean all feeding bowls with germicide and let frozen food thaw completely before feeding. Throw away any stale food and guard against chills and infection.

DISTEMPER: Once the scourge of dogdom. Whole kennels were wiped out by it and those dogs that survived it were maimed and crippled for life. We now have excellent and effective immunisation against Hardpad and Distemper (different names for the same disease), Hepatitis (Rubarth's Disease) which is transferable from the dam to her unborn litter, and Leptospiral Jaundice etc. which is carried by rats. Protection is better than cure and the vaccinations are worth every penny they cost. Puppies who have been in danger of infection can be given measles vaccine which gives them six months' immunity. This terrible disease proclaims itself in so many ways to start with that at first it is hard to recognise. If a dog, or especially a puppy, shows signs of runny eyes, a hard dry cough, vomiting, diarrhoea, loss of appetite and a staring coat the vet must be called at once. The victim should be isolated and not taken to the surgery where he can pass on the disease to all he meets there. The worst thing about this disease is that it is often only known to have been present by the sad aftermath of meningitis which causes permanent damage to the brain and blackening of the teeth, ulcerated eyes, chorea and shaking fits, convulsions and many other chronic side-effects which will be with him for the rest of his life.

EAR CANKER: The patient will hold his head on one side, scratch at it very gently and cry continuously. Close examination of the inside of the ear will show it full of black pus which has a loathsome smell, and you will hear the liquid moving about inside the ear. Canker powder with iodoform is good as the powder acts like blotting paper, drying up the liquid. Also, the iodoform kills the mite which causes the condition, and makes a healing dressing which will clean the whole thing up and sweeten the smell at once. Treatment will need to be repeated every other day for two weeks in order to effect a cure.

ECLAMPSIA : Affects bitches during lactation. They can go into fits and become unconscious. The remedy is to get to the vet without delay and have the bitch injected with borogluconate, as the making of the milk has put too great a strain on the little mother and drained all the calcium out of the blood-stream. As soon as the calcium is replaced the mother will recover miraculously but it is safer for her health if the puppies are taken away and reared by a foster or by hand.

ENTROPION : In-growing and out-growing eyelashes cause this painful condition and there is often a 'blue' eye or conjunctivitis. Corto-caps really help but if they don't, an operation is necessary and should be performed as soon as possible to save the puppy much discomfort.

EUTHANASIA : The dog's expectation of life is far shorter than our own so there comes a time when we are called on to witness his life drawing to a close. The older the dog the longer he and the owner have been together and the more attached they have become. It is a sad day for the owner when his old dog gets no further joy out of life. In fact, when life becomes painful and dreary have we the right to expect our old pals to put up with it? Far kinder to put them out of their misery as soon as life no longer holds any interest. Prolonging an ailing life is only putting off the awful day for ourselves and we are doing our pet no favours. A strong sedative should be given and the old one nursed in his master's arms until he goes into a deep sleep. The vet can then be allowed to inject the final dose into a vein and the old one will never open his eyes again. The whole process is completely painless.

FITS AND EPILEPSY : These can happen without warning—the eyes will look glassy, foam will come from the mouth, and the legs will thrash about wildly. A large towel should be wrapped securely around the dog, but be careful he doesn't bite you as he is unaware of his actions. Hold the head under the cold tap or place some ice on the top of the skull and on the back of the neck, then wait for the vet to inject a sedative. If the handle of a small wooden spoon is held between his jaws it will stop him biting his tongue. Give nothing by mouth in case he chokes.

Complete quiet for several days and a course of Vit. B complex will help restore the nervous system.

FRACTURES : If broken bones or internal fractures are suspected it is essential that the body is not moved at all, but if a child's blackboard is slid underneath the dog it will stop any movement of the bones when carrying him. Cover with a warm blanket and treat for shock with a hot-water bottle at either side and get to the vet's surgery as soon as possible as the fractures should be X-rayed. A cigar cover, slipped gently over a broken leg, will stop it jarring on the way to the surgery.

GASTRO-ENTERITIS : This is a very severe form of internal infection that needs prompt veterinary attention, a full course of antibiotics, and very careful nursing if recovery is to be possible. A no-fat diet, light food and withholding water is the recommended procedure, followed by a very slow return to normal diet and red meat.

HEART DISEASE AND HEART ATTACKS : Dogs can live for a long time with a damaged heart as long as they are dosed with the correct drugs in the correct strength. Vit. E is said to be useful in building the heart cells, and Digitalis is taken daily in order to keep the 'machinery' of the heart working. If a dog gets a heart attack the tongue should be pulled forward and a drop of brandy placed on it. Help is very necessary; the vet might give heart massage and inject coramine to help the weak heart-beats.

HEAT STROKE : Dogs should never be left in closed cars even if the sunlight is not very strong, for the faintest sun on the glass can turn a closed car into an oven. If a dog gets heat stroke the temperature of his body must be reduced without delay. He can be placed on a tray of ice or put in a bath of very cold water and his head and neck sponged continually with icy water. A very quick and effective way is to put the dog in a bag, tie it strongly inside the car and drive at great speed for a few miles with the dog hanging outside. He will probably get pneumonia but he won't die of heat stroke.

HYSTERIA : Screaming fits can be the result of distemper or eating too much white flour containing the whitening agent 'agene'. As hysteria is catching, the sooner it is stopped the better. Get the victim into a darkened room, sedate him and keep under for several days until he recovers.

INTERDIGITAL CYSTS : Painful swellings between the toes which need hot fomentations and a course of antibiotics. Bathing with a solution of warm water and peroxide is helpful.

LEAD POISONING : If a Chihuahua chews painted objects, the paint of which contains red lead or similar substances, the chances are that he will be badly affected by lead poisoning. If he has chewed any lead, a piece of washing soda should be pushed down the throat or mustard and water given as an emetic. If the victim seems in great agony, warm black treacle can be poured down his throat. A general antidote which can be kept in the house at all times is : two parts charcoal, one part magnesium oxide, one part kaolin and one part tannic acid. Four heaped tablespoonsful of the antidote should be mixed with half a pint of water and as much as possible given to the dog.

LEPTOSPIRAL JAUNDICE : Two injections at monthly intervals will give protection against this rat-borne disease which severely attacks the liver. It is shown to be present by signs of haemorrhage producing black stools. This disease is transmitted by rats through their urine. Yearly booster doses are advisable.

MANGE : Sarcoptic or red mange is caused by a mite which burrows under the skin, lays its eggs and then returns to the skin again in order to burrow elsewhere. The skin becomes red and terribly itchy. The dog is driven frantic and damages the skin through violent biting and scratching. The cure is to follow the life-cycle of the mite and treat accordingly. At the first sign of any trouble, bath the dog in a mange dressing—Kurmange, Tetmosol (I.C.I.), or any other substance suggested by your vet as new cures are being found all the time. Two days later repeat the whole process, and again three days after that. Wait a week, and then repeat the bathing once more. The female mite burrows under the skin to lay her eggs and these can be seen as little red dots in a line. When she emerges is the best time to bath the dog and then three days later when the eggs hatch out. If there are any females under the skin when the bathing is done they will escape and start the vicious circle again, so the bathing must be repeated and repeated until no more females emerge. All bedding should be burnt and the bed washed with the dressing. All woodwork should be treated with paraffin rubbed all over it and the kennel should have a sulphur candle burned in it before returning the cured dogs. Benzyl benzoate rubbed into affected areas of the dog's skin is an efficient cure but it is dangerous to cover the skin completely as it can cause death and if it gets near the eyes it could cause blindness and great pain.

Follicular or dermodectic mange is not as contagious as sarcoptic mange (which is easily transferable to humans) and appears to be a congenital disease passed on from the dam to the unborn puppies. The organisms must be present in the bloodstream of the mother as this is the only way she is connected to her puppies before birth. Follicular mange is active right at the roots of the hair and destroys the whole hair. The skin looks hard and dry like elephant skin. Treatment is long and very doubtful as the veterinary profession has no easy cure. It must be done constantly and even then the condition may not get cured at all.

MASTITIS : An infection of the milk glands that causes inflamed and very painful swellings and needs urgent veterinary attention with antibiotics. The milk could kill the puppies so they must be removed and hand fed. The only treatment locally would be hot fomentations, cooling medicine and a sedative to ease the pain. The bitch's temperature will be very high and she is unlikely to want to eat or drink.

MENINGITIS : Inflammation of the membranes surrounding the brain and spinal cord, often caused by distemper. Requires constant veterinary nursing and complete sedation before there is a hope of curing it. I kept a bitch unconscious for six weeks and gave her pheno-barbitone crushed up and dripped down her mouth and with the help of a saline drip I managed to keep her alive.

METRITIS : This often follows whelping and can be caused by retained afterbirths or dead puppies that set up an infection in the uterus. This infection can also follow the use of instruments for removal of a puppy. It usually responds to antibiotics but if the bitch's temperature gets very high the course should be continued over a longer period than usual to clear the trouble completely. In severe cases an operation to remove the womb completely may be necessary.

MUSCULAR RHEUMATISM : Very rarely found in Chihuahuas but it is a painful condition which attacks suddenly, often in the hindquarters. Junior Aspirin effects quick relief. Keep the patient warm and dry, as damp is a cause.

NEPHRITIS : Chronic disorder of the kidneys which is usually found in dogs over eight years of age. There are two kinds : non-uremic, which is the less dangerous, and uremic which causes great loss of weight, a very unpleasant ammoniac smell and complete prostration. The non-uremic kind can be helped by giving barley water to drink and a fish or white meat diet. There is no cure for the uremic type which will end in death.

OBESITY : If your dog is too fat you are giving him too much food and too much starch. Change to a non-starch diet and give raw meat at the rate of half an ounce to each pound bodyweight and reduce this by half until your dog's weight is back to normal. This will add years to your Chihuahua's life.

POISONING : Washing soda pushed down the throat is a first-aid remedy to make a dog vomit to get rid of most of the poison he has swallowed. Under LEAD POISONING is a recipe for a general antidote to give when a dog has taken poison. The best remedy, of course, is to keep all poisons, e.g. rat poison, slug death, ant killer and household poisons, out of reach.

PROSTATE GLAND ENLARGEMENT : As the enlargement of this gland presses against the rectum it can cause constipation. Castration or removal of the testicles causes the glands to waste away and is an effective solution to the problem, which can occur in a dog after it is six years old.

PYMETRIA : A highly dangerous condition of the womb which causes it to swell up and fill with pus and the bitch may have a temperature in the region of 105°F (40°C) or even higher. The case is of the most urgent nature and calls for an immediate hysterectomy—complete removal of the womb.

RABIES : Known also as hydrophobia—inability to swallow water accompanied by a craving for it. Thanks to the stringent quarantine laws in this country, all cats and dogs coming in from abroad have to spend at least six months in a quarantine kennel in solitary confinement. This dreaded disease is rife in some parts of Europe and is gradually being brought nearer the coasts on the other side of the Channel. It is carried by bats, foxes and other wild animals. The disease is transmitted by a rabid dog biting another animal or human who may not show evidence of the attack for six to eight months. The victim is wracked with such violent spasmodic convulsions that death occurs in a very short time. The victim becomes completely mad, froths at the mouth and attacks whoever comes into contact with him. Vaccinations for dogs over six months of age have proved effective in other parts of the world, and all animals going into quarantine are now vaccinated as soon as they arrive. There was a time when even the vaccine was not available in this country—so nervous were the authorities that it could go wrong. The cure is almost as painful as the disease as it entails daily injections deep into the stomach. It is to be hoped that stupid pet lovers who try to smuggle dogs and cats into this country will be punished far more severely, even so far as to refuse them entry at all and having the object of their wicked behaviour put to sleep and not quarantined at this country's expense.

RICKETS : This is a disease of puppyhood and is due in the main to a lack of calcium and a serious deficiency of Vit. D which is needed to convert the calcium in the blood to make the bones and teeth grow strong. Phosphates are also necessary and it is important that all the minerals and vitamins that are needed for growth and development are not only present in the diet given to the puppies but that the mother herself is given adequate supplies while she is carrying her litter.

RINGWORM : A fungus disease of the skin that can be transmitted to humans and vice versa. The signs of ringworm are round bald spots ringed with a thin red line. It can be cured by dressing with Stockholm tar or linseed oil and creosote mixed together in equal parts and painted on with a long-handled paint brush. The worst part of this disease is the unsightly bald skin it leaves behind and several beauty baths and oil applications will be necessary to clear the skin of the applications. Burn bedding and spray all floors and woodwork with a fungus killer and ventilate well.

SCALDING : If boiling liquid is spilt on your Chihuahua, stand him in a sink and keep soaking him and drenching him with cold water to wash away the hot liquid. Corrosive chemicals should be washed off in the same way.

SHOCK : Shock can occur as the result of road accidents, stings, bites, scalds and burns. To treat the dog, cover him completely with a blanket and put hot-water bottles at each side of him and place the whole on an electric blanket or heated pad. The idea is to keep up the body heat at all costs. If the gums look pale and the heart beats slowly it may be because of internal haemorrhaging, and glucose-saline solution can be dripped into the mouth or, if possible, given by a hypodermic syringe. Saline solution is made up of one level teaspoonful of salt and one desertspoonful of glucose dissolved in a pint of warm water. Very sweet tea or coffee can be given but on no account give alcohol or other stimulants.

SPAYING : If a bitch is not needed for breeding and is in daily contact with male dogs it may save a lot of trouble if she is spayed. If she has had a litter so much the better as it won't be so likely to make her fat. A bitch that carries an hereditary condition for some serious fault is also better spayed so that she can't be mated indiscriminately.

STINGS AND BITES : Remove bee stings from the skin with a tweezer and cover with blue bag, bicarbonate of soda mixed to a paste with cold water, or any special anti-histamine cream or spray available. On eyes, mouth, tongue or lips use bicarbonate of soda or T.C.P. in a mild form. Wasp stings do not get left behind but keep on stinging, causing shock. Dab with vinegar, lemon juice or a cut onion.

SNAKE BITES will only be from an adder in Great Britain. As their bites can be lethal, rush the victim to the nearest hospital or doctor's surgery for special snake serum. Permanganate of potash can be supplied as a first-aid device but the serum is the only real answer or cutting the bite across, sucking out the poison and applying a tourniquet in order to keep the poison localised. It is vital that the poison does not spread, so as little movement as possible is indicated. The pain of the snake bite is intense so treatment for shock will be necessary.

SUNSTROKE : Because of their Mexican background, Chihuahuas don't seem bothered by the sun, but in the event of an attack the whole body should be plunged into icy-cold water, ice-bags should be held on the head for a long time and the patient kept in a darkened room under sedation for as long as possible.

TARTAR ON TEETH : Any accumulation of tartar means that the dog is not being given enough hard food in the way of bones and hard biscuits which help to keep the teeth clean. Severe cases can be cleaned with a tooth scraper but this is a job for the expert and with a struggling little Chihuahua the chances are that the teeth are likely to be pushed out altogether. There is a new method available whereby jets of water are sent against the teeth and such is the force behind them that even the worst tartar is removed without fear of the teeth being loosened.

TICKS : Mostly found where sheep are kept. Ticks attach themselves to the skin and suck the blood until they expand to a tremendous extent. Surgical spirit applied on a cotton-wool bud will make them release their hold and they should be burned immediately with a lighted match or put on the fire before they can attach themselves again. Dogs who live in the country should have a regular check made for ticks on the face, ears and armpits. At the same time the ears should be examined and if any little grains like red sand are found in the folds, this will be the harvest mite and prompt attention with insecticide is indicated.

WARTS : Excrescences that appear on the skin of ageing dogs and can be cauterised by a vet or treated with daily applications of castor oil which if used long enough will dry them up.

X-RAYS : It has been confirmed that too long exposure to X-rays can cause cancer so care should be taken to see that they are not used unless absolutely necessary.

Useful Contents for a Medicine Chest

Assorted widths of bandage
Cotton wool and cheap cotton waste
Thermometer
Surgical and nail scissors
Borax
Bicarbonate of soda
Permanganate of potash
Epsom salts
Flowers of sulphur
Zinc oxide
Boracic powder
Fuller's earth
Canker powder
Tooth powder (smoker's)
Insect powder
Savlon ointment
Bottle of Cetavlon
T.C.P.
Hydrogen peroxide (for wounds and stopping bleeding)
Cough mixture
Milk of Magnesia
Friar's Balsam (for inhaling)
Glucose
Travel-sickness pills

Junior Aspirin
Penbritin (Penicillin)
Rhubarb tablets
Raspberry leaf tablets
Garlic tablets
Honey
Nestlé's milk
Worm tablets
Cod-liver, olive and halibut oil
Mange dressing
Benbow's Conditioner
Virol
Eye drops and dropper
Gentian violet
Eye ointment
Tannic acid for burns
Arrow root, kaolin mixture or slippery elm food (for treating diarrhoea)
Hypodermic syringe
Bottle of calcium gluconate
Kitten's feeding bottle or tube (for hand feeding)
Tweezers
Safety pins and reel of fine elastic (for tying on bandages)

WARNING : All old liquid medicines should be destroyed by pouring down the sink and washing out the bottles thoroughly. Old tablets should be burned. Old medicines will have surely lost their healing powers but not their ability to poison.

Clubs

The Kennel Club, founded in 1873, is the ruling body in Great Britain. It controls all shows, breeding of pedigree dogs, breed clubs, general canine clubs, obedience-training clubs and field trials. The address is: 1–4 Clarges Street, Piccadilly, London W1Y 8AB.

After 1st April, 1976 all pedigree litters that are intended for registration must be *recorded* at the Kennel Club within one month of birth. This must be done on a new green form which is headed 'Application for Recording of a Litter—Kennel Club Form 1'. Breeders should apply for a stock of these forms and complete them in accordance with instructions. The completed form should be sent back to the Kennel Club (before the litter is one month old) with the fee of £1 which covers the whole litter, however large. This is an entirely new concept and calls for the signature of the owner of the stud dog used in addition to the breeder's signature.

On receipt of the form the Kennel Club will issue the breeder with a 'Litter Pack' containing the appropriate number of application forms for the 'Basic Register'. The breeder or subsequent owner of the individual puppies will then have to send the relevant form back to the Kennel Club to be put on the 'Active Register' when the dog is to be bred from, exhibited or exported; this will also cost £1.

A Class I Registration can only be given to a dog if both its parents have been registered. When dogs are sold they must be transferred to the new owner, using a Kennel Club Transfer Form for the purpose. All dogs exported should be accompanied by an Export Pedigree, which will consist of three generations and costs £10 plus £2 for the Transfer Fee. Before an Export Pedigree can be issued, male dogs need to be examined by a veterinary surgeon to make sure that both testicles have descended.

The Kennel Club issues a *Gazette* every month and a *Stud Book* once a year. To gain an entry in the *Stud Book* a dog must win 1st, 2nd or 3rd in Limit or Open Classes at championship shows. Dogs cannot be shown before the age of six months and no unregistered dog may be entered at any show under the auspices of the Kennel Club.

The *American Kennel Club*, 51 Madison Avenue, New York, NY 10010, U.S.A., acts in the same way as the English Kennel Club but for American-bred dogs.

The *Société Centrale Canine* is a controlling body in Europe for France, Holland, Belgium, Scandinavian countries, Switzerland, Italy and Spain; it also operates in Germany although there is an official German Kennel Club.

The British Chihuahua Club was founded in 1949 and caters for smooth coats and long coats and holds three shows a year, two Open and one Championship.

The Long-Coat Chihuahua Club started in 1965 when the two coats were separated by the Kennel Club and two separate sets of C.C.s were on offer at Cruft's Dog Show that year. Their shows are held for long coats only.

Other Breed Clubs of Interest
As breed club officials change so often, it is advisable to contact the Kennel Club for names, addresses and telephone numbers of current secretaries and treasurers in order to join any of these breed clubs :

Scottish & Northern Chihuahua Club
The Scottish Chihuahua Club
The Midland Chihuahua Club
The South Western Chihuahua Club
The Chihuahua Club of Ulster
The Chihuahua Club of Ireland
The Smooth-Coat Chihuahua Club (founded in 1974 to promote the smooth-coat Chihuahua only)

References

Title	Author	Publisher
Observer's Book of Dogs	Hubbard	Warne & Co
The Complete Chihuahua	Delinger	Delinger, USA
Kaufmann's Complete Chihuahua	Howell, Kaufmann, Rosina Casselli, Anna Vinyard, Merrick, and Milo Delinger	Howell Books, USA
This is the Chihuahua	Maxwell Riddle	TFH Publications
This and That About Chihuahuas	Chas H. Wall	Buddy Press, Canada
Chihuahuas	Hilary Harmer	Foyles
The Chihuahua (Popular Dogs)	Thelma Gray	Hutchinson
Pet Chihuahua	Tressa Thurmer	All-Pets, USA
The Complete Chihuahua Encyclopedia	Hilary Harmar	John Bartholomew
The Complete Dog Book	Official Publication of the American Kennel Club	Doubleday & Co, USA
Dogs in Britain	Clifford Hubbard	Macmillan & Co
The Dog	Catherine Fisher	Evans Brothers
The Life, History & Magic of The Dog	Fernand Mery	Grosset, USA
Practical Dog Book	Ashe	Simikin Marshall
The New Book of the Dog	Robert Leighton	Cassell & Co
Hutchinson's Popular Illustrated Dog Encyclopedia		Hutchinson
Know About Dogs	Holmes and Fiennes	Young World
Puppies & Dog Care	Wendy Boorer	Hamyln
Prize Dogs	Marples	Our Dogs
Showing Your Dog	Leslie Perrins	Foyles
Toys (Toy & Miniature Breeds)	Stanley Dangerfield	ABCO
All About the Yorkshire Terrier	Mona Huxham	Pelham Books
The Spirit of Mexico	Beryl Miles	John Murray
The Conquest of New Spain	Bernal Diaz	Penguin Classics
The Complete Dog	Mona Huxham	Peter Way
Livre D'Or du Chien	Société Centrale Canine	Société Centrale Canine, Paris, France
Dogs & Their Management	Mayhew, Sewell and Cousins	Routledge
The Daily Life of the Aztecs	Jacques Soustelle	(Paris, 1955)
Aztec Thoughts & Cultures	Leon-Portilla	
Ancient Mexico (Pre-Hispanic Cultures)	Frederick Peterson	Geo. Allen & Unwin
Five letters of Hernando Cortés	Translated by J. Bayard	Morris, London
History of the Conquest of Mexico	William H. Prescott	(New York, 1844)
Compendio de Arte Mesoamericas & The Mexican National Museum of Anthropology	Ignacio Bernal (Director)	Ediciones Lara
Mexico	Miguel Aleman	(Mexico, 1970)
Mexico Before Cortéz	J. Eric Thompson	(New York, 1932)
Codex Florentino	Fray Bernardino de Sahagun	Biblioteca National Florence
Codex Magliabecchiano	Unknown Mexican author. Presented to the City of Florence by Antonio Magliabecchi in 1714 but known in Spain since 1601.)	(Brought to light in the Biblioteca National Florence, Italy by Miss Delia Nuttall in 1890)
The Book of the Life of the Ancient Mexicans—An account of the rites, etc. in the original Spanish. (Unfortunately I have been unable to trace Vol II which gives Miss Nuttall's translation.)	Delia Nuttall (This work was published by the Fund for Archaeological Research in Mexico and placed at the disposal of the Dept. of Anthropology by the University of California by Mrs Wm Crocker and Mrs Whitelaw-Reid.)	Californian Press, Univ. of California, Berkeley, USA (1903)
The Ancient Maya	Sylvanus G. Morley	Stanford University, California, (1947)
Maya Cities & Temples	Paul Rivet (founder of the Musée de l'Homme)	Elek Books

Lords of New Spain	Alonso de Zorita	Weidenfield
Origens de los Mexicanos	Alonso de Zorita	(Mexico 1941)
Mexico	Michael Coe	Thames & Hudson (1962)
Historia General de los Cosas de la Nueva España	Fray Bernardino de Sahagun	(Mexico 1956)
Historia de Tlaxcala	Diego Muñoz Carmargo	(Mexico 1949 Edn)
The Everyday Life of the Aztecs	Dr Warwick Bray (Lecturer in American Archaeology, University of London, England)	Batsford, London & Putnam, New York
Diego Rivera's Mexican History illustrated with his frescoes in the National Palace, Supreme Court of Justice, Del Prado Hotel, Cardiology Institute, Ministry of Education and elsewhere in Mexico	R. S. Silva	Sinalomex Editorial, Mexico City
Article on ancient dogs in which the author describes the mummifying of dog, a dog skeleton and the Mill Hill dog and also pictures ancient Egyptian dogs.	Dr H. A. Arkell	London Illustrated News, p. 782, 23rd June, 1956 issue
Cemeteries of Abydos containing an article on the dog cemetery and the mummified remains of dogs	Main work by Edward Neville but the article concerned was written by Dr Kathleen Haddon in 1910 after she had unwrapped the mummified remains of a tiny dog thought to have been an ancestor of the Chihuahua but proved by Dr Haddon to be that of a ten-week-old puppy.	Egyptian Exploration Society's Fund (1910)
Life of Christopher Columbus	Clement R. Markham	(USA)
Christopher Columbus and The New World	F. Young	(Oxford)

LIST OF CHIHUAHUA CHAMPIONS

Champion Smooth-coat Dogs

Name	Born	Colour	Sire	Dam	Owner	Breeder
Rozavel Diaz	17.3.53	Red	Salender's Darro Pharche	Rozavel La Oro Sena de Oro	Mrs T. Gray	Owner
Denger's Don Armando	17.2.53	Black & tan	Pepito IX	Denger's Dona Carmencita	Mrs D. Wells	Mrs G. Horner
Rozavel Gringo	19.5.54	Cream	Ch. Rozavel Diaz	Rozavel La Oro Memoria de Oro	Mrs T. Gray	Owner
Cisco Kid of Winterlea	17.11.54	Red & white	Scott's Si Si Boy	Bigo's Zoranna of Winterlea	Mrs M. Mooney	Owner
Jose Alfarez of Wytchend	17.1.53	Red	Ch. Rozavel Diaz	Mixcoac	Mr A. Martin	Mrs A. Ellis-Hughes
Rozavel Francisco	4.10.54	Gold	Salender's Darro Pharche	Rozavel Irra Pettina	Mrs T. Gray	Owner
Irish Ch. Seggieden Jupiter	16.3.54	White	Am. Ch. Allen's Snowball	Pearson's Angela La Ora	Lady Margaret Drummond-Hay	Owner
Don Silver of Wytchend	19.4.56	Red & fawn	Dalhabboch Grosart's Corky	Donna Rita of Bendorwyn	Mr T. Hutchison & Mr D. Cady	Mrs A. Ellis-Hughes
Dalhabboch Rio Tinto King	6.3.56	Cream	Seko King of Dalhabboch	Veronica-Vi Dalhabboch	Miss D. Russell-Allen	Owner
Irish Ch. Seggieden Tiny Mite	18.4.57	Cream	Irish Ch. & Ch. Seggieden Jupiter	Faye of Bendorwyn	Lady Margaret Drummond-Hay	Owner
Brownridge Native Gold	21.3.58	Black & tan	Brandman's Modelo's Memory	Ch. Brownridge Jofos Paloma	D. Cady & T. Turner	Mrs J. Rawson
Rozavel Humo	16.8.56	Blue-fawn	Ch. Rozavel Francisco	Rozavel Shaw's Constance	Mrs T. Gray	Owner
Pedro of Yevot	7.5.58	Fawn	Emmrill Buck's Peppie	Jofos Christina	Miss M. Tovey	Owner
Chitina's Majestic Sprite	19.9.59	Black & tan	Mabelle Pepito	Mabelle Conchita	Mrs D. Garlick	Miss Turner
Seggieden Little Heracles	28.2.59	Red	Ch. Cisco Kid of Winterlea	Seggieden Cassiopaea	Mrs M. Mooney	Lady M. Drummond-Hay
Rowley Silver Cloud	5.2.60	Cream & gold	Seggieden Zeus	Ch. Rowley Emmrill Lolita	Mrs M. Rider	Owner
Simchalas Bartholomew	23.9.59	Fawn & black	Simchalas Gay Kim	Simchalas Evana Orchide	Mrs L. A. Busson	Owner
Rozavel Aguardiente	30.7.63	Red & white	S. A. Ch. Rozavel Mexican Idol	Ch. Rozavel Trace of Silver	Mrs T. Gray	Owner
Jofos Jim Dandy	5.5.62	Black & tan	Jofos Pim	Jofos Robeena	Mrs J. Forster	Mrs M. Watts
Rozavel Chief Scout	30.3.64	Blue–fawn	Ch. Rozavel Wolf Cub	Rozavel Star Sapphire	Mrs T. Gray	Owner
Kaitonia's Don Armando	16.9.63	Silver sand	Ch. Kaitonia's Little Jo	Kaitonia's Rosabelle	Mrs K. Stuart	Owner
Jolengra Dandini	3.10.63	Tan & white	Greveny Herodero	Jolengra Allaja	Mr J. Shipley	Owner
Weycombe Antonio	20.12.60	Fawn & white	Lippens Cracker Bang	Lippens Treacle	Mr G. R. Down	Owner
Kaitonia's Wee Jo Jo Zuma	19.9.60	Gold, black mask	Kaitonia's Don Perro	Kaitonia's Little Gem	Mrs K. Stuart	Owner
Kaitonia's Little Jo	26.3.62	Cream	Ch. Kaitonia's Wee Jo Jo Zuma	Kaitonia's Dona Anita	Mrs K. Stuart	Owner
Kaitonia's Tony Jo	22.3.61	Golden-fawn	Kaitonia's Rano Kaoki	Ch. Kaitonia's Meronelle Vendereuse	Mrs K. Stuart	Owner

Rozavel Large as Life	Blue–fawn	30.4.61	Rozavel Big Bad Wolf	Ch. Rozavel Bienvenida	Mrs T. Gray	Owner
Irish Ch. Seggieden Mighty Dime	White & cream	4.8.61	Ch. Seggieden Tiny Mite	Seggieden Brynkerth Gretchen	Lady M. Drummond-Hay	Owner
Kaitonia's King Bee	Fawn	7.10.64	Ch. Kaitonia's Little Jo	Kaitonia's Sabina	Mrs K. Stuart	Owner
Rozavel Blue Flagship	Blue	11.1.65	Rozavel Blue Flag	Rozora Santa Monica	Mrs T. Gray	Mrs H. Pitt
Rozavel Cadbury	Brown & tan	1.3.66	Rozavel Trader Vic	Rozavel Alicante	Mrs T. Gray	Owner
Josalie Anstories Silver Star	White	22.9.63	Anstorie Hsaigo Magnus	Anstorie Fortunemark White Angel	Mr J. Lockey	Mrs Martin
Rowley Copyrite	Fawn, black mask	12.6.65	Ch. Perito of Sektuny	Ch. Rowley Ruby of Dalehaven	Mrs M. Rider	Owner
Lilycroft Son of Fortune	Red	28.11.64	Lilycroft Good Fortune	Alonquin Carmella	Mrs J. Gagen	Owner
Rowley Uvalda Winston	Black & tan	17.7.66	Ch. Rowley Perito of Sektuny	Uvalda Lady	Mrs M. Rider	Mrs Payne
Lilycroft Ballyduff Timothy	Black & tan	18.6.65	Ch. Emmrill Fudge	Lilycroft Katrine	Mrs J. Steinmetz	Mrs Docking
Truxillo Rowley Algernon	Black, white toes	8.5.68	Ch. Rowley Uvalda Winston	Ch. Rowley Ruby of Daleavon	Mr & Mrs Motherwell	Mrs M. Rider
Totland Hamilton of Hamaja	Cream	25.10.67	Carlo of Dapplemere	Totland Topaz	Miss Peggy Wood	Mrs M. Greening
Molimor Anyako Astronaut	Fawn, black mask	22.9.69	Ch. Rozavel Chief Scout	Orteja Prima Dona	Mrs Moorhouse	Mrs Mitchell
Molimor Rozavel Talent Scout	Blue–fawn	15.1.68	Ch. Rozavel Chief Scout	Rozavel Marbellup Carabella	Mrs M. Moorhouse	Mrs T. Gray
Lilycroft Trotabout	White & red	3.4.69	Ch. Lilycroft Trotter	Ch. Lilycroft Penny Lane	Mrs J. Gagen	Owner
Salsom Don Carlos	Fawn	26.4.66	Kemple's Little Strutter	Kemple's Perrila	Mr & Mrs Carlyon	Owners
Rozavel Pewter Model	Blue–tan	7.1.68	Ch. Rozavel Chief Scout	Rozavel Perrinola	Mrs T. Gray	Miss Boyt
Rowley Prime Minister	Fawn–sable	4.1.68	Ch. Uvalda Rowley Winston	Rowley Fairy Tale	Mrs M. Rider	Owner
Maidenslea Antonito	Gold, black mask	5.11.67	Ch. Rozavel Chief Scout	Valdamas Telullah	Mrs J. Rees	Mrs D. Hughes
Kingsmere Merry Mascot	Blue and fawn	21.11.68	Ch. Rozavel Chief Scout	Kingsmere Georgiana of Dum Dum	Mrs J. Kings	Owner
Jofos Kittie's Little Jo	Red-fawn, black mask	15.12.66	Culberson's Muggins II	Payne Daisy Mae	Mrs J. Forster	Mrs Culberson
Hobart Boulton of Boutique	Gold	15.2.56	Seggieden Mighty Guinea	Seggieden Winkle	Mrs M. Hall	Owner
Edgebourne Cock A Hoop	Red & white	30.6.68	Edgebourne Escudo	Seggieden Wee Lizzie	Lt Com & Mrs Egerton Williams	Mrs V. Preece
Dalhabboch Alfie	Black & tan	8.11.65	Donamarie's My Friend Flicker	Andrea of Buddletown	Miss D. Russell-Allen	Owner
Ardick Mystic Ash	Blue-fawn	9.5.67	Ardick Witch Doctor	Ardick Zsa Zsa of Glenjoy	R. Dick	Owner
Larkwhistle Macaroon	Cream	13.9.69	Pedmore Pearl Button	Rozavel Perinola	Mrs J. Bruton	Miss Boyt
Nixtrix Whizzby	Red & white	17.12.70	Ch. Kingsmere Merry Mascot	Nixtrix Gee Whizz	Mrs E. F. Nicholl	Owner
Maidenslea Aristo	Gold	18.12.70	Ch. Maidenslea Antonito	Maidenslea Khnumt	M. Oliver	Mrs J. Rees
Oljon Carbon Copy	Black & tan	13.3.71	Truxillo Copy Prince	Pedmore Night Ride	Mrs Harris	Mrs Shaw
Apoco Ballybroke Billy Bunter	Fawn, black mask	1.7.70	Ch. Ardick Witch Doctor	Ballybroke Sowat Foxtrot	W. Stephenson	Mr & Mrs Foote

Champion Smooth-coat Dogs—contd.

Name	Born	Colour	Sire	Dam	Owner	Breeder
Carlinder's News Boy	10.8.70	Black & tan	Maidenslea Revaldo of Yevot	Adoram Iona	L. A. Oliver	M. Oliver
Goldsborough King Midas	3.2.71	Fawn & golden	Ch. Kingsmere Merry Mascot	Clewcarn Violetta	Mrs E. I. Foster	J. Leonard
Molimor Bronzel	3.4.71	Brown & white	Molimor Jofos Memphis	Molimor Floralspa Bronzetta	Mrs M. Moorhouse	Owner
Lilycroft Trotter	30.9.62	Red	Lilycroft Tiny Tim	Alonquin Nicoletta	Mrs J. Gagen	Owner
Rozavel Peterkin	7.7.66	Sable	Rozavel Blue Flag	Rozoro Marie Elena	Mrs Braun	Mrs T. Gray
Oljon Bineite Honey Boy	29.12.66	Cream	Pedmore Saturday Night	Montezuma Bonny April	Mrs Harris	Miss M. Betts

Champion Smooth-coat Bitches

Name	Born	Colour	Sire	Dam	Owner	Breeder
Bowerhinton Isabela	6.9.52	Red & white	Denger's Don Carlos	Denger's Dona Maria	Mrs Fearfield	Mrs Horner
Brownridge Jofos Paloma	22.3.53	Cream	Bowerhinton Chico of Belamie	Jofos Millinita	Mrs J. Rawson	Mrs J. Forster
Am. Ch. Kelsbro Dugger's Spice	19.12.53	Choc & tan	Dugger's Colonel Meron	Sweet Celinda Sue	Mrs K. Stuart	Mrs C. Dugger
Maria Carmello of Wytchend	17.1.55	Golden red	Ch. Rozavel Diaz	Mixcoac	Mrs Ellis-Hughes	Owner
Adela of Bendorwyn	8.2.54	Fawn	Belanie Zequi	Jofos Lucia of Bendorwyn	Mrs Benvie	Owner
Rozavel Mantilla	19.5.54	Fawn & white	Ch. Rozavel Diaz	Rozavel La Oro Memoria de Oro	Mrs T. Gray	Owner
Rozavel Shaw's Violet	11.12.53	Blue, white & tan	Kibbe's Little Cinco	Little Darling	Mrs T. Gray	Mrs M. Shaw
Bowerhinton Ollala	13.6.56	Cream	Ch. Rozavel Francisco	Bowerhinton Carmencita	Mrs M. Fearfield	Owner
Rowley Emmrill Lolita	17.5.57	Red	Emmrill Son-ko's Red Rocket	Jofos Driada	Mrs M. Rider	Mrs M. Huxham
Rozavel Uvalda Jemima	25.1.58	Tricolour	Ch. Rozavel Humo	Uvalda Jofos Moomin	Mrs T. Gray	Mrs M. Payne
Rozavel Bienvenida	31.10.58	Fawn	Ch. Rozavel Diaz	Ch. Rozavel Platina	Mrs T. Gray	Owner
Kaitonia's Meronella Venderesse	13.10.56	Brown	Emmrill Son-ko's Red Rocket	Nellistar Arrieta	Mrs K. Stuart	Mrs H. Morgan
Rozavel Platina	15.10.57	Fawn & white	Ch. Rozavel Humo	Rozavel Jofos Onlyone	Mrs T. Gray	Owner
Kaitonia's Lulubelle	2.8.58	Blue & tan	Kaitonia's Don Pedro	Kaitonia's Twinkletoes	Mrs K. Stuart	Mrs Gowing
Ellicia of Bendorwyn	23.5.58	Black & white	Primo of Belamie	Jofos Lucia of Bendorwyn	Mrs D. Benvie	Owner
Winterlea Snow Queen	2.9.58	White	Irish Ch. & Ch. Seggeden Jupiter	Bigo's Zoranna of Winterlea	Mrs M. Mooney	Owner
Jofos Victoria of Sillwood	19.4.58	Fawn & white	Montezuma Travata of Wytchend	Evana Perdita	Mrs Wakefield	Mrs J. Forster
Lippens Koko of Yevot	20.6.60	Choc & tan	Ch. Pedro of Yevot	Lippens Hsiago Solano	Miss M. Tovey	Mrs P. Blake
Dalhabboch Sweet Honesty	1.10.60	Pale fawn	Luce's Little King Blue of Dalhabboch	Ch. Dalhabboch Sweet Primrose	Miss D. Russell-Allen	Owner
Rozavel Amorosa	18.7.60	Golden	Ch. Rozavel Humo	Rozavel Karlena's Bambi	Mrs G. Kesper	Mrs T. Gray

						Owners
Nita of Glenjoy	Bridle-brown	1.10.59	Dalhabboch Yonder He Goes	Pepita of Glenjoy	Mr Turner & Miss Massey	
Evana Peppermint of Edgebourne	Black & tan	6.7.61	Jofos Pim	Jofos Tarahumara	Lt Com & Mrs Egerton-Williams	Mrs B. Evans
Rozavel Trace of Silver	Red, white markings	27.1.62	St Erme Sorreldene Brandts Brandy	Ch. Rozavel Platina	Mrs T. Gray	Owner
Rozavel Youngelve Pixie-Poo	White	25.10.60	Rozavel El Padre	Youngelve Petinkie	Mrs T. Gray	Mrs E. Young
Rowley Ruby of Daleavon	Fawn	14.7.61	Jofos Pim	Evana Sari	Mrs M. Rider	Mrs Anderson
Johara Jezebel-Mi-Tu	Golden	20.12.65	Johara Samson	Johara Coco Tu	Mrs V. Riley	Owner
Kittalah Connies Star	Fawn & white	13.12.65	Greveny Herodero	Kittalah Barralicia Dusty	Mrs G. Hayes	Owner
Larkwhistle Vanilla	Cream	5.3.66	Ch. Rowley Perito of Sektuny	Rozavel Perrinola	Miss E. J. Boyt	Owner
Maidenslea Nephithys	Red-gold & white	21.6.66	Maidenslea Revaldo of Yevot	Maidenslea Mary Poppins	Mrs Meldrum	Mrs Rees
Rozavel Brass Buttons	Gold & white	23.5.68	Pedmore Pearl Buttons	Rozavel Abinkie	Mrs T. Gray	Owner
Rozavel Silver Shadow	Blue-fawn	29.4.68	Ch. Rozavel Large as Life	Rozavel Skylark	Miss E. Boyt	Mrs T. Gray
Lilycroft Penny Lane	Red, black mask	1.10.66	Lilycroft Honey Bov	Lilycroft Sheena	Mrs J. Gagen	Owner
Lanelea Mexican Cream	Cream	1.4.10	Lanelea Rockefella	Totland Tadorna	R. H. Pearson	Owner
Maerlake Tansy	Fawn & white	1.1.69	Maerlake Red Pepper	Maerlake Misty Violet	Mrs C. Robinson	Owner
Myavon Penny Blue	Blue-fawn	14.9.68	Rowley Uvalda Winston	Rowley Miss Muffet	Mrs Motherwell	Mrs Kennard
Rowley Sweetie Pie	Sable	17.6.69	Ch. Rozavel Chief Scout	Ch. Rowley Josephine	Mrs Rider	Owner
Stoberry Delcharchi Melinda	Blue-silver	2.11.66	Ch. Rozavel Chief Scout	Delcharchi Golden Oriole	Mr & Mrs Roberts	J. Parker
Hayclose How Pretty	Red & white	7.7.66	Hayclose Husky	Brettleton Chikeeta	Mrs Davies	J. Stott
Queenelms Celia	Cream	30.3.67	Seggieden Pooka	Queenelms Titania	Miss Gaffiki	Owner
Rowley Clarissa	Fawn	12.6.65	Ch. Rowley Perito of Sektuny	Ch. Rowley Ruby of Daleavon	Mrs. M. Rider	Owner
Rowley Lansdahlia Candytuft	Cream	3.6.66	Ch. Rowley Perito of Sektuny	Lansdahlia Sally Ann	Mrs Lansdale	Mrs M. Rider
Winterlea Blue Blue Tu	Blue-fawn	—	—	—	Mrs Mooney	Mrs Moorhouse
Candyfloss of Wytchend	Cream	19.7.65	Hsaigo My Boy Lollipop	Juliea of Wytchend	Mrs Ellis-Hughes	Owner
Kaitonia's Dona Veleta	Choc & cream	14.8.62	Ch. Kaitonia's Wee Jo Jo Zuma	Kaitonia's Minitura	Mrs K. Stuart	Owner
Valdama Honeysuckle	Cream	10.5.62	Valdama's Figaro	Valdama Snowdrop	Mrs Ashton	Owner
Eugenie of Yevot	Chocolate	7.8.63	Gaviola of Yevot	Cosita	Miss M. Tovey	Owner
Heathtop Titania	Cream	31.1.60	Ch. Pedro of Yevot	Pentrebach Perky Pet	Mrs M. Edwards	Owner
Snowdrop of Glenjoy	Fawn	9.12.62	Hacienda Gomez of Glenjoy	Talaloc Tamina	Mrs V. Jones	Mrs Turner & Miss Massey
Rozavel Hasta La Vista	Red & white	12.5.61	Rozavel Big Bad Wolf	Rozavel Huesteca	Mrs T. Gray	Owner
Rowley Josephine	Fawn	23.4.64	Ch. Rowley Perito of Sektuny	Rowley Ruby of Daleavon	Mrs. M. Rider	A. Green
Kaitonia's Little Josefina	Cream	14.8.62	Ch. Kaitonia's Wee Jo Jo Zuma	Kaitonia's Dona Anita	Mrs K. Stuart	Owner
Kaitonia's Golden Girl	Golden	9.8.60	Ch. Seggieden Tiny Mite	Fullani Paberlina	Mrs K. Stuart	Owner

Champion Smooth-coat Bitches—contd.

Name	Colour	Born	Sire	Dam	Owner	Breeder
Truxillo Miss Cadbury	Brown	7.7.67	Ch. Rozavel Chief Scout	Truxillo Rowley Sovereign	Mr & Mrs Motherwell	Owners
Clandon Mulgawood Peppercorn	Black & tan	15.1.70	Wingreen Poppet's Delight	Mulgawood Mixed Spice	Mrs Goodwin	Owner
Totland Tia Francesca	Sable	16.8.69	Totland Foxcub Zapangu	Totland Kepsi Cokernut Ice	Miss P. Wood	Owner
Strondour's Valdama Sweet Memory	White	15.4.65	Valdama Figaro	Valdama's Snowdrop	Mrs Walker	Mrs Ashton
Sternroc Baby Cham	Cream	28.11.64	Ch. Seggieden Mighty Dime	Sternroc Seggieden Pimpernel	Mrs Cross Stern	Owner
St Erme Pussy Cat	Gold & white	23.12.65	Rozavel Prairie Wolf	Tejuana Tilly Lily	Mrs Hallam	Mrs St Erme Cardew
Cluneen Red Velvet	Red & white	16.3.65	Talaloc Tambo	Mountalbion Twinkletoes	Mrs E. Banks	Owner
Winterlea Twinkle of Mingulay	Apricot	22.11.65	Winterlea Rozavel Blue Flash	Dusk of Mingulay	Mrs Mooney	Mrs Stevenson
Molimor Zillah	Gold & white	22.8.70	Ch. Molimor Rozavel Talent Scout	Molimor Zenith of Glenjoy	Mrs Moorhouse	Owner
Salsom Contessa	Fawn	28.11.68	Kemple's Little Strutter	Kemple's Perrila	Mrs Lawson	Mr & Mrs Carlyon
Mulgawood Lady Fern	Cream	6.10.70	Ch. Jofos Kitties Little Jo	Winworth Mulgawood Lady Tirza	Mrs Watson	Owner
Rowley Coronet	Golden	16.11.69	Ch. Rowley Courtier	Ch. Rowley Kismet	Mrs M. Rider	Owner
Goldsborough Tiny White Lady	White	10.7.70	Ch. Seggieden Mighty Dime	Clewkarn Violetta	Mrs E. I. Foster	J. Leonard
Nikoli Starlight	Blue & fawn	15.6.72	Ch. Maidenslea Aristo	Adorum Iona	M. Oliver	Owner
Molimor Talentina	Blue & fawn	28.12.72	Ch. Molimor Rozavel Talent Scout	Molimor Grageo Salome	Mrs Moorhouse	Owner

Champion Long-coat Dogs

Name	Colour	Born	Sire	Dam	Owner	Breeder
Nellistar Schaeffer's Taffy Boy	Red & white	23.3.54	Am. Ch. Schaeffer's Captain Boy Blue II	Lindsay's Little Sister	Mrs C. M. Erskine	Mrs. D Lindsay-Schaeffer
Cholderton Little Scampy of Teeny Wee	White, fawn markings	24.2.57	Am. Ch. Meron of Teeny Wee	Lacher's White Fluff	Mrs M. Bedford	Mrs K. Lacher
Rowley Perito of Sektuny	Deep cream	15.9.58	Ch. Rozavel Francisco	Pixie of Sektuny	Mrs M. Rider	Mrs Pearce
Rowley Umberto	Red	19.6.59	Ch. Rozavel Humo	Ch. Rowley Emmrll Lolita	Mrs M. Rider	Owner
Duniver's Angel's Ace	Golden–fawn	21.3.61	Carlitos of Yevot	Duniver Angelita of Glenjoy	Mrs C. R. Burt	Owner
Rozavel Wolf Cub	Sable	30.4.61	Rozavel Big Bad Wolf	Ch. Rozavel Bienvenida	Mrs T. Gray	Owner
Emmrill Fudge	Red–sable	12.12.61	Ch. Rowley Umberto	Emmrill Candy	Mrs M. Huxham	Owner
Winterlea Lone Wolf	Sable	14.4.63	Ch. Rozavel Wolf Cub	Winterlea Orozco Texas Rose	Mrs M. Mooney	Owner
Rozavel Alphonso Zapangu	Sable	1.8.64	Ch. Rozavel Wolf Cub	Geneau Babe Belle	Mrs T. Gray	Mr B. Mitchell
Deodar Winterlea Wolf Whistle	Sable	12.7.64	Ch. Winterlea Lone Wolf	Winterlea Carann Donna Gigi	Mrs R. Borthwick	Mrs M. Mooney
Rowley Courtier	Red	3.3.63	Ch. Rowley Perito of Sektuny	Rowley Zarah	Mrs M. Rider	Owner
Aztec Star Golden Glory	Fawn	12.1.66	Aztec Star Black Knight	Aztec Sun Star	Col & Mrs V. D'Oyly Harmer	Owner
Ballybroke Ryanlea Wee Babycham	Red & white	5.3.53	Anstorie Sirius	Anstorie Seggieden Tiny Tip Top	Mrs J. Foote	Mrs A. Murray
Kaitonia's Canberra Billabong	Red-sable	8.7.65	Mickleton Marbellup Mr Pepys	Rediviva Sylvia Minx	Mrs K. Stuart	Mrs Colburn-Hart
Pequena Little Caesar	Silver & white	8.2.65	Serrano of Yevot	Montoya Roma	Mrs O. Frei-Denver	Mr & Mrs F. Griffiths
Dekobra's Danny Boy	Fawn and white	27.8.65	Dekobras Midnight Dan	Chitina's Little Darling	Mrs Steinmetz	Owner
Montezuma Mr Chips	Apricot	17.10.65	Pancho of Dapplemere	Montezuma Rediviva Sunshine	Mrs H. A. Horton-Hall	Owner
Venico Momento	Sable & white	30.10.65	Ch. Deodar Winterlea Wolf Whistle	Venico Deodar Pussy Willow	Mrs Wilson	Mrs E. Nicholl
Chitinas Nixtrix Prince Charming	Golden–tan, black mask	16.6.67	Chitina's Peregrine	Nitrix Windmill Za Za Zoe	Mrs D. Garlick	Mrs E. Nicholl
Kingsmere Abraxas Michael Angelo	Sable	6.10.67	Rozavel Palomino	Abraxas Rozavel Gracia	Mrs J. Kings & Miss Drummond-Dick	Miss V. Drummond-Dick
Lilycroft Forever	Blue-fawn	1.10.66	Lilycroft Honey Boy	Lilycroft Sheena	Mrs J. Gagen	Owner
Venico Widogi Mr Whippy	Cream	3.6.67	Ch. Montezuma Mr Chips	Crestview Good Companion	Mrs E. V. Nicholl	Mrs J. Fraser
Winterlea Roving Minstrel	Sable	8.11.66	Ch. Winterlea Lone Wolf	Winterlea Carann Donna Gigi	Mrs M. Mooney	Owner
Nixtrix Boo Boo Bear	Golden, black mask	28.7.68	Chitina's Peregrine	Nixtrix Windmill Za Za Zoe	Mrs E. Nicholl	Owner

Champion Long-coat Dogs—contd.

Name	Colour	Born	Sire	Dam	Owner	Breeder
Rowley Magic Circle	Pale fawn	7.7.67	Ch. Rowley Umberto	Lansdahlia Talaloc Twinkle	Mes M. Rider	Mrs Lansdale
Rozavel Pirate Flag	Black	21.1.66	Rozavel Blue Flag	Rozavel Platina	Mrs T. Gray	Owner
Taydors Galloping Major	Black & tan	25.5.67	Duniver Colonel Bogey	Taydors Arosa	Mr & Mrs Taylor	Owners
Johara Peregrine	Black & fawn	18.5.67	Johara Velena Tinto Star	Johara Red Squirrel	Mrs V. Riley	Owner
Johara Ponsonby	Fawn & black	18.2.69	Johara Paddington	Johara Red Squirrel	Mrs V. Riley	Owner
Kimanchi's Golden Eagle	Sable	30.12.68	Kimanchi's Crest O'Wave	Kimanchi's Shot Taffeta	Miss E. Pantin & Miss I. Fairs	Owners
Rozavel Blue Feathers	Blue	4.2.69	Ch. Rozavel Large as Life	Rozavel Black Limelight	Mrs T. Gray	Owner
Truxillo Prince Consort	Cream	2.3.68	Ch. Rowley Courtier	Ch. Truxillo Rowley Sovereign	Mr & Mrs G. Motherwell	Owners
Winterlea Knockenjig Royal Star	Honey	13.7.69	Winterlea Delcharchi Dolphin	Knockenjig Lindina Jaunty Judy	Mrs M. Mooney	Mrs Peters
Knockenjig Roving Gipsy	Golden	27.2.70	Ch. Venico Momento	Knockenjig Lindina Jaunty Judy	Mrs Peters	Owner
Larkwhistle Quill	Fawn	13.4.71	Ch. Rozavel Blue Feathers	Larkwhistle Teresa	Miss D. Slark	Miss E. Boyt
Rozavel Real Wolf	Pale fawn	22.4.68	Ch. Rozavel Wolf Cub	Dorrow Miss Pinky	Mrs T. Gray	Mrs Ponsford
Rozavel Sea Scout	Black & tan	16.11.67	Ch. Rozavel Chief Scout	Ch. Rozavel Mermaid	Mrs J. Bruton	Mrs T. Gray
Taydors Sergeant Blackie	Black & tan	15.11.70	Ch. Taydors Galoping Major	Taydors Pollyanna	Mr & Mrs Taylor	J. R. Speak
Kimanchi's Modern Trend	Sable & silver	24.12.71	Ch. Kimanchi's Golden Eagle	Kimanchi's Black Cherry	Miss E. Pantin & Miss J. Fairs	Owners
Kinos Zapelle	Cream	17.5.70	Dresden Rockefella	Stansaker Flamenco	Mrs E. I. Foster	Mrs P. Atkinson
Nixtrix Beau Brummel	Red & white	29.10.70	Ch. Rowley Magic Circle	Ch. Nixtrix Puffa Puffa Bear	Mrs E. F. Nicholl	Owner
Redyak Honey Ball	Golden	25.6.69	Chitinas Peregrine	Dorrow Snowflake	Mrs Currie & Mr A. Wight	Mrs K. Yates
Widogi Playboy	Cream-sable	5.2.71	Molimor Anyako Astronaut	Widogi Miss Otis	Mrs J. Fraser	Owner
Winterlea Star Shine	Red with blaze	24.1.72	Ch. Winterlea Knockenjig Royal Star	Stillponds Bright & Gay	Mrs M. Mooney	Owner
Raygistaan Toy Train	Pale golden	12.3.72	Raygistaan Gold Train	Zaleti Piaco Xicola	Mrs E. King	Mr B. King
Whisky Galore of Bill Top	Sable	4.9.71	Gameland's Caramel Fudge	Gameland's Gin Fizz	Miss T. Williams	Mr Tipton

Champion Long-coat Bitches

Name	Born	Colour	Sire	Dam	Owner	Breeder
Int. Ch., Am. Ch. and Ch. Aztec Son-ko's Ita Star Dust	28.7.59	Golden–fawn	Carter's Little Ko-Ko Boy	Champagne Lady of Son-ko	Col & Mrs V. D'Oyly Harmer	Mrs D. Baese
Pequeno Miney	11.11.61	Golden–sable	Am. Ch. Bradshaws Pequeno Belleza	Pequeno Bradshaws Tomasa	Mrs O. Frei-Denver	Owner
Rozavel Mermaid	2.5.63	Sable	Ch. Rozavel Wolf Cub	Rozavel Marineria	Mrs T. Gray	Owner
Lansdahlia Talaloc Twinkle	4.12.62	Red–sable	Ch. Rowley Perito of Sektuny	Talaloc Tangara	Mrs Lansdale	Mrs Goodchild
Hayclose Harrison	22.12.63	Golden–fawn	Ch. Duniver Angel's Ace	Parabar Roseleta	Mrs J. Stott	Owner
Pequena Maria	13.5.64	Black, fawn & cream	Ch. Rowley Perito of Sektuny	Ch. Pequeno Miney	Mrs O. Frei-Denver	Owner
Rowley Kismet	14.10.63	Sable	Ch. Rowley Perito of Sektuny	Rowley Queen of the May	Mrs M. Rider	Owner
Winterlea Secker Samantha	27.10.64	Sable & black	Ch. Winterlea Lone Wolf	Mickleton Mantilla	Mrs M. Mooney	Mrs Teasdale
Chitina's Cuddles	2.3.64	Cream & white	Chitina's Dinky Gem	Chitina's Du-Bonet	Mrs D. Garlick	Owner
Deodar Honey Dew	13.12.62	Golden	Ch. Rowley Perito of Sektuny	Deodar Ginger Quill	Mrs S. Borthwick	Owner
Rozavel Fine Feathers	4.8.64	Blue, fawn & white	Ch. Rozavel Humo	Rozavel My Fur Lady	Mrs T. Gray	Owner
Emmrill Meringue of Aes	5.9.66	Sable & white	Ch. Emmrill Fudge	Xepherine of Aes	Mrs M. G. Huxham	Mrs O. Har-bottle
Ranji's Carmenchita	16.4.66	Black & tan	Ch. Emmrill Fudge	Simchalas Maggie May	Mrs M. V. Kemp-son	E. Helm
Rozavel Astra	29.9.65	Blue & fawn	Ch. Rozavel Chief Scout	Rozavel Good As Gold	Mrs T. Gray	Owner
Taydors Gitana	1.5.66	Tan	Ch. Duniver Angel's Ace	Taydor's Dorrow Trudy Pru	Mr & Mrs W. Taylor	Owners
Wingreen Aphrodite	19.11.64	Pale cream	Wingreen Poppet's Delight	Cream Cracker of Elsdyle	Mrs P. Jennings	Owner
Aztec Star Wolf Goddess	14.11.67	White & red	Aztec Star Brave Wolf	Aztec Star Cocoa Goddess	Col & Mrs V. D'Oyly Harmer	Owners
Kaitonia's Canberra Kavra-Katta	8.7.65	Black & white	Mickleton Marbellup Mr Pepys	Rediviva Sylvia Minx	Mrs K. Stuart	Mrs D. Colburn-Hart
Kimanchi's Honey Bee	1.3.66	Sable	Ch. Rowley Umberto	Kimanchi's Golden Tansy	Miss E. Pantin & Miss E. Fairs	Owners
Knockenjig Anyako Lone Star	13.11.64	Fawn–sable	Ch. Winterlea Lone Wolf	Anyako Muna	Mrs Peters	Mrs Mitchell
Nixtrix Puffa Puffa Bear	16.6.67	Red	Chitina's Peregrine	Nixtrix Windmill Za Za Zoe	Mrs E. F. Nicholl	Owner
Rozavel Tarina Song	3.7.67	Sable	Rozavel Pirate Flag	Tarina Melody	Mrs T. Gray	Mr & Mrs Grevett
Rowley Crown Jewel	22.11.68	Red–sable	Ch. Rowley Courtier	Rowley Bridget	Mrs M. Rider	Owner
Rowley Petticoat Line	7.7.67	Pale fawn	Ch. Rowley Umberto	Lansdahlia Talaloc Twinkle	Mrs M. Rider	Mrs Lansdale
Rozavel Tarina Do-Re-Mi	6.10.68	Chocolate-brown	Ch. Rozavel Chief Scout	Tarina Honeybun	Mrs T. Gray	Mr & Mrs Grevett
Chitina's Beautinas Chocolate Drop	7.11.68	Red–sable & white	Chitina's Peregrine	Chitina's Glamour Puss Jill	Mrs D. Garlick	Mrs Latham

Champion Long-coat Bitches—contd.

Name	Born	Colour	Sire	Dam	Owner	Breeder
Raygistaan Fieldhill Sparkle	14.10.67	White, black points	Ch. Venico Momento	Deodar Gay Donna	Mrs E. King	Mrs Wilson
Raygistaan Rumbunny	26.5.66	Red	Ch. Rozavel Wolf Cub	Raygistaan Deodar Honey Bunch	Mrs E. King	Owner
Chitina's Peregrina	31.12.68	Tan & white	Chitina's Peregrine	Ch. Chitina's Cuddles	Mrs D. Garlick	Owner
Limmerlease Suki-Sue	26.5.71	Fawn	Fancy Fare	Limmerlease Wild Silk	G. Farmer	Mrs E. D. Skellon
Pequeno Sockitoem Tammy	24.4.70	White & chocolate	Pequeno Didly	Pequeno Witchytoo	Mrs O. Frei-Denver	Owner
Rowley Royal Gem	6.10.71	Pale fawn	Ch. Rowley Magic Circle	Ch. Rowley Crown Jewel	Mrs M. Rider	Owner
Rozavel Larkwhistle Nutkin	13.4.71	Sable	Ch. Rozavel Blue Feathers	Larkwhistle Theresa	Mrs T. Gray	Miss E. Boyt
Twinley Golden Melody	26.12.71	Red-sable, white trim	Tarina Cobbler	Twinley Aztec Star Garnet Goddess	Mrs A. Block	Owner
Rowley Lansdahlia Candytuft	-.3.66	Cream	Ch. Rowley Perito of Sektuny	Lansdahlia Sally Ann	Mrs M. Rider	Mrs Lansdale
Danchis Peach Blossom	18.9.67	Cream	Chitina's Peregrine	Kemple's Bridget	Miss Hawkins	Owner
Chitina's Little Cuddles	31.12.68	Tan & white	Chitina's Peregrine	Ch. Chitina's Cuddles	Mrs D. Garlick	Owner

Index